FAMILY AND CIVILIZATION

BACKGROUND

Essential Texts for the Conservative Mind

FAMILY AND CIVILIZATION

Carle Zimmerman

edited by James Kurth

with an introduction by Allan C. Carlson

Wilmington, Delaware

Zimmerman, Carle Clark, 1897–1983.

    Family and civilization / Carle Zimmerman ; edited by James Kurth ; with an introduction by Allan C. Carlson.—2nd ed., rev. and abridged.—Wilmington, Del. : ISI Books, 2007.

        p. ; cm.
        (Background series)

        ISBN: 978-1-933859-37-8
        Originally published: New York : Harper, 1947.
        Includes index.

        1. Family—History. I. Kurth, James. II. Title. III. Series: Background series (Wilmington, Del.)

HQ503 .Z56 2007   2007937165
306.85/09—dc22   0801

ISI Books
Intercollegiate Studies Institute
P.O. Box 4431
Wilmington, DE 19807-0431
www.isibooks.org

Book design by Beer Editorial and Design

Manufactured in the United States of America

CONTENTS

Introduction to the 2008 edition

Allan C. Carlson

HAVING TAKEN A BREAK FROM planning the World Congress of Families IV, an international assembly that took place in 2007 and focused on Europe's "demographic winter" and global family decline, I turned to consider again Carle Zimmerman's magnum opus, *Family and Civilization* (1947). And there, near the end of chapter 8 in his list of sure signs of social catastrophe, I read: "Population and family congresses spring up among the lay population as frequently and as verbose as Church Councils [in earlier centuries]." It is disconcerting to find one's work labeled, accurately I sometimes fear, as a symptom rather than as a solution to the crisis of our age. Such is the prescience and the humbling wisdom of this remarkable book.

With regard to the family, Carle Zimmerman was the most important American sociologist of the 1920s, '30s, and '40s. His only rival for this label would be his friend, occasional coauthor, and colleague Pitirim Sorokin. Zimmerman was born to German-American parents and grew up in a Cass County, Missouri, village. Sorokin grew up in Russia, became a peasant revolutionary and a young minister in the brief Kerensky government, and barely survived the Bosheviks, choosing banishment in 1921 over a death sentence. They were teamed up at the University of Minnesota in 1924 to teach a seminar on rural sociology. Five years later, this collaboration resulted in the volume *Principles of Rural-Urban Sociology*, and a few years thereafter in the multivolume *A Systematic Source Book in Rural Sociology*. These books directly launched the Rural Sociological Section of the American Sociological Association and the new journal *Rural Sociology*. In all this activity, Zimmerman focused on the family virtues of farm people. "Rural people have greater vital indices than urban people," he reported. Farm people had earlier and stronger marriages, more children, fewer divorces, and "more unity and mutual attachment and engulfment of the personalit[ies]" of its members than did their urban counterparts.

Zimmerman's thought ran sharply counter to the primary thrust of American sociology in this era. The so-called Chicago School dominated American social science, led by figures such as William F. Ogburn and Joseph K. Folsom. They focused on the family's steady loss of functions under industrialization to both governments and corporations. As Ogburn explained, many American homes had already become "merely 'parking places' for parents and children who spend their active hours elsewhere." Up to this point, Zimmerman would not have disagreed. But the Chicago School went on to argue that such changes were inevitable and that the state should help complete the process. Mothers should be mobilized for full-time employment, small children should be put into collective day care, and other measures should be adopted to effect "the individualization of the members of society."

Where the Chicago School was neo-Marxist in orientation, Zimmerman looked to a different sociological tradition. He drew heavily on the insights of the mid-nineteenth-century French social investigator Frederic Le Play. The Frenchman had used detailed case studies, rather than vast statistical constructs, to explore the "stem family" as the social structure best adapted to insure adequate fertility under modern economic conditions. Le Play had also stressed the value of noncash "home production" to a family's life and health. Zimmerman's book from 1935, *Family and Society*, represented a broad application of Le Play's techniques to modern America. Zimmerman claimed to find the "stem family" alive and well in America's heartland: in the Appalachian-Ozark region and among the German- and Scandinavian-Americans in the Wheat Belt. More importantly, Le Play had held to an unapologetically normative view of the family as the necessary center of critical human experiences, an orientation readily embraced by Zimmerman.

This mooring explains his frequent denunciations of American sociology in the pages of *Family and Civilization.* "Most of family sociology," he asserts, "is the work of amateurs" who utterly fail to comprehend the "inner meaning of their subject." Zimmerman mocks the Chicago School's new definition of the family as "a group of interacting personalities." He lashes out at Ogburn for failing to understand that "the basis of familism is the birth rate." He denounces Folsom for labeling Le Play's "stem" family model as "fascistic" and for giving new modifiers—such as "democratic," "liberal," or "humane"—to the "individualistic" family model favored in the Chicago School's theory. Zimmerman explains that the modern "intellectual . . . cannot see or understand" familism because he is commonly "a non-participant in the family system." As Zimmerman concludes on the last page of the book: "There is a greater disparity between the actual, documented, historical truth and the theories taught in the family sociology courses than exists in any other scientific field."

Zimmerman wrote *Family and Civilization* to recover that "actual, documented, historical truth." The book stands as an extraordinary feat of research and interpretation. It sweeps across the millennia and burrows into the nature of otherwise disparate civilizations to reveal deeper and universal social traits. To guide his investigation, Zimmerman asks: "Of the total power in [a] society, how much belongs to the family? Of the total amount of control of action in [a] society, how much is left for the family?" By analyzing these levels of family autonomy, Zimmerman identifies three basic family types: (1) the trustee family, with extensive power rooted in extended family and clan; (2) the atomistic family, which has virtually no power and little field of action; and (3) the domestic family (a variant of Le Play's "stem" family), in which a balance exists between the power of the family and that of other agencies. He traces the dynamics as civilizations, or nations, move from one type to another. Zimmerman's central thesis is that the "domestic family" is the system found in all civilizations at their peak of creativity and progress, for it "possesses a certain amount of mobility and freedom and still keeps up the minimum amount of familism necessary for carrying on the society."

So-called social history has exploded as a discipline since the early 1960s, stimulated at first by the French *Annales* school of interpretation and then by the new feminist historiography. Thousands upon thousands of detailed studies on marriage law, family consumption patterns, premarital sex, "gay culture," and gender power relations now exist, material that Zimmerman never saw (and some of which he probably never even could have imagined). All the same, this mass of data has done little to undermine his basic argument.

Zimmerman focuses on hard, albeit enduring truths. He affirms, for example, the virtue of early marriage: "Persons who do not start families when reasonably young often find that they are emotionally, physically, and psychologically unable to conceive, bear, and rear children at later ages." The author emphasizes the intimate connection between voluntary and involuntary sterility, suggesting that they arise from a common mindset that rejects familism. He rejects the common argument that the widespread use of contraceptives would have the beneficial effect of eliminating human abortion. In actual practice, "the population which wishes to reduce its birth rate . . . seems to find the need for more abortions as well as *more* birth control."

Indeed, the primary theme of *Family and Civilization* is fertility. Zimmerman underscores the three functions of familism as articulated by historic Christianity: *fides, proles,* and *sacramentum*; or "fidelity, childbearing, and indissoluble unity." While describing at length the social value of premarital chastity, the health-giving effects of marriage, the costs of adultery, and the social devastation of divorce, Zimmerman zeros in on the birth rate. He concludes that "we see [ever] more clearly the role of *proles* or childbearing as the main stem of the family." The very act of childbearing, he notes, "creates resistances to the breaking-up of the marriage." In short, "the basis of familism is the birth rate. Societies that have numerous children have to have familism. Other societies (those with few children) do not have it." This gives Zimmerman one easy measure of social success or decline: the marital fertility rate. A familistic society, he says, would average at least four children born per household.

Given current American debates, we should note that Zimmerman was also pro-immigration. In his era Anglo-Saxon populations around the globe had turned against familism, rejecting children. Familism survived in 1948 only on the borders of the Anglo-Saxon world—in "South Ireland, French Canada, and Mexico"—and in the American regions settled by 40 million non-English immigrants, mainly Celts and Germans. However, "when the doors of immigration were closed (first by war, later by law [1924], and finally by the disruption of familistic attitudes in the European sources themselves), the antifamilism of the old cultured classes . . . finally began to have effect." In short, "within the same generation America became a world power and lost her fundamental familistic future."

Rejecting the Marxist dialectic, Zimmerman asserts that the "domestic family" would not be the agent of its own decay. When trade increased or migration occurred, the domestic family could in fact grow stronger. Instead, decay came from external factors such as changes in religious or moral sentiments. The domestic family was also vulnerable to intellectual challenges by advocates for the atomistic family.

Zimmerman was not optimistic in 1947 about America's or, more broadly, Western civilization's future. Drawing on his work from the 1920s and '30s, he finds signs of continued family health in rural America: "Our farm and rural families are still to a large extent the domestic type"; their "birthrates are relatively higher." All the same, he knew from the historical record that the pace of change could be rapid. Once familism had weakened among elites, "all the cultural elements take on an antifamily tinge." He continues:

> The advertisements, the radio, the movies, housing construction, leasing of apartments, jobs—everything is individualized. . . . [T]he advertisers depict and appeal to the fashionably small family. . . . In the motion pictures, the family seems to be motivated by little more than self-love. . . . Dining rooms are reduced in size. . . . Children's toys are cheaply made; they seldom last through the interest period of one child, much less several. . . . The whole system is unfamilistic.

Near the end of *Family and Civilization*, Zimmerman predicts that "the family of the immediate future will move further toward atomism," that "unless some unforeseen renaissance occurs, the family system will continue headlong its present trend toward nihilism." Indeed, he predicts that the United States, along with the other lands born of Western Christendom, would "reach the final phases of a great family crisis between now and the last of this century." He adds: "The results will be much more drastic in the United States because, being the most extreme and inexperienced of the aggregates of Western civilization, it will take its first real 'sickness' most violently."

In the short run, Zimmerman was wrong. Like every other observer writing in the mid-1940s, he failed to see the "marriage boom" and "the baby boom" already stirring in the United States (and with equal drama in a few other places, such as Australia). As early as 1949, two of his students reported that, for the first time in U.S. demographic history, "rural non-farm" (read "suburban") women had higher fertility than in either urban or rural-farm regions. By 1960, Zimmerman concluded in his book *Successful American Families* that nothing short of a social miracle had occurred in the suburbs:

> This Twentieth Century . . . has produced an entirely new class of people, neither rural nor urban. They live in the country but have *nothing* to do with agriculture. . . . Never before in history have a free urban and sophisticated people made a positive change in the birth rate as have our American people this generation.

By 1967, near the end of his career, Zimmerman even abandoned his agrarian ideals. The American rural community had "lost its place as a home for a folk." Old images of "rural goodness and urban badness" were now properly forgotten. The demographic future lay with the renewed "domestic families" replicating in the suburbs.

In the long run, however, the pessimism of *Family and Civilization* over the family in America in the second half of the twentieth century was fully justified. Even as Zimmerman wrote the elegy for rural familism noted above, the peculiar circumstances that had forged the suburban "family miracle" were rapidly crumbling. Old foes of the "domestic family" and friends of "atomism" came storming back: feminists, sexual libertines, neo-Malthusians, the "new" Left. By the 1970s, a massive retreat from marriage was in full swing, the marital birthrate was in free fall, illegitimacy was soaring, and nonmarital cohabitation was spreading among young adults. While some of these trends moderated during the late 1990s, the statistics have all worsened again since 2000. Zimmerman was right: America is taking its first real "sickness" most violently.

Any solution to our civilization's family crisis, he argued, must begin "in the hands of our learned classes." This group must come to understand the possibilities of "a recreated familism." Accordingly, it is wholly appropriate for this new edition of *Family and Civilization* to appear from ISI Books in 2008. Zimmerman wrote the volume at the height of his powers of observation and analysis and as a form of scholarly prophecy. The times cry out for a new generation of "learned" readers for this exceptional book.

It is important, too, to remember Zimmerman's discovery that it had proven possible in times past for a "familistic remnant" to become a "vehicular agent in the reappearance of familism." Hope for the future, Zimmerman concludes, "lay in the making of [voluntary] familism and childbearing [once again] the primary social duties of the citizen." With the advantage of another sixty years, we can conclude that here he spoke the most essential, and the most difficult, of truths.

1

INTRODUCTION

N O PROBLEM IS MORE INTERESTING and vital to us than that of the family. The child is born into a family and sees the world through its eyes. His introduction to civilization is through the family. At first he is only a child in a system of social relations consisting of a unity of husband and wife, parent and child. Later he learns that there are relatives (grandmothers, aunts, uncles, cousins, etc.) who are closer to him than other people. In time he acquires the idea of friends, and then of strangers. Then he learns that he secures his status through his family. He is an American, an Englishman, a Chinese because he is born into a parental unit that belongs to those nationalities. His parents belong to a certain community and so does he, and they are subject to its rules and privileges. He can and must go to the schools of his community.

As the child grows up, he founds a family of his own where the roles are reversed; instead of remaining a child, he becomes a husband (wife), parent, leader, breadwinner, responsible person, disciplinarian, and status conferrer. In the course of a lifetime, most people play changing roles within the organization known as the family. A broad and philosophical knowledge of the meaning of this to the individual and to society is one of the first requisites of understanding the society of which he is part.

In recent years there has been considerable discussion of the family. Among serious subjects, none are given as much attention as family, government, and religion. No one of these three topics can be discussed without the other. No government or religion is without decided views on the family, and no family can get along without day-by-day contact with the rules, regulations, and ideas of the contemporary government and religion concerning what is proper, correct, and justifiable family behavior.

This recent discussion has been concerned with "family problems," "the decline of familism," the "evolution of the family," the "origin of the family," and the "changing functions" and "future of the family." It is said that a new type of family has now arisen—the conjugal family. This is supposed to be a family type in which a married pair abstain from having children, or at least give most of their time and attention to their marriage and little or none to the parent-child relationship.

However, this has not always been so. In other times and places familism has had different connotations from those set forth today. Consequently, we have many books on the family that set forth its history, its origins, its functions in different societies, and its present state. This literature, running into thousands of volumes and written in every language in which the study of social science has been attempted, offers many explanations, interpretations, histories, pseudo-histories, and arguments, but little or no agreement concerning the family.

Family Problems in Other Societies

This disagreement over the family is not new. On the contrary, it is one of the oldest arguments of history, as a few examples will show. At the height of the old Roman Empire in Western Europe, from the first to the third centuries of our era, the family relationship was a free one like ours; there were many conjugal marriages such as have recently become popular and are now highly recommended in many circles. At that time under Roman law, divorces were easy and frequent. People did not have many children. The armies were recruited from the barbarians on the edge of the empire. The government offered rewards to people for having children and tried to penalize those who did not by higher taxes, withdrawal of privileges, and so on. There were forces in public life that favored familism and forces that did not. A marriage was at most only a civil contract that had many elements of private contract about it; the latter depended on the kind of marriage chosen. A man who wanted a binding civil contract chose the *dignitas* type of marriage. If he wanted a looser relationship which meant that the children, if any, remained with the mother's family and never received rights from the father, he chose the more flexible form called *concubinatus*. A woman who married according to *dignitas* was supposed to become a mother, and the family consisted of husband-wife, parents-children, and inner versus outer relatives. In the *dignitas* marriage, the woman left her own home more completely and "cleaved to her husband." However, she brought with her a dower or marriage portion, and her family retained an interest in it; consequently the family was always to some extent tied up with both paternal and maternal relatives. The child of such a marriage came under the *potestas*, or power, of the father, was given his name, and became his legitimate heir.

The *concubinatus* marriage, although a much looser relationship, was still a real marriage, subject to legal regulation and social consequences. However, these regulations were not so broad, and the social consequences were not so great, as in the *dignitas* marriage. The child remained with the mother and inherited from her; in the later period, by means of special legal forms the child could be adopted by his blood father and given the standing of one born of a *dignitas* marriage.

And so the difference of opinion continued through the latter days of the Roman Empire. The conservative forces of the state favored marriages of *dignitas* which would produce children to replenish the number of citizens born of Roman parents. Some of the people preferred marriages of *dignitas*, with or without children, and some marriages of the *concubinatus* type, with or without children.

Toward the last days of the Roman Empire a new force entered into this argument, the Christian church. This religious organization called the mores of the Roman family "decadent" and demanded reform after reform. The church recognized marriages of one kind only, *dignitas*. It insisted on the reform of the Roman *dignitas* marriage to make it a sacred and lasting union. It was opposed to divorce and every other form of "demoralization" throughout the Roman Empire. At first the Christians were severely prosecuted for "impiety" toward the Roman gods; every time a calamity occurred, it was the fashion to blame the difficulty on the Christians and to persecute some of them rigorously. But later, some of the emperors were converted and Christianity became a legal as well as a moral force. Then came a period when disciplinary legislation regarding the family was forced upon the people by the Christian emperors.

Romanism decayed, however, and many smaller regional governments replaced the central government that had ruled over most of civilization. A new force came into power—the emperors chosen by and descended from the barbarians of northern Europe, who were migrating to the districts of the old Roman Empire. Into these small states came a new type of family, the barbarian, an organization with an outlook entirely different from that of the Roman *dignitas* and *concubinatus* families. Marriage, to the barbarians, was not a private or a civil contract. To them it was a unity of family, a blood relationship, involving rights and duties far transcending anything Roman civilization had known for almost a thousand years. Marriage among the barbarians meant that the members of a family agreed to protect their relatives in case they committed crimes, to aid them when someone did an injury to them, to help financially if they had to pay a composition or *wergild* (a type of fine), and to receive part of the *wergild* or composition in case they fined and accepted payment from another family for the actions of its members. The Roman law family came into contact with the Beowulfian type of family and society.

By this time the Roman *concubinatus* family had disappeared under the censure of the Christian church, so that three types of family were struggling for domination. One was the Roman civil law type of family, the *dignitas*, favored by the people used to Roman ways; a second was the unbreakable Christian marriage, the purified *dignitas*, favored by the bishops of the church; and the third was the barbarian trustee type, in which the household or small family came immediately under the larger family of outer relatives and clients and thus was an agent of the larger group. These types and their adherents—the Romans, the Christians, and the barbarians—struggled with each other.

The next serious change came between the tenth and twelfth centuries of our era when the governments gave way to the church. This was due partly to failures in the ability of governments to rule, and partly to a series of severe economic catastrophes that swept over Western society in the ninth and tenth centuries, bringing governments into disrepute. In large measure, however, this was undoubtedly due to the constant education carried on by the church, which insisted that only one type of family was capable of measuring up to the law of God as set forth by the church fathers from St. Augustine to Pierre Lombard and St. Thomas Aquinas.

For two or three centuries after this the only conception of the family in Western society, at least officially, was that of a family united under the aegis of the church, an unbreakable unit subject to all the rules and regulations of canon law. In most districts, however, the trustee barbarian family, shorn of most of its legal power, continued to rule much of the actual family life. Furthermore, within the church there were several heretical groups, Manicheans in particular, who wished to consider the family more in the Roman civil light as a secular and semiprivate institution than as a sacramental union of the church family or one subject to the clannish rules and regulations of the trustee barbarian family.

This general situation lasted for several centuries, during most of which time people gradually came to accept the Christian type of family outlined by canon law as *the* family. But underneath all this there was still a strong feeling of localism or "home rule," a spirit carried over from the trustee family type outlined by barbarian law for all northern Europe when the church first came into contact with the northern infidels. Finally, beginning with the Bohemian revolution which followed the death of John Huss in 1415, and the Lutheran movement about a century later, three conceptions of the family emerged again. One was the home-rule idea, a revival of local and familistic custom, more or less of the trustee type; another was the secular conception, which held that the family was an agent of the state, a civil contract, in which divorce by law should be considered; and the third was the original Christian family specifically set forth by canon law after long analysis of the spirit and conceptions of the Gospels by the church councils and canon-law doctors.

The Rise of the Private Contract Conception of the Family

These conflicting ideals of the family were at loggerheads with one another for several centuries. The rising national states were able to capitalize for themselves both on the home-rule conceptions in the remnants of the trustee family and on the spirit of secularism, which considered the family as a civil contract, although a serious and very holy arrangement. The church seriously discussed these proposed changes in the family at the Council of Trent, a long series of conferences following 1530. It stood by its original interpretation of the Christian family as one founded upon an unbreakable sacrament of marriage, entered into under the surveillance of the church, and with the free consent of the married partners. The Protestant Revolution and its doctrine, insofar as it concerned the family, offered one of the most serious challenges to the original Christian church. From that time until the French Revolution following 1789, the family was considered a holy arrangement created under God's influence, but not one of His original sacraments.

In the meantime, however, a number of "thinkers," the eighteenth-century rationalists, began to set forth from the standpoint of pure secular speculation a new conception of the family, one of private contract, with only limited civil consequences at the most. This group of men wrote mostly in French, but it also included a number of Germans and certain prominent Englishmen like Locke and Hume. Their idea, varying according to the thinker, held chiefly that the family was a private agreement between a man and woman, restricted by the state for public reasons, but having only limited civil functions. John Locke thought these functions were procreation, education, and inheritance after execution of which the marriage could, and should if wished, be dissolved at will. This was an idea distinctly different from the previous medieval conception of the family as an act designed by God, or by the all-powerful secular state, or by the all-embracing group of related persons, the clannish trustee family.

These ideas of the family as a private contract remained more or less pure speculations until the French Revolution, particularly during the period from 1793 to 1798. During this time an attempt was actually made, largely in law and completely in fact, to make marriage and the family such an agreement. This purely private conception of the family was followed, during the next century or so, by other experiments which attempted to do the same thing with parts of the Western family. One of these was a series of reforms in nineteenth-century America that endeavored to make divorce a pure reaction of the will of the local judge and to release women from legal responsibility in the family. Examples of the thinking of this period are the omnibus divorce clauses and the *feme sole* conception of married women. The *feme sole* idea looked upon the married woman as a single woman and, when carried to its full meaning, released her from the *manus* or common union with her husband. It resulted, in fact, in a form of social organization almost identical with that light sort of family popular under the early days of the Roman Empire, the *concubinatus*. A third experiment with the private family occurred during the Russian Revolution, following 1917, when the will of the parties concerned became, for a number of years, the dominant factor in the family. For a time a divorce action did not even require the consent of the other party, so that any marriage arrangement was merely an agreement which could be canceled at will by the unilateral wishes of either party. This practice was prevalent in France between 1794 and 1799, but never was so widespread as in the demoralization of Russian life during the 1920s.

A fourth experiment in the private contractual conception of the family is being carried on today, chiefly in America. Here it is more or less understood by all concerned that unless one party in the marriage disagrees, or appears before the judge and fights the case, all the old legal family safeguards are discarded. It used to be understood that the public would refuse a divorce to a married couple if one of them had condoned the act (permitted conjugal relations after the act was known to be committed), recriminated the act (done the same thing or similarly violated the marriage bond), or colluded the act (agreed to permit the violation in order to make a divorce possible). Those safeguards have now disappeared and the public has left the family restrictions largely to the enforcement of judges far away from the actual jurisdiction of the couple. Unless the parties themselves bring the evidence into court, a judge in Arkansas, Nevada, or several other states grants divorces almost automatically to persons who may reside as far away as Maine, Alaska, or South Carolina. The private contractual marriage and family have become established in the United States, although winked at by public opinion and the law. With only the partner's consent or his inability or unwillingness to make a public scandal, and particularly in the absence of children, anyone can get a divorce at will in America now, after a few weeks' temporary residence under a false jurisdiction. Of course, if the lawyers learn that the client can afford to pay more, the divorce will be more expensive.

The Rise of Family Sociology

In the midst of this conception of the family as a private institution, as opposed to a group regulated by the church, the clan, or the state, there arose a school of sociology that has devoted itself to studying the family. The first great writers in the school were a Swiss jurist, J. J. Bachofen, who about 1861 published a book called the *Mother-Law* or *Das Mutterrecht*; an English jurist, Henry Sumner Maine, who in the same year published *Ancient Law*; and an English sociologist, Herbert Spencer, who in his treatises on sociology paid considerable attention to the place and role of the family in his evolutionary schemes for interpreting the whole history and destiny of mankind. There had been one or two earlier works, such as that by Unger in Germany about 1850; but after this time there was a deluge of books devoted either wholly or partly to history, law, and ethnology, which gave an entirely new interpretation of the family. The new ideas gained headway and spread, so that practically all writers on the social sciences "found" the conclusions true for their studies. Some examples of this are the reaffirmations by many historians that most of the fantastic tales reported by Herodotus (b. 484 B.C.)—stories of Amazonian women and of the purchase and sale of marriage partners—were true of early Greece and other areas of the Mediterranean he had not seen.

The chief ideas developed by this new school of family sociology may be listed and criticized as follows:

These principles emphasized the fact that the family had a definite beginning, an original type, that could be determined. In contrast to the Platonic conception that origins could hardly be calculated or, if approximated, were to be discovered in a systematic examination of historical processes, the new school launched into an immature conception of the rise and destiny of the family. In doing this, they postulated straight-line evolutionary theories of the family, extending from its theoretical origin until the present and on into the future. Instead of developing a conception of numerous families to fit numerous conditions, as Plato in *The Laws* (III) suggested several forms of government to fit the changes in the state, they postulated an onward sweep of man with an ever-changing, never-repeating system of family types.

To find this origin, these family sociologists had to imagine a primitive man. The hundreds of studies, then available, of isolated and disappearing primitive groups in faraway islands of the Pacific gave them the idea that here was original man in his pristine archaic social organization. From him they could learn the origin of the family. From nineteenth-century Europe they could learn its progress. By taking a sight between these two observations, they could plot and predict the development of the family for centuries to come. Consequently, the smaller isolated peoples became the main observational stage for understanding the family of highly cultured and civilized man. The "unknowns" in this series of evolutionary observations were the far past and the future; the "known" was the nineteenth-century family. Hence, the deciding issue was what had happened to the family, or what was imagined to have happened in the past, in far-off places, among peoples different in nature, in nurture, and in total psychosocial experience from the fairly recent north European barbarians and Romanized peoples who constituted Western civilization.

Neglect of History

In developing this scheme, they got into a quandary. What of history? What about the Council of Trent, the Lateran Council? What about Pierre Lombard, St. Thomas Aquinas, barbarian law, the Corpus Juris Civilis of the Roman Empire, St. Augustine, Manicheanism, early Roman codes, the Roman Twelve Tables, the early Roman *gens* organization and rule, the Greek family of Plato, Aristotle, Demosthenes, Xenophon, the law cases of the late Greek orators, the family in Pericles' time, the family as seen by Thucydides and Herodotus, the family of Hesiod and his brother Persus, or, most important, the families of the Homeric period? What about the origin and development of canon law in the Latin church; the experience of canon law in the Greek Orthodox, Slavic, and Byzantian churches? How about the Slavic barbarian family; the family brought into Europe by the Mongol invasions; the family of the heroic legends of all European peoples, whether Beowulfian England or the other great folk creations of northern Europe? How about the Vedic hymns, the Ramayana and Mahabharata, and the history and legends of China? How about the different types of families in the old Hebrew works?

These are a few of the many highlights in the family that belong to the actual history of our people, five and ten thousand years ago. How could these family sociologists handle these data in their sweeping, one-way, linear schemes of development and change in our family system? What about these facts that we *know* are part of our lives?

To these questions the family sociologists until this date have largely had three, and only three, answers—"skip it," "mix it up with something else, misinterpret it, and call it the same thing," or "forget it."

Neglect of Logical, Meaningful, and Causal Analysis

Finally, these family sociologists have in most cases abstained from a careful logical and causal analysis of the factors involved in the family. Aristotle's dictum that if children did not love their parents and family members, they would love no one but themselves would have caused them to stop and realize that, in the absence of strong external forces, no human society could long exist. If they had observed this fact carefully, that the attachments basic to human society all arise and take their orientation from the human family, they could have found the key to an understanding of family types. In the absence of strong central governments, a condition in which most of human society has existed off and on for centuries, familism as a key to the internal strength of social groups must have played a much greater role in social order than in other periods. Such a logical analysis would have enabled them to see at once that the family was differentiated fundamentally from time to time as to its sovereignty. What differentiating roles does the family have to play in social order in societies which have many or in those which have few other agencies interested in social order—in livable human conditions?

With this logical thought in mind, they could have seen that periods like that of nineteenth-century Western society, with its strong governments, its abundant codes of laws, and its multiple agencies for the control of human beings, were relatively minute times in history, minor segments compared with the longer centuries in which strong national governments and statute laws were unimportant in the day-by-day life of peoples. This thought would have led them to examine more closely the forms of rule and order in the "common law" periods of societies. They would have picked the period in Greece when statute law and strong states ruled, contrasted it with similar periods in Rome immediately preceding and during the empire period, and with the modern period after the Protestant movement when the secular state rose to power again.

If this had been done by the family sociologists, they would have found a meaningful relation between the type of family and strong central governments and abundance of statute law agencies for social control. They also would have found meaningful relations between the conditions in periods—such as our own Dark Age, from the fifth to the tenth or twelfth centuries, the early or Homeric period in Greece and the Roman period prior to the first law code, the Twelve Tables—in which all these strong governments and statute law social-control agencies did not exist, and the strength, sovereignty, and role of the family in those periods. In other words, they would have found in each society that there were periods in which the trusteeship for social control and order, and the very existence of society, were held in family hands—the trustee family times. They would have discovered "in between" periods when, throughout the developments of several centuries, the trustee periods were giving way but the strong modern governments had not yet completely established themselves. Logically, they would have compared similar periods in several societies, such as the Greek from the ninth to the fifth centuries B.C., the Roman from the Twelve Tables code to the formation of the empire, and modern society from the first stirrings of the Protestant Revolution and the embryonic start of "sovereign" states. These periods extended from the first revolts against localism until the times when law and order became completely a state function. They would have discovered in these periods a mixed family type, partly one and partly another. They would have discovered the domestic family periods, as these will be called hereafter in this work.

Finally, these family sociologists would have seen that the abundance of law and order agencies and the multiplicity of external bonds holding societies together during the periods of statute law and strongly developed central governments made the internal cohesion of family groups less and less necessary as a unified social force. These would then naturally become periods of the emergence of the individual, the social "atom," the atomistic family periods.

Then if the family sociologists had gone a little further, they would have concluded that the facts of sociology are *acts with meaning* attached to them. A sum of money paid to a wife for the weekly budget is the same act as money paid another woman for other purposes, but sociologically these have entirely different meanings. In the one case, the payment means a home, loyalty, privilege, responsibility, status, children, obligations to rear these children according to fixed rules and regulations, and oftentimes, when we become as attached to them as if they were part of our own bodies, giving them to die for their country, because we also gave them status as citizens by giving them our names, our status, our rights, privileges, and responsibilities. In the other case, the act has a transient meaning, one that is ephemeral and of no possible comparable significance.

Reversing the situation, the family sociologists, with their broad and sweeping generalizations about society, would have seen that they had based most of these theories upon the classification together of acts without their attached meanings, and which in their essence had the most violently opposed and differing meanings. The family sociologists have assumed that these widely separated acts had the same significance and meaning because they "appeared alike." Such is the type of thinking in the wife-purchase theory, one that is attributed to certain types of societies in the alleged evolution from wife-stealing to wife-purchase and finally to romantic love marriage. They would have realized that all that was involved in the "proof" of this theory was the fact that in some societies men give economic goods to their wives' families before taking a wife from that family. This could mean either the purchase of a woman or an economic condition antecedent to the consummation of a marriage union between two families, not unlike an engagement ring, a settlement upon a wife, a dowry, or any other specific form of exchange of gifts within and between families and marriage partners upon the entering of those close social relations that marriage and familism entail.

The neglect of logic and meaning was a symptom of, and also a condition antecedent to, the fact that these family sociologists have not given us a thorough causal analysis of the changes in the human family. We do not have today any comprehensive analysis of familism in terms of cause and law, two basic reasons for the existence of a science of sociology. Cause and law, two factors sometimes related and sometimes not, are the primary differences between a record of social events concerning the family and the existence of a science of sociology. If logic and meaning be neglected, we cannot have an analysis in terms of cause and law.

In the field of the family there are numerous haphazard generalizations about the breaking-up of the family and its influence upon human behavior. Yet we have no significant causal analysis of why the alleged break-up of the family occurs. Most sociologists attribute it loosely to the industrial system, which they claim does not require family unity any longer; yet they do not find the industrial system opposed to the family. But on the other hand, the human characteristics which they allege are being destroyed by the break-up of the family evidently need familism, if this causal analysis is true. Thus we have, on the one hand, an institution which is breaking up because it is not needed and, on the other, a great many juveniles who are breaking up because they do not have the proper family backgrounds. The family is, therefore, both needed and not needed. The two brief analyses of cause, one entirely separate from the other, cite two types of needs, one human and the other industrial, one unimportant (industrial) and the other important (human), as reasons for antithetical attitudes about the family and the distinct behavior of the family.

This argument will not be continued further here. It is evident that logical, meaningful, and causal analysis of the family has not been carried far by the modern family sociologists. Nowhere has it been suggested that the family might be a changing element in social change—a result at one time, a cause at another.

The Purpose and Plan of This Work

To fill in these discrepancies, to bring history, logic, meaning, and causal analysis into family sociology—these are the purposes of this work. History must be brought into family sociology, not as isolated and meaningless events, but as integrated interpretations of the why and wherefore of family behavior.

The aim is to discuss the family in its relation to civilization, with four standards or ideals as to what constitutes a perfect sociological analysis. First comes *criticism*. Are the previous theories of the family valid, once they have been dragged out and examined in the cold light of day? Second, what has been the previous *history* of the "civilized" family? Is it a derivative of people and family systems of the Homeric and Beowulfian types, or is it related more to the Trobriand Islanders cited by Malinowski and Folsom or the hundreds of small primitive isolated groups brought into the analyses of Westermarck, Spencer, and others? Third, there is *thoughtful* analysis. Can the family be examined from the same analytical point of view applied to social problems by the great fathers of thought, Socrates, Plato, and Aristotle? When they took up a problem for discussion, they always examined the relations between the matters discussed in all their possible implications. No idea could have any definitive meaning for them until it had been searchingly criticized from all points of view. Fourth is *causal* examination. Is the family a cause of development and change in civilization, or is civilization a cause of variations in the family? Or do both influences work? If so, when and how?

These four points of view—criticism, history, thoughtful analysis, and causal examination applied to the family—form the basis, the point of view, and the *raison d'être* of this work.

The family as a social institution is part of the life of everyone. We are here as the result of the family, we are the products of families, most of us create families of our own, and when we die those families bury us and mourn our passing. If we have done good while here, this is remembered and worshipped. If we have not done good, this is excused and forgotten. If one is in trouble, the family is the first to help and the last to condemn. If one does not create a family of his own, he or she lives in a world where family law and family mores sharply define the most important phases of conduct.

Most of the sentiment and emotion of the world is centered about the family or is of a family nature. God is the Father, and His chief representative in this world is the Son. The work of the Father and the Son is called "divine." Father-love and mother-love and "Honor thy father and mother" are three subjects that are always taken seriously. Homer's Greeks made their gods a quarrelsome trustee family. Our ancestors in Beowulf's time made their devils (Grendel and his mother) a feuding trustee family, just like some of those in our own Southern highlands today.

Yet when one starts to write about the sociology of the family, he finds that the elementary concepts of the subject have been the objects of diverse interpretation and bitter controversy. What is the family? What influence does or should it have upon human character? What is its future? What attitude should the intellectual class have toward it? Does it merit condemnation or praise? All these questions and many more have been the subjects of violent debate.

On one side are the persons who wish to consider the family as a group which must continually justify itself by overt acts. To them the family is a contractual group. If it fails in any particular time or situation, then it is outmoded and will or must pass away. On the other side are the pro-family people who consider the family as an institution not to be questioned any more than life itself. To them the family is a natural group like the swarm of bees or colony of ants. Every age has its sophists and its Socratics. This is mentioned here because Socrates was accused of impiety and leading Athenian youth astray by being a sophist. In defending his teacher and describing the relation between Socrates and his son, Xenophon, in *Memorabilia*, wrote one of the most, if not the most, human parental documents in existence.

These two groups which take sides about the family may be called the family negationists, on the one hand, and the familists, on the other. Both are idealists, but both cannot be right. The family negationists are opposed to any concept of a dominant-submissive family inculcating order, security, and organization in society. [J. K.] Folsom calls one group democratic and implies that the other is not. However, Folsom misses the whole point, since the problem is not one of democracy. This same type of argument is as old as human history, whereas democracy, in the sense of a very limited domination of collectivity over the individual, is a new thing, a form of social organization that requires much more familism than Folsom's negationism.

Certain words are given good or bad meanings at various times. One can hardly express meaning without arousing undue emotion. Up until and after Andrew Jackson's time, the word *democracy* produced a disagreeable effect in the United States. Two unpopular words now are *dominant* and *submissive*. As used here they have the following nonemotional significance. A group is a power organization. A family, a community, or a state has social power. This power may be limited, or it may, as in the totalitarian state, be great. The power of the modern family, contrasted with what it has been at other times, is not great. The power of the present family is limited largely to domestic functions and an attempt to keep harmony among the children until they know better and can do this for themselves. Nevertheless, family power today is much greater than that of other organizations, excluding the state and its all-embracing political agencies. Each power organization tends to polarize itself into dominant and submissive agencies or persons or transpersonalized figures such as parent and child, leader and led. This does not imply autocracy or oppression, because those terms are descriptive of how power is *used* and not of what is *possessed*. In the family, for most purposes, any member can become the dominator and the others the submissors. A vigorous baby or an adolescent can dominate a family in wholesale fashion. Sometimes the roles change from day to day and from function to function. Some phases of the family become transpersonalized in that the state or the community calls upon the parent to do things and holds him responsible. In this case the parent, and most often the wife, but oftentimes the child, represents the transpersonalized family power in carrying out family missions.

This discussion between the family negationists and the familists has a bearing on sociology in that a nomographic or law-seeking science attempts to get at the facts with meaning. It seeks to evaluate and explain the family as an integral part of society, not to criticize or to blame it. The purpose is neither to defend nor to attack the family. If the family is a necessary and natural institution, little that is said here can bring it into disrepute. If the family, as the negationists claim, is a private contractual form of human relationship, the result of a particular and passing type of social organization, the most spirited intellectual defense could not long delay its end.

Family Sociology and the Idea of Progress

During the nineteenth and early twentieth centuries, while family sociology was developing as a separate social discipline, certain characteristic ideas dominated social thinking. Some of these were theories of continuous evolution in one direction; ideas that social groups are contractual, man-made, incidental, and nominalist in nature; the conception that a social science has as its main duty to unfold the social process, to look back upon its past and into its future; and finally, that the active social scientist was to help in the negation of all social forms or institutions that were out of place, were obstructions, or were not on the right track. Social science was to eliminate archaic anachronisms, to battle against cultural lag, and to guide the social process toward a newer and better society.

Beneath all this, of course, was the attitude that social science was "scientific" and looked only for the facts. But who could deny the obvious progressive one-way evolution which everyone saw about him and believed in as an article of faith? The idea of progress toward an ultimate good was adopted as the sole field of the devotees of continuous movement in one direction, nominalism in social relations, and negation of the older family types. As Plato sought the ultimate good in social relations, so did these family sociologists; but, unlike Plato, they never gave the "good" a sound logical and historical analysis. The family sociologists were unwilling to give any credit to a theory of the good or desirable, to anyone who would have suggested limits to the constant movement towards nominalism, contractualism, and negation in family bonds.

During this period, and up until the present confusion, the main integrative theories of family sociology were centered around the evolutionary, or continuous-movement-in-one-direction, school of thought. Since continuous movement in one direction involved the shucking off or negation of familistic bonds, the dominant sociological family theories were of this nature. Some held that we must find the perfect happiness or ultimate good in easy divorce; a second group, that we must free the family from patriarchism; a third, in eliminating the burdens of child-rearing; a fourth, in securing the proper sex adaptation between partners; a fifth, in increasing individual happiness by the proper mating selection and practices; and many others in various eliminations and reforms. All of these ideas have as their fountainhead the evolutionary school of thought, which has stolen good intentions and scientific analysis, mixed them with progress, and claimed them as the sole property of the school of continuous change in one direction, as regards the family.

This movement in the field of the family is not new or unique to this last century. In some respects, it has been under way ever since, or even before, the twelfth or thirteenth centuries and has had some manifestation in every century since that time. It had a firm beginning with the rise of nationalism and the Protestant conception that the family bond was holy but not a sacrament. It led through the philosophical conception of the eighteenth century that the family was a union based upon private contract with only incidental, but necessary, civil implications. The nineteenth- and early twentieth-century schools of family sociology, with their consistently negative attitudes toward the binding and displeasing aspects of the family unit, were but the wholesale development of centuries of previous thought which in a smaller way had the same attitude toward familism.

Thus modern thinking about the family, other than the scholasticism of the Christian church, has been largely a product of the Reformation and has attributed to the family all those elements of nominalism and contractualism so prevalent in institutional thinking since that period. Just as John Locke, J. J. Rousseau, Thomas Paine, and a number of the Founding Fathers of our own nation could hold that the social compact—government—if it became unsatisfactory to the body of the people could be abolished for a new form, so the developing school of family negationists could hold that unsatisfactory family types had been, are being, and will continue to be abolished. This does not deny the existence of a strong minority who have held to absolutism in both social and family compacts; but the prevailing schools of thought have been, as far as the family is concerned, negationists and evolutionists.

Negation and evolution in the theory of family sociology have held that progress, or the constant linear or stair-step movement toward human betterment, consisted in the dropping of family bonds and the perpetual creation of new types of families. This has been extended in family philosophy to include a *world theory* and a *world history* of the family, extending the doctrines back into the dawn of life and forward to new conditions as yet only in the offing. The great works in family sociology by Maine, Bachofen, Lubbock, Spencer, Starcke, Westermarck, McLennan, Engels, Bebel, Howard, and many others present, support, and operate upon the hypotheses of linear negation of the family. Such is also the case, with some variation and with negligible exceptions, down to the active or implied statements in all current works.

However, as we shall show in this work, disintegration of the family into contractual and noninstitutional forms is so devastating to high cultural society that these atypical forms can last only a short while and will in time have to be corrected. The family reappears by counterrevolutions. All of these facts strike directly at most of the family sociology which seeks to hold that the "unrestrained individual" is the end of society and the family his private agent.

2

FAMILY TYPES AND CIVILIZATION

I N THIS CHAPTER, THE AIM is to classify the family of civilization into types, to show the principle and logic of this classification, and to make some preliminary remarks about the structural mobility of these families or types in civilization changes.

Family Typology

Type, in the sense used here, means the idealized conception of a form. In this analysis, the ideal or typological method developed by Le Play and set forth systematically by Max Weber is used. Not all families at any given time are of the type specified as characteristic of that age. In Homeric Greece we find that the trustee family is typical. This same family appears later as the dominant form in Europe after the Roman decay. However, in Homeric Greece and in Europe of the Dark Ages there were numerous types of families. Nevertheless, the idealized form which the people felt was best fitted to their situation was the trustee family. In the absence of strong reasons to the contrary, that form continually appeared, recreated itself, and rose to power. Today, when we use the term atomistic family, we do not imply that all families are of the atomistic or conjugal type. All our actions, however, assume that this form is dominant.

A few years ago a young girl, member of one of the trustee families in the Southern Appalachians, while not yet at the age of consent, went out at night with a notorious character in the neighborhood, against her father's will. When she returned, her father attempted to administer corporal punishment, as was the custom of the community. She killed her father and was sentenced to life imprisonment for murder. Her case became a cause célèbre and many people rushed to her financial aid. They assumed that the atomistic family conceptions should play the dominant role in this case. The people in the neighborhood who passed judgment on the case still held to the old Beowulfian conceptions of our ancestors, that kin-murder and parricide are the most heinous of offenses.

It is not our purpose to pass judgment upon this case. It merely shows that antithetical family systems can exist side by side.

Most classifications of the family do not tell us how the family functions or what it really means. They classify the whole by alleged characteristics of parts. They do not get at the fundamental issue concerning the family, its power or ability to function and its field of action.

To meet this problem a new classification is used which combines the power of the family as a social unit with the social functions the society delegates to the family. Of the total power in the society, how much belongs to the family? Of the total amount of control of action in the society, how much is left for the family? What role does the family play in the total business of society? These are the real problems. If we want to marry or to break up a family, whom do we consult, the family, the church, or the state? If we are in need, to whom do we go, the family or the community? If we violate a rule, who punishes us, the family or the state?

This leads us to the logical conclusion that there can be three main family types. One is the trustee family which has the most power, the widest field of action, and the greatest amount of social control. The completely opposite type is the atomistic family, which has the least power and the smallest possible field of action. An intermediate type is the domestic family, in which the balance of power is distributed between the family and other agencies.

The family as an institution and as an aggregation of persons can assume three potential forms: maximum strength, middle strength, and maximum weakness. These may be called respectively the trustee, the domestic, and the atomistic or individualistic families. The polar types are those of maximum strength (trustee) and maximum weakness (atomistic). The central type, that of middle strength (domestic), has some mixture of the characteristics of both of the other types. When the family attains maximum strength it tends to break up of its own accord, mainly because of internal incompatibility and its failure to satisfy either family needs or individual desires. If it breaks up because of internal incompatibility, the result is generally the splitting of the trustee family into several similar families or the destruction of part of its power by the state. If it breaks up because of its failure to satisfy the needs of individualism, it is generally modified by the state by a reduction of its power and it moves toward the middle, or domestic, type.

In the same manner, the extremely weak family (atomistic) also can break up because it fails to carry on the necessary family functions or because it fails to satisfy the needs of individualism. If the atomistic family fails to satisfy the necessary family functions, the state helps to break it up, through legal fiction or positive law, and to move it toward the middle type or domestic family. When it fails to satisfy extreme individualism, the atomistic family is broken up by the individuals, oftentimes with the aid and blessing of the state, and the end result is temporary family negativism, nullification, or nihilism. When the state permits the weakened or atomistic family to break up completely, the state loses a certain amount of power in one of its subordinate units and this must be supplied through tutorship (the fiction of the state as parent) or through public support of aged and infirm adults in case they do not need juvenile tutorship and are incapable of existing as unattached individuals.

This gives us great contrasting periods in family law, those long centuries when the state was trying to break down the overstrong trustee family, and the alternate periods when the state was trying to build up or cure the overweakened atomistic family. Thus from the twelfth to the fifth centuries

B.C. in ancient Greece, the general temper of law reform of the family was to destroy and weaken the power of the great family (trustee type) of the Homeric Age. A similar period came in the Roman Empire from the time of the Code of the Twelve Tables (placed by Mommsen at 451 and 450 B.C.) down probably to the time of Augustus, the first emperor, who reigned from about 30 B.C. to 14 A.D. At that time, a new temper of family law set in, signalized by the two laws *Leges Julia de adulteriis* and *de maritandis ordinibus* (18 B.C.) and *Lex Papia Poppaea* (9 A.D.). However, this is only an arbitrary time, as social changes move over long periods. This period in Rome was one in which the old powers of the *gentes* were almost completely destroyed. A third similar period of legislation against the older family came from the twelfth or thirteenth to the end of the eighteenth centuries in Western society, during which time familism as outlined by St. Thomas Aquinas lost most of its power through the rise of the conceptions of absolute divorce and the contractual nature of social organization. This again is purely an arbitrary time limit and could be moved either way, according to the point of view of the student and the century concerned.

Whereas these three periods were long ones, in which the states or the governments, because of popular pressure, were more or less trying to break down the extreme power formerly in the hands of the trustee family type, they have each been succeeded largely by long periods in which the state tried to build up and protect the weakening family. In the case of the Greeks, in spite of the fact that the fifth century B.C. was the Sophist period, the general spirit soon changed to help the family with its problems of maintaining itself against the growing individualism. In Rome from the time of Augustus to that of Constantine, continuous attempts were made by all types to build up the family or to have the state or the public fill in where the family failed. Constantine (306–37 A.D.) abolished the laws against celibacy and reduced the penalties for small families, particularly the laws of succession and citizenship. Justinian (527–65 A.D.) did away with all traces of the Augustinian family reform code. All privileges of parenthood were abolished. The typical feeling of Justinian's time can be characterized by the philosophy of Sozoneme in his *Ecclesiastical History*. Here he held that the number of people increased or decreased according to Providence and not according to any human wish.

In modern society, of course, affected by the colonization of the New World and the Industrial Revolution, as well as by the population spurt of the ninetenth century, this same movement to strengthen the family has gone on, gaining its widest headway since the last two wars and the belief that population decay was menacing the very existence of the states themselves.

These details will be discussed at length in the later chapters on the respective cultures. The important point now is to tell what is meant by these three family types—trustee, domestic, and atomistic.

The Trustee Family

The *trustee* family is so named because it more or less considers itself as immortal, existing in perpetuity and never being extinguished. As a result, the living members are not *the* family, but merely "trustees" of its blood, rights, property, name, and position for their lifetimes. The family is supposed to have existed and to continue to exist forever, so that the individual is subject to family duties first of all, if the family needs him. This type of family has the greatest degree of power it ever held, amounting in extreme cases to the right of life or death over its members. That is, in case of parricide or matricide, the family, being the punishing power and the main local manifestation of *total* power, can put the individual to death, sell him into slavery, or banish him as an outcast to make his living, if he can, as a pirate or a robber. In the early Roman family this was known as "giving to the gods," which meant simply that the individual was killed in the name of one of the gods. The offense did not necessarily have to be as bad as parricide, because many of those families considered economic offenses against the family, such as destroying a cornerstone of the family lands or menacing the future of the family, as serious offenses often ending in death.

Another extreme power in the hands of this trustee type of family arose out of the common responsibility of the family to another injured family for the crimes of its members. This is known in early law as *passive solidarity*, which means that each member must either pay a part of the damages arising out of the actions of another member, or help deliver him up for fine, banishment, death, or other punishment. The obverse of this is an extreme form of responsibility known under the law as *active solidarity*, meaning that an injured member of one family must call on other members, through the family, to help him secure revenge or justice for wrongs done to him. In later days we see these laws in our own highland families where each family member is expected to take part in feuds against other families; if a member of one family has injured a member of another family, many may be killed in the resultant feud. In the old days, these laws existed in periods of dominance of the trustee family under the name of *active and passive solidarity for blood vengeance.* Later these same types of solidarity existed for collecting money or property damages.

In this trustee family, rights, except for a minimum of biological needs that can hardly be collectivized, belong primarily not to the individual but to the family. The family passes or imputes these rights to the individual. The state is a unity of families and looks to the family to govern, protect, support, discipline, and take responsibility for its members. The state is a unity of *gentes* or *genos.* There is hardly any appeal from the family to the state, because the current conception is that the family business does not concern the state. If a person violates the governing power, this act of treason becomes family treason and can result, and many times has, in complete banishment of the family. The individual lives within and for his family, once his few biological needs are satisfied. The family council, generally an informal meeting of relatives, decides on a head, or a process of automatic selection is used. The person selected is given responsibility and power not in *himself* but as *family head.* He often holds the most extreme power when carrying out family responsibilities and purposes, but as an individual he is extremely weak because he is also only a family member and, as such, has only the limited rights of any other member.

Here is one of the great sources of the most common misinterpretations of the early or allegedly primitive family, the patriarchal power attributed to the early family by Henry Sumner Maine. According to Maine, the family began with a patriarch. The evolution of the family was from this patriarch to the individual, from status to contract. This same misinterpretation is found in most generalizations about the Roman family in which it is assumed that there was an absolute *patria potestas*. The high power which the head of the *early* Roman family alone had was not the power of husband over wife or parent over child. It was the power given to the family head, acting as trustee, *only* for the purpose of carrying out the public or social responsibilities delegated to the family at that time.

The Domestic Family

The *domestic* family is a middle type, arising out of modifications of the trustee family or being revived by governmental or religious sanctions from the atomistic type. The domestic family is the most common type in this world. It satisfies to some extent the natural desires for freedom from family bonds and for individualism, yet it also preserves sufficient social structure to enable the state or body politic to depend upon it as an aid in government and as a source of the extreme power needed by states in carrying out their functions. It is particularly necessary in the imperialistic or militaristic state, or in a state (like Sweden) in an imperialistic and militaristic world of states. These are most common in civilized society. To date they are about all we have known. This domestic family possesses a certain amount of mobility and freedom and still keeps up the minimum amount of familism necessary for carrying on the society.

In highly dynamic societies (those which flourish and die like organic things, as Spengler would have us believe), the domestic family has always been a transitional one, lasting several centuries before the onset of the atomistic type. In static societies it has lasted much longer, oftentimes not perceivably being replaced by the atomistic. Consequently, in a dynamic society it is a changing organism, varying from the period of the first great breakdown of trustee powers through the complete emergence of the almost free person or individual in the atomistic type. Probably in different societies the limits of this time are varied, but it can generally be set apart by the great onslaughts against *active* family solidarity in matters of criminal law, through the decline of the *passive* solidarity of the family in its responsibility to the state. The end of *passive* solidarity marks the almost complete emergence of the individual before the law. Thus, the history of the domestic family includes a long series of changes in this decline of *passive* solidarity, leading to the rise of conceptions of absolute divorce. The trustee family has largely only repudiation, or a family-decided divorce. The domestic family has a middle type of divorce, such as *a mensa et a thoro* (from bed and board only). Absolute and free divorce, when it is popular, is more of a trait of the atomistic times and families, although fundamentally all types of families provide some escape from impossible situations.

It must be made clear that we are speaking here of family *types* and more or less dividing history according to the type which is predominant. All three types—trustee, domestic, and atomistic—are prevalent in any country at any time. Illustrations in contemporary America are the urban family—chiefly Protestant, although spreading among the Catholics—which is almost completely atomistic. Our farm and rural families are still to a large extent the domestic type. The trustee type exists in remnants in our highlands in the Eastern and Southern United States.

It is rather unfair to the trustee type to mention only the degenerate cases which come to our attention in popular literature today. Many of our old Southern families, as well as the New York and Yankee colonial types, are of the trustee make-up, but they are not written up in the newspapers or current literature because of their feuds and blood vengeance or their cohesiveness in exacting a living in a parasitical manner from contemporary public relief activities or small crime.

This second type of family is called domestic because it arises under conditions when trade sets in and when the freeflowing of values, lands, goods, and persons is essential to commerce. The beginnings of extended commerce among the Greeks led to the gradual envelopment of the trustee type in the domestic. The same thing happened in Rome at about the time of the Twelve Tables, when commerce, which was to lead to the Punic Wars and the Roman Empire, began to blossom forth as a major activity. It also occurred in modern society when the Renaissance called forth a revival of trade, and the old anticommercial laws against interest, profits, and commerce had to be abrogated.

The rise of the commercialization of the manor, when the British manorial lords wanted the lands enclosed for sheep raising instead of the crop-growing and subsistence activities of the people, had to have some new form of family organization in order to make arrangements for the enclosure of the fields, an action which went against common rights of the masses of small farmers. The villeins held the largely hereditary rights to the positions and fruits of the manor.

This was domestic because the dominant thought now appearing was that the domestic or home-residing and -living family owned the family property and could give clear titles to it, despite the rights of future members. Obviously, no one would enclose a piece of property if the descendants of the persons who made the agreement would come back and reclaim the property again. If the property belonged to the living members of the family, absolute sale or disposal of it could be achieved in one way or another.

It should be pointed out that ownership of property was a series of rights and that the man on the manor, the hereditary tenant, while not owning land in *fee simple* as we think of it in America today, still held rights in the produce from the land, and, in a limited sense, held owner-ship to the property. His family ownership was in conjunction with that of the lord and others who shared in the proceeds.

The domestic family includes in its major conceptions of the family those members of the domestic group who are living and who influence decisions about family living, family behavior, and family property. In the domestic family, in order to make property free for alienation, the legal fiction of extreme *patria potestas* creeps in again. In order to free the head to give title to the property, the fiction is developed that the head is absolute owner, lord of all he owns, and the remainder of the family, wives, children, slaves, and property are under him. They are under his hand or *manus* (in Rome, *potestas* was used for children and later a new term *dominum* was developed for property), or *covert* (under his cover, or incapable of acting or even having a jurisdiction except with and through him; this practice was Anglo-Saxon). This unintentionally gives the husband arbitrary power, something not intended by the law, so that since the early Twelve Tables and since early medieval Anglo-Saxon common law, there have been constant revisions taking away this patriarchal power inadvertently granted the family head.

This is another of the sources of misinterpretation of the family as having originally been a despotic thing and of the idea that human progress has been directed from despotism toward equality. The conception of arbitrary power being given the head at the beginning of the rise of the domestic family was legal fiction. This was intended for the freeing of property and not to give the head of the family *other* power incompatible with the gradual movement toward the rise of the organization of the state as an aggregate of individuals. The state wishes to have only enough family power left as is needed to achieve the functions of government.

The Atomistic Family

This family type is called *atomistic* because of the rise of the conception ·
that, as far as is compatible with the successful carrying-on of society, the individual is to be freed of the family bonds, and the state is to become much more an organization of individuals. Atomism as a theory of the physical nature of the universe arose with the onslaught of the Greek atomistic family, having first been set forth fully in the works of Leucippus and Democritus in the fifth century B.C. This type of family was most prevalent in times of individualism, such as after the fifth century B.C. in Greek culture and after the reign of Augustus in Rome, and it certainly became exceedingly prominent in the eighteenth and nineteenth centuries of our time.

If the trustee family represents the great family, measuring greatness in terms of legal and social power and responsibilities given the family, the atomistic family represents the great individual, measuring individualism in terms of legal and social power and responsibility given the individual.

In trustee times, the family was held responsible for the individual and the individual was held accountable to the family. In atomistic times, the individual is held responsible for himself and he alone is accountable to the state, or through the state to other persons.

In trustee times, the family was sacred. Thus the early *gentes* of the Romans was a sacred thing, with its conceptions of common origin and common god or religious deity. The same applied to the conception of the Homeric family. Acts against the family were antireligious acts. Refusing to accept family responsibility, such as the call to leadership, or to help in the pursuit and punishment of those who had committed acts against the family, was profanity. People really felt that way and acted accordingly.

This same sacredness (*fidelitas*) appeared again in the trustee family when it gained ascendancy after the decline of the old Roman Empire. The family was the major social value of the people. Among the French and German barbarians many of the old practices similar to those of the Homeric days and the times of the *gentes* before the Twelve Tables rose to the forefront again. *Fidelitas*, a family principle, dominated the whole society, as [Pitirim] Sorokin has shown in his analysis of the life from the eighth to the fourteenth centuries of our era.

On the contrary, in the atomistic period, the individual becomes sacred. This may be measured in the rise of the conception that the illegitimate child must not be excluded from full social position because of the illegitimacy of his origin. Thus, in later Greece, illegitimate children were admitted to citizenship. And during the atomistic period in Rome, children were easily legitimized because of the shortage of population and the conceptions that children were necessary for inheritance and for political preferment or action.

The study of illegitimacy by the League of Nations makes quite a point of the fact that when the Christian church gained power, its attempts to purify the family mores transformed the legal and social position of illegitimate children.

"Concubinage was disavowed and, to bring about its disappearance, the Emperors introduced various restrictive measures preventing illegitimate and legitimate children from being placed on the same footing." This statement in the League of Nations publication refers to a sort of free marriage, known as *concubinatus*, which became popular among the well-to-do Romans during the empire. It was theoretically a monogamous institution (publicly recognized successive polygyny), because a man could not legally have two *concubinati*, or a wife and a *concubinatus*. It was not as respectable as *dignitas*, except in smart circles. A wife had a warmer degree of affection (*dilectus*) in the *dignitas* than in the *concubinatus*. The children of *concubinatus* were not under the father's *potestas*, but they were under a sort of maternal *potestas*. They must support their mother and, since the husband could not acquire the property of the *concubinatus*, they would naturally inherit it. *Concubinatus* was used frequently when men wished family life for a period of time, as when they set out to rule a province but did not want later complications over inheritance, children, or *potestas*. Thus, the problem of the major source of illegitimate children was solved by considering them products of an inferior type of marriage.

In spite of this way of doing things, which is rather different from ours, it is clear that the children who in our society would be illegitimate were given a much higher social standing in atomistic times than in the trustee period in the Roman Empire. This is an index of the sacredness now attached to the person, as contrasted with the family.

In our society the rise of the atomistic family has been associated with movements in every jurisdiction in the United States, and in most European states, to ease the laws against the illegitimate, who under old common law was *filius nullius*, or a child of no one. Under that condition, his rights were few. As Blackstone wrote in 1765:

> I next proceed to the rights and incapacities which appertain to a bastard. The rights are very few, being only such as he can *acquire*; for he can *inherit* nothing, being looked upon as the son of nobody; and sometimes called *filius nullius*, sometimes *filius populi*. Yet he may gain a sirname by reputation, though he has none by inheritance. All other children have their primary settlement in their father's parish; but a bastard in the parish where born, for he hath no father. . . . The incapacity of a bastard consists principally in this, that he cannot be heir to any one, neither can he have heirs,

> but of his own body; . . . A bastard was . . . incapable of holy orders
> . . . but this doctrine seems now obsolete. . . . A bastard may, lastly,
> be made legitimate, and capable of inheriting, by the transcendent
> power of an act of Parliament, and not otherwise. (*Commentaries*,
> 19th ed., London, 1832, 378–79.)

Today this harsh law has been almost completely changed. In America by 1939, two states, North Dakota and Arizona, held that all children were the legitimate issue of their natural parents. All states permitted legitimization by the acts of one or both parents. If the parents married later, the child became legitimate, although nineteen states required acknowledgment by the father. Parents are now responsible for the support of their children. This illustrates how today, in the period of the atomistic family, the individual has become sacred.

As the League of Nations study shows, in most modern countries the position of the ordinary illegitimate (as contrasted with the illegitimate born in adultery or incest) has come to resemble more and more closely that of legitimate children. The position of the illegitimates born in adultery (parents married to others at time of birth of child) and in incest (parents of forbidden degrees of marriage, such as of the same uterus) has also been moved toward the higher status, but not so far as the plain illegitimate (where parents are marriageable under the law, but are not married).

Thus the atomistic family is essentially the one found in societies where law and custom bring the individual, as far as possible, out from under the *covert*, the *manus*, the *potestas* of the family and make him the agent of the government, the one responsible directly to the law, and bound least to family obligations. The family, particularly in the classes where atomism has proceeded farthest, begins to be conceived merely as an association or, as the Chicago School of Sociology has popularized it, as a group of interacting personalities. It is not different from any other group of interacting personalities, even though it has the "life history" tag attached to each personality. The atomistic masses of the people, those freed from the restraint of custom and religious ideas, begin to think of the family as a private contract.

A marriage contract differs from a civil contract in that the five following provisions have in the past affected it:

1. It cannot be rescinded nor can its fundamental terms be changed by agreement of the parties concerned.

2. It results in status. Marriage, so far, makes a man husband, a woman wife, and children legitimate and entitled to national and other status of parents. Private civil contracts do not involve the parties in these ways.

3. The husband and wife, and even children, have their legal identities merged for common-law purposes, and common law is still the basis of most of our legal system.

4. It is not a contract in the sense of the Fourteenth Amendment to the Constitution, forbidding the legislation impairing the obligation of contract. (Changes in marriage laws, retroactive for earlier marriages, are not illegal or unconstitutional because of this.)

5. It differs as regards the statutes of limitations.

The present conception in the atomistic family is to make the marriage contract, as far as possible, a private or semi-civil contract. It follows naturally the course of the "Social Compact" school (1500–1800) which first differentiated clearly as to the *nature* of the family compact (and the national compact) and all other compacts. Then, in the revolutionary period at the end of the eighteenth century, the national or state compact became nullifiable like all other compacts. This was in French Revolutionary thinking and that of the South during our Civil War. Now inevitably we approach the period when the marriage compact is considered to be the same as any other compact. This is the ultimate implication of the characterization of the family as "merely a group of interacting personalities."

This gives us the general nature of the atomistic family conceptions, which will be made clearer as the discourse proceeds.

Summary

The following outline of the three types of families found in the cultures of high civilization is for the purpose of introduction only. As we proceed, further details and specifications will be made clear. At present, what has been said about them may be presented tabularly as follows:

Trustee Family	Domestic Family	Atomistic Family
	Greece	
Homeric period (to the end of 9th century B.C.	8th century B.C. to 5th century B.C. (to ascendancy of Sophism), Hesiod to Pericles.	From Sophism to end of classical Greece, where it joined with Roman atomistic family.
	Rome	
From the earliest tribes to the period of the Twelve Tables Code about 450 B.C.	From the Twelve Tables to Augustus (B.C.–A.D) to the *Leges Julia de Adulteriis* and *de marit. ordin.*	Augustus to Justinian (527 A.D.; tending to break up between Constantine and Justinian).
	Modern Western Society	
6th to 12th century A.D. (rise and dominance of canon law over the barbarians and remnants of Hellenic-Roman culture.	13th through 18th centuries (breaking up of conceptions of St. Thomas, rise of absolute divorce, domination of Protestant Revolution and capitalism).	From the 18th century rationalists to date. (Now probably breaking up.)

Trustee Family	Domestic Family	Atomistic Family

Main Conceptions of Property Ownership

Primarily to the family in perpetuity, the living members having its use only during their lifetime.	To the living family, primarily to the male head, so that alienation could be encompassed and trade become prominent.	Largely to the individual separate from the family. Marriage does not necessarily involve property transfer. Children get right to own income early.

Main Conceptions of Criminal Responsibility

Active and passive solidarity of the large family and clan for the actions of its members.	Passive solidarity of household members for all minor law violations but tending toward individual responsibility.	Practically individual responsibility (John Doe and Richard Roe).

3

FLUCTUATION OF THE FAMILY BOND

A CONSIDERATION OF THE THREE family types involves an analysis of the strength of the marriage bond. What are the inner forces holding the family together? How do they vary in strength? What are the outer forces and how do they vary in strength? No matter what may become of the family, what preconceptions are placed in the marriage formula as an indication of the intentions of the couple, or the couple and their families, who are joined by the marriage contract or bond? What about divorce? Is it possible? Is it used?

The family bond is a general title uniting all these various characteristics. Relations between husband and wife, parent and child, and the inner versus the outer relatives are a part of this, and yet they do not express it altogether. As an organization the family assumes peculiar meanings from time to time. These meanings express the whole organization of the separate parts and the complete integration of society insofar as society is organized about or reflected in the family.

Trustee, Domestic, and Atomistic
Conceptions of the Family Bond

The trustee family is founded on the conception of a uniting of personalities. Property, names, rights, theory of common origin, psychosocial beliefs (religious worship)—everything becomes the same. Under the "law," the husband and wife are responsible for each other, cannot ordinarily give evidence against each other, and husband, wife, and children belong to each other. Love is given the full meaning of delight, sacrifice, and sensual unity. The family may have its internal quarrels (an accompaniment of all close-knit organizations of any size), but against the outside world it is a unity. Divorce is more or less unthought of, only repudiation or separation being allowed by the mores. Marriage, repudiation, separation, and acceptance or rejection of a new member become formal legal actions carried out before a family council. The conception of marriage and the family bond is as near that of actual organic unity as human beings can make it.

In the domestic family all these trustee ties tend to become looser. In any given society, families of distinctly freer patterns exist side by side with others trying to preserve the older scheme of mutual life. A conception of separate property for man and wife begins to appear, but does not develop very far. Different forms of marriage begin to appear which are not so binding as before but still considered as arrangements made for life. Beliefs and rights of the parties start to differentiate. The social rules, according to which a man and his wife, or other relatives, are mutually responsible for a common crime, begin to change, so that a man may no longer be hanged alone for an offense committed jointly with his wife. Thus there could be no recurrence of the episode in thirteenth-century England in which a husband was hanged while his wife went free, although they had mutually forged a charter. Both would now be punished.

The husband begins to lose coresponsibility and also his right to exact punishment and to protect himself. Divorce becomes possible, though disreputable, and love loses some of its sacrificial meaning. Husband and wife are theoretically united for life but, if unbearable, the unity can be broken.

In the atomistic family, the whole series of conceptions loosens. Common property, common names, common rights, common theories of origin and psychosocial beliefs begin to break up. The idea of the strength of the marriage bond has moved from the conception of absorption and mutual guardianship to that of a loose contractual partnership, the terms of which are subject to constant review. Husband, wife, and children no longer "belong" to each other in any real sense. They are not fundamentally responsible for each other (allowing for the differences in capacity of minors). Interfamily suits are permissible, and, to some extent, each member is accepted as capable of giving evidence in the courts against the others. Love comes to mean sensual union only, although the fiction is maintained that the partners should have two conceptions of love. *Copula carnalis* is no longer held to be a specific family function, and its meaning inside the family changes. This is not to say that in the other family types sex relations outside of the family do not exist. But such as do exist are considered ignoble and "declassing." In the trustee and domestic families, public persons would not remember their concubines in their wills, as Aristotle remembers his to the amount of one drachma in addition to his previous gifts.

Absolute divorce increases, becomes very prevalent, is no longer considered declassing. The "cause idea" of divorce is extended to include "mutual consent." However, in contrast to the Roman atomistic society, others, such as ours, still partially maintain the fiction of an "innocent" party and a "guilty" one. At times the Roman atomistic family kept up the fiction of an injured and a guilty party; at others, depending upon the emperor, the matter of divorce was just what the parties concerned wished. Under the *concubinatus* or lesser form of marriage, dissolution was achieved openly, by consent, and with no idea of "cause" other than consent ever sought.

The Decline of the Graeco-Roman Family Systems

The Greek and Roman family systems went through the same basic stages as has the modern Western family system. Together, they illustrate the forms of the family found to be inherent in civilization.

The words, forms and types, are used here instead of cycles. This analysis has shown that there are three fundamental types of families, depending upon the amount of sovereignty, independence, home-rule, strength, and influence allowed them—the trustee, the domestic, and the atomistic. These three types, based upon the strength and independence of the family, are the only possible main forms, if we discount the minor variations which differ from country to country and from region to region and do not affect the fundamental forms. Movements of the family are from type to type, generally from the contemporary form to the one nearest it. Thus, normally, the trustee type becomes the domestic, or vice versa if it is making a "backward" movement toward family solidarity and strength. The family, like any other social institution, moves slowly and with minor changes, not great ones. The Greek trustee became the Greek domestic and the Roman did the same. The atomistic could come only after the domestic had achieved its full development.

The only possible cases evident in history of rapid changes in the family have been the reverses resulting in Eastern and Western Europe after the downfall of the Roman civilization. Here, the demoralized atomistic family of the old empire, both in East and West, was thrown into contact with great groups of new barbarians who belonged to trustee families. In the West these were largely the German and English barbarians of Northern and Western Europe. In the East, the Greek Byzantine family fell under the influences of Eastern "primitives," primarily the Slavs and Balkan barbarians, but also the Arabs and others who were included in the Mohammedan groups. There in each case a weak family system of the atomistic type came into contact with a dominant element of the trustee type. The Greek family, described by Polybius about 200 to 150 B.C., developed and weakened as noted by Plutarch down to the end of the empire, when it was thrown into contact with the hill tribes, the Slavs, the Mongols, and the unspoiled groups of "Pelasgians" still left in pockets of the Mediterranean area. The family of the West, described by the church fathers, was thrown into the hands of the Germans as recounted by Gregory of Tours. The whole Roman world family system, founded in its later stages upon Manicheanism or the cult of "eat, drink, and be merry, for tomorrow you die," fell into the hands of a new ruthless series of primitive groups, the "Scourges of God," as Attila and his followers were called.

Out of this, in the tenth and eleventh centuries in the West and about two centuries later in the East, came the domestic family, a compromise between the Roman atomistic and the old North European barbarian. The change from the original Roman atomistic at the beginning of this period to the domestic after the tenth century was not an immediate shift into the trustee, but first a compromise, in which the atomistic was enveloped by the trustee of the most primitive, blood vengeance sort, and then a final compromise, under the aegis of the church, which resulted in the domestic type.

Polybius gives a vivid description of the decline of the Greek family system:

> In our time the whole of Greece has been subject to a low birth-rate and a general decrease of the population, owing to which cities have become deserted and the land has ceased to yield fruit, although there have neither been continuous wars nor epidemics. If, then, any one had advised us to send and ask the gods about this, and find out what we ought to say or do to increase in number and make our cities more populous, would it not seem absurd, the cause of the evil being evident and the remedy being in our own hands? For as men had fallen into such a state of pretentiousness, avarice, and indolence that they do not wish to marry, or if they married to rear the children born to them, or at most as a rule but one or two of them, so as to leave these in affluence and bring them up to waste their substance, the evil rapidly and insensibly grew. For in cases where of one or two children, the one was carried off by war and the other by sickness, it is evident that the houses must have been left unoccupied, and as in the case of swarms of bees, so by small degrees the cities became resourceless and feeble. About this it was of no use at all to ask the gods to suggest a means of deliverance from such an evil. For any ordinary man will tell you that the most effectual cure had to be men's own action, in either striving after other objects, or if not, in passing laws making it compulsory to rear children.

This statement applies to the period 200 to 150 B.C. It bears out what we know from other evidence, that the family of Greece had been progressively deteriorating since the fifth century B.C., and that the actual decline in numbers, owing to the failure of the family to function sufficiently in a reproductive sense, had suddenly claimed the attention of the Greek world by the beginning of the second century. Before that time, slavery and foreigners had filled in the gaps. The rural districts of Macedonia had had sufficient population to create the Hellenistic world through the conquest of Philip II and Alexander, in the middle of the fourth century B.C. However, these conquests had exhausted their numbers. Since then under Antigonus Gonatas and his successors in Macedonia, attempts had been made, some successful, to build up Macedonia, and by the time of the wars between Rome and Macedonia in Polybius' time, this revival had been sufficient to influence Macedonia in the wars against Rome. This led to their defiance of Rome, contrary to the rest of Greece.

Similarly, Theodor Mommsen writes in his *History of Rome*:

> What ideas as to divorce prevailed in the circles of the aristocracy may be discerned in the conduct of their best and most moral hero, Marcus Cato, who did not hesitate to separate from his wife at the request of a friend desirous to marry her, and as little scrupled on the death of his friend to marry the same wife a second time. Celibacy and childlessness became more and more common, especially among the upper classes . . . we now encounter even in Cato . . . the maxim to which Polybius a century before traced the decay of Hellas, that it is the duty of the citizen to keep great wealth together and therefore not to beget too many children. Where were the times, when the designation 'children producer' (*proletarius*) had been a term of honor for the Romans?"
>
> In consequence of such a social condition the Latin stock in Italy underwent an alarming dimunution, and its fair provinces were overspread partly by parasitic immigrants, partly by sheer desolation.
>
> . . . the giddier the height to which riches arose, the deeper the abyss of poverty yawned—the more frequently amidst that changeful

world of speculation and playing at hazard, were individuals tossed from the bottom to the top and again from the top to the bottom. The wider the chasm by which the two worlds were externally divided, the more completely they coincided in the like annihilation of family life—which is yet the germ and core of all nationality . . . and not until the dragon seed of North America ripens, will the world have again similar fruits to reap." (IV, 489–92) (This statement in the end, written a century ago, identifies America and Rome as to fundamental sociological aggregates.)

This analysis by Mommsen introduces a number of social traits characteristic of the periods of emergence of the atomistic family. These are the increasing development of extrafamily sex life; the decay of the mores of the upper-class families; the rise of sexual abnormalities; the increasing refusal of women to be sedate in an unsedate world; the emergence of purely romantic conceptions of love, which finally became dominant; the decline in the seriousness with which adultery is considered; the purely formal adhesion to the moral code; the increased popularity and frequency of absolute divorce and separation; the rise of celibacy and aggravated birth control; the displacement of the older populations, at first near the cities, later in the further hinterlands; the replacement of the native populations by immigrants, slaves, and non-natives; the development of an antagonism to the whole system of values upon which the society formerly operated; the enlargement of the class struggle; and, finally, positive social antagonism to the old domestic family system and the family among the whole masses of the people.

These are some of the traits associated with the development of the atomistic family in Greece after Pericles, and in modern Western society after increased familistic reaction toward the strictness of the Protestant Reformation was worn away by the growing secularism of modern life. That Mommsen saw these in Rome is understandable. He could have found the same traits developing in Greece between the Persian and the Peloponnesian wars, and in modern Europe of the eighteenth century. However, Mommsen himself in this work did not cover the time of complete domination by the atomistic family of the whole culture—a movement whose tempo increased in Rome after Augustus and spread to the farthest limits of the empire. Consequently, what he saw was the decay in Rome, in its immediate surrounding districts, and in some of the larger Italian cities where the provincial societies followed quickly in the footsteps of Rome. His reactions to the change in the urban districts at the heart of the empire were those to be expected of a man of Mommsen's type who, in the first half of the nineteenth century, studied this period of Roman society carefully.

Thus, when analyzed, Mommsen in his minute inspection of that great civilization shows that the correlation of Roman civilization with the three family types—trustee, domestic, and atomistic, as outlined in this present study—ran true to form.

4

FROM LATE ROMAN TO TRUSTEE FAMILISM

THE FOURTH AND FIFTH CENTURIES A.D. saw the large disruption of atomistic familism and the beginning of its replacement by domestic family ideas and then by trustee family rule. The history and sociology of this change is very involved and controversial. It was associated with the breaking-up of the Roman Empire, particularly in the West. This break-up was to be both preceded and followed by the rise of Christianity as the dominating "spirit" of European society and the growth of barbarian rule. It was also marked by the appearance of the feudal system, in which the masses were tenants, personally free, but bound to the soil of large rural landholders—feudal lords.

The agents in this change were provincial magistrates, feudal lords, rural bishops, Christian emperors, and barbarian chieftains. The powers they used were written law, unwritten law, moral suasion, and physical force. The causes lay in those sets of conditions which led to the break-up of the Roman Empire. Illustrations of these conditions are the decline of commerce and city life, the decay of contractual obligations (the replacement of these by feudal arrangements based upon *fidelitas*), and the reappearance of localism and provincialism (in opposition to the city as the milieu of the common man), rather than the empire and world concept that had hitherto existed. In this new localistic rural world of decayed spiritual forces, only trustee familism could take over until civilization, first in the shape of the church and later as the integrated national state, could function effectively. The first attempt at reform was domestic familism, but that gave way to trustee doctrines, particularly in the Western Empire and Western and northern Europe.

The classic statement to the effect that the people in the empire had no perspective on the totality of the change the world was undergoing is made by James Bryce: The people did not expect the empire to fall and even the barbarians with the possible "exception of the Mongol, Attila" wanted it to continue. (*The Holy Roman Empire*, Ch. III.)

If the agent were the provincial magistrate, he wanted order and security in his locality. Furthermore, he had to get along with his people. This meant that the magistrate or the feudal lord, through the power they exercised over the tenants, had a decided influence on all matters of family control. At first the magistrates and the lords could be different persons; later they merged. The feudal lord wanted serfs on his estates; he did not want the population to act without consideration of the interests of the estate. Marriage, divorce, inheritance, entering the army or clergy were largely by and through his consent. He wanted sufficient people to till his fields, yet did not want to be burdened with too many during years of famine. Every agent, whether provincial administrator, feudal lord, rural bishop, Christian emperor, or barbarian ruler, wanted about the same things—order, rule, controlled familism, and security in his region. Consequently, all came to the same general point of view—the free individualism and disrupted familism of the atomistic period in Rome must cease.

In this situation, the moral doctrines of domestic familism of the Christian church gradually took hold among the leaders, and the conception of the family as a sacrament and lifelong unity of persons became more and more dominant. Under these conditions, society hoped to escape some of the disruption coming from within and without the empire. Each secular agent had either a material or an administrative gain in mind. The religious agent had as a goal the conversion of society away from the sins of the flesh. The emperor wanted taxes and soldiers; the local administrator wanted help in securing them; the lord wanted his fields tilled. The objectives of all coincided. Thus, a series of separate purposes met to create a general sociological change which had as an ultimate effect the recreation of moralistic familism from individualistic decay. Over a period of two centuries, this confused picture rectified itself; but Western society was not very orderly or peaceful for several centuries more.

As far as the family was concerned, the next result of the change was a return to family rule for most matters affecting the masses of the population. In the barbarian-ruled districts, blood vengeance grew in popularity. For several centuries numerous family quarrels and enmities occurred that now seem as absurd to us as the stories in the Homeric epics. On the feudal estates matters not settled by the dependent families themselves were handled by feudal lords, according to a growing set of common laws or local customs. In the districts where the bishops were powerful, adjudication by a bishop or priest according to a growing canon law was the rule when matters got out of family hands. The bishops had increasing trouble with the willfulness of blood vengeance-bound trustee familism of the chiefs and lords. Remaining Roman law, used by Augustus in his attempts to build up familism, replaced many of the former economic sanctions by physical sanctions. These consisted, for example, of physical punishment or sentence to a monastery until signs of repentance appeared. Eventually Western society took on essentially the same aspect that it had in Homeric and early Roman days. Whatever may be the causes or interpretations, the universe of the common man became his family and his local community.

The situation was very complicated and confused, differing somewhat in the Eastern Roman Empire from the Western, where the barbarians took over earlier and where Roman law was more sadly mutilated than in the East. Important factors everywhere were the inroads of the barbarians, the decay of city life, and growth of feudal estates. The free common man moved down to the condition of serf, in most cases; the slave categories moved up toward personal freedom (*servii tradscriptiae*). Most persons became bound to the soil and questions of marriage were decided largely in relation to their effect upon the estate. Thus marriages had to take place largely among the group bound to the same feudal estate, so that on each estate familistic groups grew up, bound by semi-familistic ties—*fidelitas*—to the lord. The condition of trustee familism developed very rapidly in a few generations.

Family Life among the Barbarians

An important influence was the trustee organizational nature of the barbarian families. The barbarians included the new peoples south of the Rhine and the Germans and others to the north. Some of these stayed in northern and Eastern Europe; others, under constant pressure, migrated west. From the point of view of the Christian bishops, these barbarians were roughnecks pure and simple. In analyzing its own experiences with the family at this time, the church itself says (translating freely):

> The last period of the patristic age (church fathers after Augustine) gives an abundant harvest (of the experiences of the church with family doctrines). However, this was not the period of great heresies which required further extensions of family principles, nor of leaders of great genius capable of extending family philosophy. The period was more favorable to spreading the doctrine because the great invasions of the Roman Empire by the barbarians forced the church to take up the task of educating and adapting the new peoples to the church theories. (*Théologie Catholique*, Vol. IX, Part III, Columns 2077–87)

There were various types of barbarians. The Germans were the nearest to the Western Empire, but north and east of them were Slavs, Avars, Bulgars, Magyars, Mongols, Huns, and Goths. All of them had in common a trustee type of family of the most primitive type, in which blood feuds, incessant warfare, and primitive conditions prevailed. The small families existed, but they too were grouped into larger community organizations. Some of the more civilized groups—particularly the Jugoslavs—had still larger organizations like the *gentes* of the Romans and the phratries of the Greeks. At first, most of them were not settled civilized people with high standards of living, from the economic point of view, as were the residents in the Roman Empire. Family life was rather pure. Birth rates were high, but famine and incessant warfare, coupled with miserable living conditions, did not always permit rapid growth of population. The barbarians were a violent people when they intermingled with the old Roman society, best described by the words applied to Attila, King of the Huns (434–53 A.D.): "scourges of God." The family was of the most primitive trustee type, similar to the earliest Greek and Roman types before peaceful settlement of disputes, rather than blood vengeance, helped them prepare for the periods of Greek and Roman statehood.

They came into the empire in different waves and at different times, from the third century on. Some became good settlers, auxiliary soldiers within the legions, or peaceful agrarians. Others were more violent, although there is an argument as to how much they destroyed the Western Empire and how much it decayed of itself. In any case, they did become part of the empire. Their tribal system of settling disputes and their cruder ways became part of this civilization. The great migrations took place from the end of the fourth to the end of the sixth centuries A.D. Among our ancestors we number the barbarians of northern Europe. They had the most primitive form of trustee familism, based upon the trustee concept of justice. Blood vengeance, family solidarity to punish miscreants for crimes against the family, family unity to defend or deliver up members who committed crimes against other families, and common responsibility to family members to help secure protection, vengeance, justice, etc., were widespread. Thus again our European history saw the upswing of the trustee family into a position of dominance. Not since long before Solon in Greece and the Twelve Tables of Rome had society been so completely at the mercy of the unregulated militancy of blood-grouped familism. The other agents in the revival of familism (church, emperors, provincial magistrates, feudal lords of Roman origin) would have been content with a return to domestic familism similar to that in Rome in the days of Cato the Censor. But these groups were largely overwhelmed by barbarian familism and the violence of its familistic quarrels.

The Family Mind of the Christian Church

The moral agent in the revision of the family was the Christian church. There are probably few subjects more thoroughly discussed in our literature than the breaking-up of the Roman Empire and the rise of the Christian Church. The empire did break up. The church rose first as a moral force and later became a combined spiritual and secular power. The church was against social decay, whether in Rome or among the barbarians, whether within the church (the heretics) or without (among the pagans). Without quoting at length from the church fathers, we can give their attitude toward the Roman decay in a few words.

We need no better description of the period than that given in Revelations in our own New Testament. Here the New Babylon is Rome:

> I saw a woman sit upon a scarlet coloured beast full of the names of blasphemy;
>> And upon her forehead was a name written, MYSTERY, BABYLON THE GREAT, THE MOTHER OF HARLOTS AND THE ABOMINATION OF THE EARTH;
> And the woman has seven heads;
> These seven heads are mountains (the seven hills of Rome);
> And an angel came down from Heaven having great power;
> And he cried with a strong voice BABYLON THE GREAT IS FALLEN;
> Come out of her, my people, that ye not partake of her sins and receive of her plagues;
> Alas that great city;
> For in one hour so great riches has come to nought;
> The light of a candle shall shine no more at all in thee;
> The voice of the bridegroom and the bride shall be heard no more at all in thee;
> For Heaven hath judged the great whore which did corrupt the earth with her fornication. (Adapted from Revelation 18:2)

Church doctrines on marriage and the family were fairly well developed by the time St. Augustine finished his *City of God*, in about 426 A.D.

In general, after some centuries of discussion by the early fathers, marriage was held to be a sacrament to be celebrated before the church; husband and wife were one; marriage was indissoluble; and entering marriage was a serious business like joining the church. The parallel between the union of Christ and the church and the union of husband and wife was accepted as the standard of value for the family. The later fathers, after St. Augustine, had before them increasingly the problems of the barbarians. From that time on the outstanding problems of the church were those of administration. One example will show the problems faced:

> The campaign of Attila in Italy in 452 A.D. devastated the Roman armies. A large number of towns and villas had been pillaged and ruined and the captives carried away by the barbarians. The wives of the prisoners had had no news of their husbands and did not think they could live in captivity. After a certain time, finding life difficult, they had remarried. Then conditions became better and many husbands returned. In the year 458 A.D., Nicétas, the Bishop of Aquilée, went to the Church Fathers to find out what to do. It was decided according to the precedent set by Saint Basil, that the first marriage was indissoluble.

The church faced two extremely different sets of conditions. The decay of the family through atomism among the Romanized people of Southern Europe had gone as far as it had in old Rome itself. These people had been Roman since Julius Caesar "domesticated" them during the empire-making and exceedingly bloody wars of the first century B.C. Five centuries had now passed. These "Gauls" had become Romans, had lived Roman lives, had Roman citizenship, had furnished emperors for the whole empire, and later for both the Eastern and Western sections of the divided empire. They had an atomistic family, with its weaknesses, its childlessness, its inattention to family loyalty, its contractual nature, its weakened conception of the meaning of adultery, and family disloyalty. These did not fit into the conceptions of society as visualized by the bishops of the church.

The church had to decide between two family codes, although it was not completely sympathetic with either of them. From the standpoint of family life (practical indissolubility of marriage, fecundity, relative absence of divorce, dignified treatment of women) the church sympathized more with the barbarians than with the dissolute mores of the Romans. From the standpoint of ruthless barbarian behavior in interfamily feuds (reversion to blood vengeance instead of the use of transaction, composition, and amend), it favored the refined and peaceful delicacy of the Roman atomistic family. It had to make a decision between the two. The church first accepted barbarian law, hoping eventually to refine barbaric custom. The very violence of the barbarians made this compromise necessary. Essentially, it threw itself in with the new dominant element in European civilization, seeking to civilize these people by its good graces. Out of this it constructed canon law, a growing body of knowledge. The leaders found from experience that it was easier to civilize crudeness than to reform dissolution.

St. Augustine and Family Change

The family at the end of the Roman Empire can best be illustrated by taking up the works of St. Augustine (354–430 A.D.), whose writings and character have made him one of the most important influences in the foundation of the Christian church as an institution. St. Augustine is used to give a picture of family decay in Roman society; to point up the fact that the Christians themselves would have settled the matter with a revival of domestic familism; to describe the revulsion which the Christians—following in the steps of even the pagan and barbarian emperors—finally developed towards the lack of social interest in Roman society; to tell of their turning towards the moral (if uncouth and bloody) virtues of the barbarian groups in order to spread Christianity to civilize the barbarians and recivilize the Roman world.

In specific writings St. Augustine gives us a comprehensive text on family sociology in the Roman Empire, written about the time of the invasion of the Christianized barbarians (Goths from Rumania) and before the complete destruction of the Roman world by the pagan barbarians

(Vandals). These chapters on "Continence," "The Good of Marriage," "Virginity," "Widowhood," "Lying," "Patience," "Care for the Dead," and "Marriage and Concupiscence" give us the proposed solution to the problems of the family within the Roman Empire, as recommended and attempted by the Christian leaders. From these writings we can see clearly and specifically the desire of the Christian leaders to hold society together by the revival of domestic familism. What Augustus had sought to do by force, law revision, and economic sanction the Christians attempted to do by moral sanction and spiritual revival. Secondly, the other writings (*Confessions, City of God, Morals of the Catholic Church, Morals of the Manicheans, et passim*) give us a clear and unmistakable picture of familism among the pagan Romans and heretic sects as they actually existed among the Romans at that time. There can be no mistaking this evidence.

The Christian mind was as opposed to that of the popular writers of the atomistic period as was day from night. The works by St. Augustine show conclusively that the family had decayed in Roman society. Associated with it was a moral decay which made the problem of holding together and governing the empire exceedingly difficult. In this period of gradually growing demoralization and decay, three great movements and interpretations had arisen. The first had been that of Augustus and the leaders of his time. They traced their weakness primarily to family decadence and secondarily to the moral depravity of the period. They sought to cure the matter by legislation and reorganization of the social system of the state. The second movement had been the revival of Roman philosophy and pagan religion. This was best exemplified by the period of Marcus Aurelius, and by his writing and example. Marcus Aurelius placed primary emphasis on moral rejuvenation and by example sought to lead the people towards a remoralization. He devoted his entire life to the effort of committing no unworthy act. The third movement was Christianity. This placed equal weight upon familism and moral issues, and sought first by spiritual conversion and moral example, and later by legislation (the codes of the Christian emperors), to control these two forms of behavior.

The supreme good of the Christians was "life eternal," but familism was no bar to life eternal (*On the Good of Marriage*).

Whatever may have been the differing interpretations of historians in later centuries, these were the major concerns of thoughtful Romans from the time Augustus first read books on marriage and the family to the Roman senate, until 426 A.D., when St. Augustine finished his *City of God.*

St. Augustine (Aurelius Augustinus) was a Roman, although neither born nor educated in the city of Rome itself. He considered the fall of Roman civilization and the decline of the Roman city and empire a calamity. The Roman Empire was an agent of God's work. The use of Christian virtue—heavenly peace—could contribute to the reconstruction of the empire—earthly peace. The extension of the empire was a good thing. Nevertheless, even St. Augustine was weary of the prevalent form of behavior within the Roman Empire and turned toward the barbarians for examples of moral conduct. He points out all through the first books of the *City of God* that in the sacking of 410 A.D. the barbarians had been more humane in their treatment of Romans than the Romans had been with captured peoples. The reason, of course, was that the Goths sacking Rome had been partially Christianized. They did not kill those who fled for sanctuary to the churches. In his letter to Victorianus (409 A.D.) he deprecates the violence of the barbarians and implies that they must be Christianized. He believes that the capture of Christians by barbarians might end in "wonders of power and grace," resulting in the Christianization of the barbarians. Here again is the defensive note for the barbarians—he points out that the "cruelties of the barbarians" are light compared to some of the sectarian quarrels within the empire. "For what barbarian could ever have devised what they (Donatists and Circumcelliones) have done, viz., casting lime and vinegar into the eyes of our clergymen, besides atrociously beating every part of their bodies?"

The entire work of St. Augustine indicates clearly that the emphasis of the church was upon domestic familism. The revival of trustee familism as the dominant element in what civilization remained was a historical matter beyond the control of the church. The Christian ideas that man and wife were one, and that the sins of the father were potent factors in the life of the child, were purely domestic family views. They had no such trustee conception as that found in Homeric or Beowulfian society, where the sin of a Paris or the stealing of a cup could involve a whole people in warfare and bloodshed.

Conclusion

The reforms seeking to keep the Roman family from decaying, and thus undermining the empire, most probably delayed the end of this society. But by the time the Christians took up the task, the foundations of the social system were already shattered. The barbarian system was the only one that could control the rampant dissolution and even this could not do it very well. The barbarian chief or tribal group brought the trustee family system into the empire. The feudal manors, which became the next chief focal points of social organization, found that they also had to adopt this system. Family organization in Europe again returned to the condition of Homeric and early Roman times, when the world of the individual became kin, clan, lord, and *fidelitas*. The only thing carried over from the past was the Christian church, with its conception of decency, moral virtue, and the ultimate dignity of the individual.

The Christian idea was that the social system of the Romans could be recreated and saved by the development of the domestic family social organization. Within the family there were no such things as "others," because they conceived a lifelong unity of husband and wife, parent and child as furnishing a family personality with common aims and interests. Between these domestic units they conceived "all men as neighbors" and the maxim "do unto others as you would have them do unto you." But the Christian movement developed too late in the scene for it to attain the necessary control to restore the Roman Empire. Thus, in a large sense of the word, the return to trustee familism in the Middle Ages was an historical accident. No one wanted trustee familism as a permanent system of family organization; rather, it was accepted as a necessary compromise. The church had a remedy which demonstrated in time that it could hold society together without a complete return to blood responsibility and blood feud. Its ultimate development, beginning with the tenth century, required four centuries of constant effort on the part of the church. Thus, the church furnished the fundamental historical continuity between the Roman Empire aspect of Western civilization and modern Western civilization. Disregarding all else that may be said about it, the church was an institution molded in the Roman Empire. It brought to us the fundamental conceptions throughout the ages of the proper relations between man and man, as developed in the best thinking of Greece and Rome.

In one sense there are no such things as separate Greek, Roman, and Western civilizations; there are merely the Greek, Roman, and modern versions of the same Western, or European, civilization which in the past few centuries has spread from the old to the new worlds. From the beginning and until the end of the ancient world, the Greek and Roman civilizations were fundamentally of the same people. In the Greek world, the Romans constituted the invading barbarians. The north European peoples were the invading barbarians in the Graeco-Roman world. We are, therefore, a combined civilization in the same sense as are the Chinese, the Hindu, and the present Muslim cultures, all of which underwent similar invasions and transformations.

The Greek world was encompassed by the Roman, the Roman by the north European barbarian. These groups successively took up the challenge of European society. Plato, Aristotle, and Homer are as much a part of our inheritance and culture as they were of the Roman. From the beginning through all of Western history, the influence of these Graeco-Roman ideas has been carried over from one "bulge" of civilization to the next.

The carrying agent from the last expression of Graeco-Roman culture to ours was the church bishop. He came into the scene armed with a Greek education and the philosophy of a Roman, St. Augustine. He was determined to hold the world together by establishing decent standards of conduct between husband and wife, between parent and child, between neighbor and neighbor, and finally between the ruler and the ruled.

5

THE TRUSTEE FAMILY OF THE DARK AGES

B Y THE FIFTH CENTURY, ROMAN society could no longer maintain itself. A man shortage existed. As a matter of fact, except among the noncivilized barbarians, a famine of good men existed. The raids of the third and fourth centuries into Germany were primarily to secure captives—men for the armies, farms, and colonies within the empire. Islam emerged in the East and Christianity in the West as moral doctrines attempting to save civilization. Our concern here is primarily with the West, or the European-Christian society.

Both of these religions used Judaism as the vehicle for the concrete expression of their social philosophies. They laid particular emphasis upon those aspects which they thought had proved ruinous to their respective civilizations. Christianity developed as an active social force from the decay of the Roman Empire. It naturally incorporated in its tenets the best moral and political philosophy of both the Roman and Greek worlds. St. Augustine was a Roman who knew all the great writers of Graeco-Roman civilization. His *City of God* is a textbook on Graeco-Roman philosophy. He was a teacher of philosophy at Milan before he became converted to Christianity, finally rising to become Bishop of Hippo. He made selections from the writings of St. Paul and set forth a theory of the family which he thought would cure the ills of society. His three fundamental tenets were *fides* (loyalty), *proles* (children), and *sacramentum* (indissolvable unity of man and wife). His was essentially a domestic family concept. At the time he developed it, the Roman family was of the atomistic type. When Roman society failed, the trustee family became dominant.

The Christian church thus took a firm position with regard to the type of family needed by society. From this early position, based upon "the mind of God" and the experiences of Western society, Christianity took its doctrinal roots. That is to say, Christian doctrines were directly influenced by the peculiar nature of the experiences of Western society. Christianity is, in addition to everything else, a doctrine of good behavior based upon the totality of social experience of Western society. Modern Western civilization is based immediately on Roman and Greek society, transmitted through the agency of Christianity. The experience of the Christian church is that of the Western Roman world; its philosophical terminology is Greek; its vehicle of expression is Judaism; its aim is a stable society; its methods are moral and family control.

When a modern European or American reads the Greek and Roman writers—from Homer through Procopius—he sees his own forefathers in the picture at all times. Our history is the history of Rome and Greece. We are at the same time the barbarians who created Greek and Roman civilization and also the barbarians who inherited their cultures.

After the decay of the power of the state, the church became the civilizing influence. It had to conquer the mind of man before it could civilize him. The struggle was centered about family organization and family mores. Christianity, from its beginning to the present day, has maintained a constant position regarding the importance of the family. The spacious philosophy of St. Augustine (among the early church philosophers this influence was most profound) was a complete crystallization of the church's primary concern with the family. St. Thomas Aquinas and the Council of Trent were reassertions of these specific social objectives of the church. Its development, its actual effect upon history can be broken down into a number of periods of jurisdiction of the aims and ideals of the family and the power of the church to enforce these ideals upon its followers and upon the Western world.

The first stage extended from the fourth and fifth to the tenth and eleventh centuries. During this time the church power in family law and jurisdiction grew, but it shared its decisions and power with the state. For instance, in 406 A.D., although the church was against divorce and the remarriage of divorcees, the Council of Carthage defended the right of divorcees to remarry and requested an imperial law permitting this. We know from the writings of Archbishop Hinchmar of Reims (he wrote about 860 A.D.) that the state was still the dominant outside factor in family issues. According to civil law at that time, a child could not marry without parental permission.

But in the tenth and eleventh centuries, canon law had almost complete dominance over marriage. We European barbarians had become civilized again. The trustee family, at least in its exaggerated phases, was declining in the West.

The power of the church over marriage and the family was not only preserved but also enlarged and extended from the twelfth to the fourteenth centuries. This was the golden age of canon law. After that, secularism again arose. It gained complete legal power over the family during the revolutions of the eighteenth century and subsequently through the spread of secular law in Europe by Napoleon. In England secularization gained sway in the seventeenth century, ending in a great splurge in the revolution of Cromwell. In the meantime, Americans had carried this secularism of the family to the colonies. Here it flourished apace, since England was too busy with internal affairs and European wars to pay much attention to the colonies. With the American Revolution, family secularism, like other secularisms, gained headway. During the nineteenth century and until World War I, the family became an almost completely contractual institution in all Western society. After this, "compulsory" familistic laws set in widely throughout Europe, and seemed to be spreading to the European colonies.

The dominant idea of the family and the effect of these changes on the family can be measured if we give the conceptions of the family in the following general periods:

I. Family conceptions at the end of the Roman Empire and beginning of the Dark Ages.

II. Family conceptions during the dominance of canon law (tenth to twelfth centuries).

III. Canon law conceptions at the end of the golden age of canon law (fifteenth and sixteenth centuries).

IV. Secular conceptions of the family about the end of the nineteenth century.

V. Conceptions of the family in (or inherent in) the modern "all-powerful" state.

One phase of this development deserves some special consideration. Prior to Christianity, barbarian society was ruled primarily by tribal mores, as were the Chinese before Confucius and the Hindus before Manu. The *jus gentium* (law of all men) of Roman law immediately preceded Christianity. To some extent the development of Christianity into a doctrine of world religion may be viewed as an evolutionary and partly nonreversible trend. Prior to the complete domination of the Western world by this universal conception of absolute right and wrong, there was no possibility of getting all the gods—or incarnations of moral forces—to agree on an issue. In the Homeric period the gods were always quarreling among themselves; at least one god was sure to be on either side of any issue. At that time, the family of gods was conceived to be like the families of men. With Christianity the conception arose that God was always right, and that men might not be like God, but to the extent that they failed in this, they were sinners and lost. Only one right and one wrong existed in the moral sense, so to speak, and the conception of good lost some of its former pliability.

Christian Family Ideas at the Beginning of the Dark Ages

At the beginning of the Dark Ages, the church was struggling against the two forces of diffuse atomism and brutal trusteeship family conception, the one Roman, the other barbarian. The church objected equally to ideas in both conceptions. Some of the principles it set forth were as follows:

I. *Differences in religion were an impediment to marriage.* This was a stand against the decline of the Roman family into companionate marriage, and an attempt to build up a body of consistent followers who would carry out the doctrines of the church. Christians were supposed to marry Christians.

II. *Every family was to be a spiritual parenthood,* through religious vows. This was an attack upon Roman mores. Marriage was a sacrament, like baptism.

III. *Restriction of intermarriage* made it incest to marry within seven degrees. (A first cousin was fourth degree, an uncle and niece are third degree.) This was striking directly at the barbarian trustee family, which by intermarriage had created local family units so solid that incessant warfare went on due to their conceptions of family responsibility for actions of members. Thus the return was to the old Roman conception of reducing family warfare by eliminating class and tribal restrictions to intermarriage. (*Connubium* had slowly spread from the original groups and classes in the ancient city to all the tribes and classes in Italy.) Under the Roman trustee family any marriage within six degrees of relationship (the children of cousins) was *nefariae et incestiae nuptae.* Thus, the same practice was adopted a thousand years apart, for the same purpose. During atomistic family times (late Roman and now) incest is loosely defined by the secular powers to coincide with third and fourth degrees of relationship. In support of the increase in restriction by the church, the bishops quoted Leviticus 18:6—none of you shall approach to any that is near of kin to him, to uncover their nakedness.

IV. *Extreme limitations upon divorce, polygamy, and repudiation.* This was an attack both upon the excessive divorce among the Romanized barbarians, and upon the increased repudiation among the new barbarians as they came into contact with the urbanized Romans. Tertullian said that divorce in Rome had become "a fruit of marriage."

V. *Freedom of marriage from excessive family control.* This struck at the strong family control of the barbarians and was one of the attempts to meliorate barbarian law.

VI. *Development of the conception of "dos."* Dos ex marito was a gift from husband to wife and was to replace *pretium nuptiale,* or gift from husband to father-in-law. Under the trustee family, *pretium nuptiale* bound the trustee family together and was objectionable in the same way as was close inbreeding to public order. However, if *pretium nuptiale* was abandoned, there would be no economic considerations with marriage, and the newlyweds would have no property. *Dos ex marito* was a custom which eventually resulted in the development of the domestic family in replacement of the trustee.

VII. *Measures against abortion and infanticide.* Romanized barbarians were particularly guilty of abortion and the other barbarians of infanticide, when parents could not or would not accept children into the family. For the earlier idea that a child was a social being only if accepted by the parents, the church set forth the idea that all children born were social beings. They were automatically children of their mother and her husband and could not be rejected or exposed. This tried to do away with exposure, an ancient custom of the trustee family which was seriously limited also by the Romans.

VIII. *Quarrels between families were to be heard by public assemblies* (juries) *and were to be settled by composition rather than blood vengeance.* Avoidance of family feuds among the barbarians. Transaction meetings between families came to be considered courts and under the jurisdiction of the representatives of the proprietor (who also represented the Comte or King) a portion of the composition (*fredum*) was taken for the lord or king. However, this was a process of realization. The original idea was not to fall back on interfamily jurisdiction.

IX. *Testaments or wills should be introduced.* This was against barbaric family solidarity.

X. *The conception of abstention emphasized by St. Jerome was limited to the church officials, and the masses were supposed to spend their adult lives in the marriage state with children and familism as the aim.* St. Isidore (c. 560–636) made familism and childbearing for the laity a *primary* duty in the Christian way of life.

All of these reforms were suggested by the church during the Merovingian period in Europe. The Merovingian was the first empire to arise among the Romanized people in the West. Here the barbarians and the Romanized peoples were mixed together, trying to create a new society from the remnants of the old. The reforms were discussed in total or in part at the church councils of the fourth, fifth, and sixth centuries. The ten principles were not put into immediate effect, except among the more spiritual Christians. It was some centuries before canon law became the dominant power in the family. But these principles exercised a growing influence and gradually won supremacy. (They developed in written Roman law after Constantine.)

Their importance to us lies in the fact that the trustee-type family bonds of the barbarians were extremely strong, while those among the atomistic Romanized peoples of the West were exceedingly weak. Through Christianity, family bonds were to grow stronger among the Romanized peoples and to become weaker among the barbarians. Here we have a meeting of the contractual and the organic family types.

It is possible to see the contrast between family types faced by the bishops of the church if we imagine that the Homeric Greeks or the early tribal Romans instead of the northern barbarians had moved into the late empire. To illustrate the similarities among the early Romans and Greeks, marriage was a sacrament, a *rehoç*, or sacred ceremony. It was almost indissoluble and divorce was almost impossible. Such family organization, while essentially monogamic, could lead to polygamy among the head warriors, as it did in early Greece. Families controlled marriage; gifts to the father of the bride kept property in the family; the trustee idea was alive and dominant. Quarrels between families were constantly disrupting society. Infanticide and infant exposure were rights of the household head, acting for the group. Testaments and wills were unheard of. Had the bishops been confronted with early Greek and Roman familism, they would have had to face the same problems presented by the barbarian familism of the early Dark Ages, and would have had to seek a solution to these problems by adopting practically the same measures as those taken.

The ten-principle system of Christian familism was not then the dominant one in Western society. It was merely a moral ideal set forth against both Romanism and barbarianism, a critical standard of society. To the Christian, man and wife were one for life; parent and child were united until the child set up a family of his own; moral relations of the family were to be those of absolute faith and trust. Plutarch had noted that the conventional belief had arisen that the fact that brothers came from the same uterus should not influence their conduct. The Christians held that husband-wife, parent-child relations were to be regulated as though all belonged to the same spiritual body. In a society where the barbarians believed kin-allegiance to be more binding than other social obligations, the Christians held that the individual was morally responsible for his sins, and that the sole necessity for marriage was the free consent of normal adults.

The early Greek and Roman concepts were of marriage with *manus*. Later, their concept was one of marriage without *manus*. Now the Christians held for a sacramental marriage—a new form of *manus*. But the Christians, though reintroducing a form of *manus*, saw the necessity for both familism and for a social organization with claims stronger than those of the family. They were against *manus* or sacraments binding relatives together against the kin of others. The Christians wanted both a strong family and a strong civilization.

Gratian and Pierre Lombard were the two eminent churchmen whose synthesizing work had the most influence upon the development. The result was a canon law regarding the family which was as detailed on all points as a Roman law code. It combined the principles of the Roman family with those of the north European barbarian family, according to the religious doctrines of the church as developed through St. Augustine. Essentially, from the point of view of this systematization of family forms, it created the formal groundwork of the domestic family. As a result we see Western society move from dominance of the trustee type—attributable to the influence of our medieval barbarian forefathers—into a new domestic type, similar in outer organization to that of middle Rome and middle Greece.

Domestic Family Ideal (Twelfth Century)

When the entire system of marriage and the family came under jurisdiction of canon law, the principles set forth by the earlier bishops were put into effect and extended, as experience directed. The following ideas were gradually established. This movement took at least until the thirteenth century to become established.

I. *Marriage is a sacrament.* This placed marriage in the same category as the taking of holy orders. It was the same unity as the relation of Christ to the church and to humanity. Consequently, marriage was indissoluble and came completely under the jurisdiction of the church.

The principle of indissolubility had always been one of the main positions of the church. However, prior to this time in practice, a good many exceptions had been secured on the grounds that marriages were null or did not exist because of previous adultery, absence, sterility, differences in religious belief, relationship, or taking of religious vows. In practice these exceptions and nullification actions had been used as forms of divorcement. Hinchmar of Reims took upon himself the burden of breaking up these numerous exceptions.

II. *Marriage is a unity of man and wife.* Before this time marriage under the trustee family had been the uniting of two families. This still carried on but the primary conception of marriage of the church, for reasons easily understandable in terms of the family warfare which had troubled barbarian Europe for centuries, was that of a man and woman uniting under the church and of separation from their families as far as jurisdiction was concerned. This was the beginning of the development of the domestic family conception, and was again similar to the gradual changes in middle Greece and Rome. Both Pierre Lombard and St. Thomas Aquinas took the position found in Genesis 2:24:

> Therefore shall a man leave his father and his mother and shall cleave unto his wife: and they shall be one flesh.

The importance of the beginning of this conception of the domestic family cannot be overestimated. Plato in illustrating the old Greek trustee idea tells the story of a man who on his deathbed wanted to make a will. He desired to favor one and reject another of his relatives, according to their treatment of him. But the legislator replied to the man:

> Thou who canst not promise thyself a single day, thou who art only
> a pilgrim here below, does it belong to thee to decide such affairs?
> Thou art the master neither of thy property nor of thyself: thou and
> thy estate, all these things belong to thy family; that is to say to thy
> ancestors and to thy posterity. (*Laws*, XI)

This is a decidedly different picture from the conception that a man (and a woman) should *leave* his parents and cling to his spouse. When this condition occurred, trustee relationships were broken and the domestic conception of the family came to prevail.

III. *Marriage is a unity of equals, based upon consent; it is essentially unbreakable after engagement and absolutely indissoluble after* copula carnalis. This gave the family the essence of a contract between equals, but the precontract (*sponsalia per verba de praesenti*) was practically binding and the sexual union was indissoluble. Contract was part of the sacrament, so that the family was a sacred thing. The family was not contractual but had contract and, if no prohibitive impediment were found, moved from engagement to *copula carnalis* and unity for life. The influence of the outer family upon marriage was to be merely informal. On the other hand, the church held that the steps to marriage, although involving only the unity of husband and wife, were as binding as if it were a family unity. There was to be no breaking of engagements without deep reason. Our present conception that an engagement is a promise to be carried out only if still mutually agreeable was not permitted to prevail. Hinchmar of Reims held that an engagement was a conditional promise (*sponsalia per verba de futuro*) and that since consummation had not taken place there was still no sacrament, so the relation was not completely indissoluble until the *copula carnalis* had taken place. However, due to the influence of Pierre Lombard, the general feeling was that the engagement should be studied carefully, that the fiancés should make definite promises (*fançailles*) before family, friends, or preferably the priest, and that from then on the marriage was a sacrament made either *sponsalia per verba de praesenti* or *de futuro*, and not to be broken. The promises were to exchange funds and property, as in the older financial arrangements between families of the trustee type. The difference was that they were now between man and woman, rather than between families, although they were to establish an equally unbreakable arrangement. As has been pointed out before, in the trustee family a breach of engagement was a violent break in social relations and led to trouble between the families. On the other hand, during atomistic periods, except for the return of previously exchanged property, and a few useless "breach of promise" suits (primarily by designing women, but sometimes by male fortune hunters) both parties are legally free until the ceremony of marriage is completed.

Viewed in perspective, the attempts of the canonists were to establish the same sacramental family as that which existed in trustee periods, under public rather than family law, with the church taking the place of the old private family organizations.

Pierre Lombard (1100–1160) followed closely in the footsteps of St. John Chrysostom, St. Augustine, St. Ambrose, and St. Isidore and emphasized particularly the fact that free consent of the parties was the only fundamental necessity for marriage (if the parties offered no impediments to marriage). We need not go into all the hairsplitting on theological doctrine which had arisen at that time, except to point out that it was not compatible with Christian doctrine that any human person should prevent a responsible man and woman from entering the sacrament of marriage. From this, of course, arose the idea of the domestic family, split off from the family unions of the trustee variety. Of their own free will, man and wife became one. Both Pierre Lombard and St. Thomas Aquinas had a significant influence in the establishment of the *proles, fides, sacramentum* conception of the family, long held as the three foundations of the necessary perfect union.

IV. *Marriage is completely freed from family power.* This went further than the point that marriage was a unity of man and woman, which was a positive statement suggesting this idea. But a clear-cut statement on the absence of parental power strengthened and made the interdiction of parental influence decisive.

> The marriage *jure canonico* ought to be completely free from family
> power, and here, as in many other points, Pierre Lombard won out

over Gratian. Lombard is in effect the first who taught absolutely that the consent of parents is never an essential condition of valid marriage. On this point he made only two contentions: (1) the consent only of the two to be married, makes the marriage; and (2), the consent of parents to the sacrament is not for the purpose of making the sacrament, but like certain other forms, is merely to add decency and dignity to the union." (Translated from A. Esmein, *Droit canonique*, Vol. I, 158)

V. *Neither gifts from husband to wife or wife's family* (dos and donatio propter nuptias) *are necessary to marriage.* Since the couple were to be freed from their families, a payment of money to the parents of either would imply that they had a negative or positive role in the marriage. Hence, an exchange of property was made unnecessary. Funds could be exchanged between the husband and wife, but that was a personal matter and had nothing to do with the family of either. So also, the setting up of brides' property—as separate from husbands' (*donatio propter nuptias*)—would be a contradiction of the fact that man and wife became as one flesh. Hence, there was to be no separate wife and husband property but a complete joint ownership of everything, a community property between them.

VI. *Actions in nullification, where an impediment to marriage exists, involve primarily the couple, and others only from the standpoint of the facts.* The canonists had a number of conceptions which made a marriage null. They called them impediments to marriage. These ranged from being below the age of consent (fourteen years of age for men, and twelve, or the age of puberty, for girls) through differences in religion and incapacity to perform the sexual act, down to consanguinity and affinity. However, they were very careful to see that actions nullifying marriage were not used as undercover divorces of the indissoluble marriage and that the older family control did not creep in here. They had something similar to our marriage courts, but used the simpler system and terminology of the Romans, *accusatio, denunciatio,* and *inquisitio.* They wanted to be sure that any impediment which could be removed would be removed and the couple would remain married. Cases of early puberty leading to prelegal age marriage could be remedied so that in due time the marriage became valid. Differences in religion could be removed by baptism.

The Romans, once they began developing public law about marriage, recognized the old family interest and made the family members the chief and *only* accusers or denouncers. Thus the *Lex Julia de adulteriis* gave the wife and her father the exclusive right to make accusations. Even the later laws of Constantine gave the right to appear in court in family matters (*accusationes matrimonii*) exclusively to the near parents and relatives (*personae proximae et necessariae*). But the canonists were not going to tolerate family interference, so they worked out a system with many fine points, which largely prevented outer family interference.

All of these principles involved in family debate from the time of Gratian to St. Thomas Aquinas indicate that the church was now in a position in Western society where it could begin to think of breaking up the trustee family and of helping society reorganize on the domestic family pattern. From the beginning this had been the ideal of the church. From the earliest development of its doctrine it always stood between the barbarian and the late Roman family types. All the early church fathers had personal knowledge of the two great family types and had resolved on a compromise which would preserve the best in both the familistic and nonfamilistic phases of civilization. They conceived an ideal society as one in which the family did its job within the home, and outer rule remained in the hands of competent public authorities. The Christian church was to be over and above both these institutions and give the essential moral directives to both family and secular authorities.

Conclusion

In this chapter the family conception has been followed from the empire into the Dark Ages (sixth to twelfth centuries A.D.), during which Christianity was struggling with the numerous philosophies of the empire and the barbarians for family control and moral supremacy in the Western world. The family had moved from a religious institution in early Rome to the contractual and atomistic period of the empire. *Manus* was replaced by personality; a marriage of *dignitas* gave way to *concubinatus*; *patria potestas* dissolved; childlessness emerged; the empire had to force people to have children. The marriage and family bond had weakened and given way to personal liberty. Barbarians inherited the empire because there was no great body of people who felt any loyalty to the social structure, either family or state, or who could support such a structure. There were three systems of social values in the Western world of the middle of the first thousand years of our era: decadent Romanist antifamilism, barbarian primitive trustee familism, and the tenets of the Christian church, which stood for order, decency, and the salvation of society. The struggle continued for five hundred years until finally the antifamilism of the Romans and Romanized Gauls and the primitive familism of the barbarians gave way to canon law and church rule.

The contrast between the decadent family of late Roman civilization and the family reintroduced into Europe by the barbarians was extreme indeed.

The barbarian family was of the most primitive trustee type. *Mund* was *manus*, concubines were concubines, and marriage meant *dignitas*. Adultery meant death; *potestas* meant power and responsibility. Marriage was the normal state of life and included family and children. Again blood vengeance and family law prevailed, almost undisciplined by higher authority. Personal liberty was liberty within the family. Again we have the unrestrained struggle of *genos* against *genos*, *gens* against *gens*. Side by side in what was known as civilization were two of the most extreme developments of the family.

From this state of affairs, the church began to formulate a conception of public power to regulate the family. It tried to make a sacrament of marriage, to force people to marry out of their families in order to establish blood lines integrating the group, and to form interfamily lines which would lessen the antagonisms. Divorce, polygamy, and repudiation were banned to the faithful. Marriage was to be freed from excessive family control. Abortion and infanticide were interdicted. Community property was required of the faithful. For interfamily quarrels, trials were to be held before public assemblies. Testaments and wills were to be used to break up the clans.

By the twelfth century, the church achieved family power. Canon law was ready to set forth a definite number of principles. Marriage was a sacrament, a unity of husband and wife, a unit freed from legal responsibility and excessive interference by the outer families.

The conception of the family which was established at this time due to the exposition of St. Thomas Aquinas has since become the official position of the Catholic Church. It will be well to review these ideas briefly.

The state of virtue for man includes marriage for the begetting of offspring and the education and development of these offspring. A secondary end of matrimony is the mutual love and aid that the married couple give each other in the household. This is as natural and Christlike as producing children and rearing them, but it is a secondary matter. Marriage is not compulsory if persons wish to abstain from sex and devote themselves to holy orders, but outside of that marriage is more or less the natural thing. In case there is a shortage of population it is lawful from the standpoint of Christianity for the regulating organizations (state and church) to make marriage and childbearing compulsory. Marriage purely as an excuse for sexual cohabitation is a venial sin.

Matrimony is the joining of husband and wife to produce children. A perfect marriage results in the joining together of the bodies and minds of the husband and wife. Its essence is consent but a betrothal based upon dishonorable conditions (I will marry you if you promise sterility, so that I will not have children to rear) is a fault and should be broken. Children are a compensation for marriage, not a burden, because marriage rightfully considered is the choice of a way of life. This consent must be freely given and not under "the agitation of mind occasioned by danger imminent or future." Consent is a very complicated term, but the idea of the church is that the marriage should result in mutuality, constancy, and children. If this is achieved, factors of consent and compulsion, such as a father persuading his son to marry and helping him get started in life, are valid in the eyes of the church. Marriage is too important socially and individually to be reached except through the will and consent of the couple involved.

Fundamentally, *proles* and *fides* make the *sacramentum*. (Children and constancy in married life make it a grace. St. Thomas follows St. Isidore here in the arrangement of *proles* and *fides* in the order given, as opposed to St. Augustine. In this work he does not mention St. Augustine, but constantly quotes St. Isidore, Aristotle, and the Bible.) Marriages other than for *proles*, and failing the ability to have *proles*, for *fides*, are without sin, but otherwise "it is always at least a venial sin."

A careful study of St. Augustine's *De bono conjugali* leads me to the opinion that he places *fides*, or faith and constancy, above *proles* in this enumeration of the three foundations of marriage and the family. It is difficult to interpret his many statements, but this seems to be his general idea. Later writers (St. Isidore and St. Thomas Aquinas) seem to me to rearrange the sequence into *proles*, *fides*, and *sacramentum*.

The impediments to marriage are those which can be removed and do not invalidate it and those absolutely invalidating a marriage. On these St. Thomas quotes two verses, the first applying to minor or removable impediments, and the second to fundamental nullifying factors. The first is:

> The veto of the Church and holy tide
> Forbid the knot, but loose it not if tied.

And the second:

> Error, station, vow, kinship, crime
> Difference of worship, force, holy orders,
> Marriage bond, honesty, affinity, impotence,
> All these forbid marriage, and annul it though contracted.

By error, he refers to ignorance as invalidating consent. In his reference to station he is speaking particularly of slavery as making consent sometimes a matter of fear. The same general analysis applies to the other impediments.

There is a great deal more of this, because in this document St. Thomas undertakes to answer every question that has ever arisen about the family. He always seeks to answer them not with a *yes* or *no*, but according to the Aristotelian approach. To him, Aristotle is *the* philosopher. Marriage is a natural state of man and has its definite biological and social purposes and results. Consequently every question must be answered with regard to the influence it will have upon this natural state. As Aristotle showed in his *Nicomachean Ethics,* every social trait (friendship, courage, generosity) has a range of expression, the minimums or maximums of which have different meanings from the middle expression. Ordinarily friendship is a virtue, but either too little or too much of it can be a vice. This is the approach of St. Thomas to all the acts of marriage and family life, with the single exception that his relativity is to the acts influencing marriage and not to marriage and familism itself. Thus he combines the relativity of acts with the absoluteness of aims in a value system.

At the same time it must be pointed out that it is neither the trustee nor the atomistic family he is outlining to us. By his time the trustee family had been disciplined and the domestic family was typologically dominant in Western society. The family he outlines is the domestic unit integrated under the church and related to kin only in an informal manner. Thus in the course of seven or eight centuries the family system of civilized Europe had twice completely reversed its trend. It had changed from the atomistic to the trustee and then over several centuries had gradually reformed itself to the domestic. This struggle, one of the most interesting in the history of the Western family, is relatively unknown to us today. Nevertheless, it was to leave an impression upon our religious institutions, the total effects of which possibly we do not appreciate completely. The future of the family system in Western society may always be influenced by the experience the church underwent in this struggle.

6

RISE OF THE MODERN DOMESTIC FAMILY

A N OUTSTANDING CHARACTERISTIC OF THE family as set forth in canon
law at the end of the twelfth century was its relation to the church
and to religion. This was not a domestic or a state religion but a general
world conception. It had evolved in the West during the weakness of
the states and governments and the decay of the Roman Empire. There
was nothing else to discipline the rampant forces of society, no one to
protect the weak, no other moral civilizing force. Many philosophies had
struggled for supremacy; Christianity survived. The barbarian family had
to be broken away from clan influences and brought under that of the
church. Consequently, it was evident at the beginning that the domestic
type of family organization would last only so long as the masses clung
to the ideals of the church. If temporal forces and strong states could take
from the church its power, rule, and regulation of the family, then the
atomistic type could reappear. Actually, this is what did happen. States
and religious groups did rise in antagonism to Rome. Secular power rose
against the church. Thus we had the Reformation, best exemplified by
the rise of humanism and the Lutheran and Calvinist movements; the
splitting off of state churches, such as the Church of England and German Lutheranism; and finally, the secularization of family control. The
church is again in the position it occupied during the late Roman Empire.

It no longer can effect its principles, it can merely set them forth. Secular powers make family laws.

One must not assume that just because these mature principles of canon law were stated, they were immediately accepted by the families concerned. In the Middle Ages, as now, there was cultural lag—probably more so. In the analysis of the period of these changes, several centuries have been allowed. There were considerable differences between Eastern and Western Europe. During much of this time, Eastern Europe was over-run by Mongols and Muslims. The trustee families among them reemerged in the Eastern empire. Furthermore, leaving aside the differences between the countries and territories organized around the Roman law codes—as opposed to those following the alleged barbarian codes—even in Western Europe there was considerable variation. Some argued that since woman was made from man, woman was subject to man, a point of view different from that of canon law that the two parties to the marriage contract were equal and that in marriage man and woman were one. St. Thomas Aquinas held that "man is not of woman, but woman is of man." But at the same time, Humbert de Romans of the Dominican order held (in his model *Sermon to Women*) that women were better than men by nature, grace, and glory, that man was made from earth but woman was made in paradise. As the domestic family developed, there were wife-beating and subjection of women in some families, while in others women were accorded a certain amount of independence, such as trading on their own account, and so forth. The "henpecked" husband became a familiar joke.

In time, the ideas of the church on the family triumphed over trusteeism. In our late Middle Ages (from the twelfth century on) the domestic conception became increasingly dominant. The age of heroes was over. Society could no longer understand a family system like that described by Beowulf. The *Morte d'Arthur*, a similar epic poem (applying to fifth-century England but published later by Caxton), loses its original characteristics and becomes unrecognizable as an early, or primitive, epic. No longer was knighthood in flower. Great social changes took place, such as business, trade, commercial revolution, household factories, the inclosure acts, and the revival of Roman law under canon law principles. A new spirit began to dominate society. Will-making now became more and more an accepted right. The period of interest-taking, profit-making, and capitalism was under way.

Differences within Europe

These movements began earlier in Western than in Eastern Europe. The splitting of European society into two types of empires, the Eastern and the Western, kept the two regions apart psychologically for some centuries. The Eastern family remained in the trustee period longer than the Western family. This was a reversal of the earlier process. Greece had gone through the three forms of the family cycle—trustee, domestic, and atomistic—while Roman society was hardly out of the trustee period. By the time the primitive Twelve Tables were engraved for the guidance of Roman society, Pericles, the popular dictator of Athens, had already made the hetaera Aspasia the leading woman of Greece. Now Eastern Europe, while following the same familistic pattern as the West, was lagging behind the West.

Part of this difference may be due to Islam, to which this society was exposed on the Southeast. Another influence was the Mongol invasions, which affected the family system at the time the Western half of Europe was turning toward the domestic type. These Mongols were a primitive and tribal people with a trustee family organization of the most elementary kind.

However, fundamental consideration must be given also to the influence of ruralism in the large land mass which composes Eastern Europe. It is a great isolated region, lying between the Black and Caspian Seas and the Arctic Ocean, bordered on the west by the Carpathian Mountains and Pripet Marshes. Once established, a family system in this great area would be much more stable than one in the West, where communication and new ideas were constantly changing the scene. The Greek Orthodox Church, under whose religious dominion the people came, and the numerous local barbarian customs of the Slavic peoples and their invaders were the forces which established the family system in the East. There were also minor variations in and between the different countries, depending upon their geography (mountains and other forms of isolation) and upon national fortunes.

The countries in the old Holy Roman Empire and England (the empire claimed some jurisdiction over England) had changed to the domestic family by the thirteenth century. The Scandinavian group (Norway, Sweden, Denmark, Iceland) did not complete the change until the sixteenth century. Ireland, Scotland, and Wales kept their trustee family organization several centuries longer than England. From the infiltration of these peoples into our Appalachian highlands at about the end of the seventeenth century, much of this family organization developed among our own Southern highlanders.

In general, the Eastern Church took the same position regarding the family as did the Western. Throughout the Middle Ages it served as a regulative and guiding influence for the barbarian families in the Eastern sections of Europe. It sought to introduce domestic family concepts as soon as a group became Christianized. From the fall of the Roman Empire until today, the family of Eastern Europe has followed the same general trends as that of the West, although varying somewhat in the details of its development. Trustee familism among the masses gave way sooner or later to the more civilized domestic concept. In the West the change took place in the twelfth and thirteenth centuries and lasted until the Reformation. In the seventeenth and eighteenth centuries, during the era of Enlightenment, individualism of the modern atomistic family type began to develop. These changes generally occurred later in the East.

The "Humanists"

In order to understand the changes in family conceptions immanent at the end of the golden era of canon law, one must be aware of the impacts of many influences, such as the reformationists, Luther and Calvin, the attitudes of the kings and secular leaders who took over political power during the emergence of modern civilization, the appearance of public law codes defining the rights and obligations of husband and wife, parent and child, outer and inner relatives, of the arguments which bothered the church authorities and led to the long-continued Council of Trent, and the ensuing decisions of the church regarding the significance of the family bond.

Many attacks were made on the accepted thirteenth-century conception of the family. Rulers who, in the usual dissoluteness of royal courts, wanted to marry, divorce, and remarry, libertines, humanists, and pre-Reformation freethinkers all challenged the church doctrine, as did men of genius such as Desiderius Erasmus (1467–1536). Erasmus could not see anything in marriage to make him believe it was as sacred as the "Union of Christ with the Church." He could not see that the apostles of the church had mentioned marriage among the seven sacraments. He was particularly outspoken in referring to the marriage peculations of David and other Old Testament characters. Erasmus claimed that he wanted to return the church to its primitive simplicity and to abandon the growths of church doctrine which had developed. He himself helped with the publication of the New Testament so the common people might read it.

In *Notes on the New Testament,* in 1518, Erasmus took a rather critical position on the marriage of clergy, divorce, validity of the view that virginity was a higher state than marriage, and the conception of marriage as a sacrament, particularly in reference to marriage in First Corinthians 7. Later, in *Christian Marriage,* he modified these views sufficiently so as not to get into serious trouble with the canonical authorities at Rome. For this reason he is called a humanist rather than a reformationist. He also, by implication, discussed marriage in his *Praise of Folly, Familiar Colloquies,* and *A Comparison of the Virgin and the Martyr,* but his most comprehensive direct statements are in the work *Institution of Christian Marriage,* written in 1526 and dedicated to Queen Catherine of England. Erasmus often took two sides of the same question. He practiced a good deal of personal expediency, and was not unwilling to be disloyal to his supporters and friends if he thought it would help him.

In *Praise of Folly,* the general impression of the family and marriage is not very high. Erasmus, as is typical of the unfamilistic people who are always "experts" on the family, apparently had little conception of its fundamental meaning. Folly is the personification of a social force compounded of ignorance and all the vices of man. No man would run his head into the "collar of a matrimonial noose" if he had beforehand "considered the inconveniences of married life."

"Or indeed what woman would open her arms to receive the embraces of a husband, if she did but forecast the pangs of childbirth, and the plague of being a nurse?"

Consequently, folly is necessary to human life because the family is founded upon it. Birth comes from a bridebed solemnized by "my waiting woman, Madness" so you "cannot but acknowledge how much you are indebted to me."

This attitude toward the family and the obligations of life is not incidental. It runs through this whole work. The usual apologies of the hero-worshippers of Erasmus, that this is a "satire" and that he is trying to "make people laugh," are not enough. Erasmus was a moral teacher. (When he refused a professorship at Oxford, it was said that if "Oxford lost a professor, the world gained a man.") The tone of this work is identical with those of Plutarch and Aulus Gellius. It was presented at a time when the issue was not that between the atomistic and the domestic families, but when moral leaders of Europe were arguing that state control of familism, as opposed to control by Rome, would lead to a revitalization of the family and the moral improvement of society.

Whatever good Erasmus may have stated to exist in the family pales into insignificance when compared with his stated views of the absolute baseness of human nature. (For further amplification, see "The Uneasy Wife," "The Young Man and the Harlot," or any one of a dozen smaller essays in *Familiar Colloquies*.) He veered sharply from the moral doctrines of both the Protestant and the Catholic Churches. In essence, his views upon the family were physical rather than moral. The harlot was told to reform "to avoid syphilis." The uneasy wife broke the bedchamber over her philandering husband's head in order to make him physically unattractive, and so forth. Consequently, his views on state regulation of marriage and against celibacy of the clergy are in themselves of no particular importance. They were factors in the revolt of the intelligentsia of that period against the old conceptions of familism. The movement toward the atomistic family was as inherently a part of the sixteenth century as it was of Greek society in the fifth century B.C., or of the moral confusion among Roman leaders in the second century before our era.

Erasmus presages a revolt against all existing institutions.

> It is Folly that in varied dress, governs cities, appoints magistrates, and supports judicatures; and, in short, makes the whole course of man's life a mere children's play and push-pin diversion.

Of course such a man would not stand by Martin Luther and would let Berquin, his French translator, go to the gallows without rising to his defense. This from a man who wanted to "improve" the masses by translating and popularizing the New Testament.

The Reformationists

Erasmus's argument that marriage was not a sacrament struck deeply at former conceptions. From St. Augustine on, the theory of the church had been based upon this idea and the scholastic view promulgated in canon law of the tenth to twelfth centuries had been built around it. The Protestant Reformation, which began about the time of Erasmus, challenged this sharply. The Protestants were willing to admit only three sacraments—baptism, communion, and taking church orders. Marriage is not on this list. The reformers spoke clearly on the subject of marriage. Luther spoke a great deal on marriage. In 1522 he had already published, at Wittenberg, his views on marriage in his sermon *von ehelichen Leben*. He pointed out in this that in the preceding century the church had let a great many people take holy orders without giving them useful duties or occupations in the church, and that essentially this had harmed the family. Luther represented the north European family spirit. He idealized the humble home, with father, mother, and children carrying on their daily duties. In his sermon *von ehelichen Stand* in 1529 he appeared to consider marriage almost a sacrament instituted by God, the most dignified of all the conditions of man. He held that it ought to be regulated by the state. He cited the proverb "many countries, many costumes." Each state has its own marriage customs as well, and these should be regulated by them. Marriage belongs in the category of exterior things, such as clothing, food, houses, etc., and since exterior things are regulated by states, marriage ought also to be regulated by them. He recognized that from the standpoint of religion marriage has a high value and put it above virginity and continence. Marriage is *the* religious state, he held. He advocated the secularization of marriage, the abolition of religious orders, and doing away with celibacy of priests.

Most of Luther's ideas on the family are given in his *Commentaries on the Psalms*. Regardless of all that may be said pro and con about Luther, he was not, like Erasmus, a sophistic playboy. His intentions were of the most serious nature—to reform existing mores, to help in the development of nationalism in northern Europe and to do away with what he considered "popish errors." In discussing Psalms 127 and 128 he states clearly (adapted):

> Marriage is to be unquestioned. It is God's way of life. So also are the children to marriage. Everyone should marry. Procreation and subsistence go together. God will take care of the family people with children and a few exceptions do not disprove God's way. When men are strong and able they should marry. Strong families make strong societies. But the head of a family should not rule according to his own "fancy" but in the light of established Christian principles of family equity. Marriage and children mean work and suffering to raise the family. But this is the way of life, "a sacrifice unto God." Fundamentally, "prosperity" in a society and strong familism go together. The "idle bellied" who abstain from matrimony and familism are the very "Antichrists." The familistic person must count upon non-economic rewards. He must have need of "faith." The government and the family should work together to the same ends. Marriage is a social institution and not merely individual pleasure.

Luther's aim was to strike directly at the sins and omissions he saw about him. He thought that partial divorce under church law was a recent and harmful invention. At that time the church had a form called *divortium quoad torum,* which meant separation from bed and board. It means that the couple had no more conjugal duties, that they could live separately and be freed from all secondary obligations which derived from living together. Luther and his followers advocated absolute divorce for adultery and malicious desertion. Later they added cruelty as a cause, calling it essentially a form of desertion, as was a refusal of conjugal duty. These became quasi-desertions, and were included in full divorce.

Luther held that human nature was essentially bad and that men needed marriage to hold them in check. He himself married and led a very devoted conjugal life. Marriage was given by God to hold man honestly from concupiscence. Luther's ideas can be given succinctly.

1. Sex is bad, but in marriage for the faithful (including priests) God makes it good.

2. Marriage is obligatory for the Christians: Multiply and inherit the earth.

3. Marriage is not a sacrament, but a divine institution.

4. Marriage can be dissolved:

    a. Annulments in case of impotence because no marriage existed. (There is no marriage without *copula carnalis.*)

    b. Divorce for adultery.

    c. Divorce for refusal of conjugal duty.

    d. Divorce for diversity of religious faith.

    e. Separation for bad character of one, and in case of no reconcilation after a year, divorce.

5. Marriage should be regulated by secular authorities, the state.

6. Marriage should not take place without parental consent, although this may be given afterwards.

7. The extreme degrees of affinity and consanguinity set up by the church (to break the trustee family—see preceding chapter) were reduced to three degrees (just beyond first cousins) but mainly by the followers of Luther. (Much of this had already been done in a preliminary way in the fourth Lateran Council.)

Calvin and the other Protestant leaders followed essentially the conceptions of Luther regarding marriage. Calvin was particularly concerned that religious leaders should marry. He favored divorce for differences in religious faith, abandonment, and incompatibility (*inconvenienta in conversatione*). This led later to a long argument at the Council of Trent, where the views of Calvin were attacked by the Cardinal of Lorraine.

Calvin, who wrote at length on the subject, could not see that marriage was a sacrament unless every word in the Bible made the act it mentioned a sacrament. He thought the church had taken jurisdiction over marriage in order to gain temporal power. He attacked the libertines, both within and without the church, whom he accused of destroying marriage and the family.

A number of canon law professors also joined in the criticism of current doctrines of the family as set forth by canon law. Most prominent of these were Melchior Kling, Erasmus Sarcerius (not the humanist), and Basile Monner. All these wrote about the middle of the sixteenth century (1553–64). Monner held that marriage is honorable and sacred but that the church had gone too far in prohibiting the clergy from marrying. However, marriage is neither a sacrament nor a spiritual thing. It does not confer grace; it is common to all men, believers or not, *res plane politica*; and if God instituted it, he did it as a magistrate only. Matrimony belongs under civil, not canon law. Consent makes marriage, but not the consent of the parties alone; it should include that of the parents. There is not only a natural law, but there is also a family law (*gens* law), divine law, civil law, ancient canon law, and customary, or common, law. Above all, there is reason. All must be considered. Monner attacked Luther on polygamy. He advocated as principal grounds for divorce: adultery, desertion, impotence, heresy, cruelty, and misconduct of wife before marriage. These are for absolute, not partial divorce. The innocent party to the divorce, the one securing the divorce, can remarry.

It is not the purpose of this work to go into the ideas which motivated the religious and secular leaders of the Reformation and the resulting argument which split up the church, but simply to point out that this period was one in which most of the ideas dominating the Middle Ages were challenged sharply, among them most of the conceptions of the family bond.

The Council of Trent

These criticisms of the former doctrines of marriage and the family, along with other Reformation criticisms, led to the Council of Trent, a sort of general session of leaders in the Catholic Church, which lasted, with interruptions and different sessions, from 1536 until 1563. Out of this came a reaffirmed conception of marriage, representing the views of the Catholic Church leaders. The conclusions concerning marriage are as follows:

1. Marriage is a sacrament (the essence of holiness.)

2. Monogamy is the only permissible type. (Luther had given his consent to one secret case of polygyny.)

3. Continence is a higher state than marriage. (Luther had placed marriage above celibacy and virginity.)

4. Marriage is and makes a semipublic institution.

   a. All previous clandestine marriages are valid.

   b. No future marriage can be valid without three witnesses.

   c. Marriages by males under eighteen and females under sixteen are void without parental consent.

   d. Marriage is to be preceded by a publication of bans.

   e. It is to be contracted before a priest who is acquainted with the previous facts about the couple, as far as feasible (*proprius parochus*).

5. The conditions of marriage are to be investigated by the "semi-public" before the sacrament is permitted.

   a. See 4d on banns.

   b. See 4e on *proprius parochus*.

   c. The priest is to question the couple as to "consent."

   d. Great discretion is to be used in marriages of *vagi* (vagabonds, or those without fixed domicile).

   e. The facts of the marriage are to be written down in a church book or registry and to be jealously guarded by the priest (aids to future investigation).

6. Mixed marriages (Protestant-Catholic) can exist, but:

a. The Catholic must be left free to remain in Catholic worship.

b. The Protestant must not object if the Catholic tries to convert the Protestant.

c. The children are to be raised as Catholics.

7. Rape could not result in marriage unless the person raped was freed from the attacker and gave consent of her own free will. Rape was now a partial impediment to marriage. (The previous emphasis had almost ceased to make rape an impediment to marriage.)

8. Persons who forced marriages for pecuniary reasons, bringing about forced consent, were condemned. These were feudal authorities, secular judges, and ambitious parents. Marriage is to rest in the feelings of the married. Earlier, this had been agitated against feudal excess, and now it was against "divine right of kings."

9. The impediments arising from consanguinity, affinity, and spiritual relationship were discussed. These had been eased in the Fourth Lateran Council in 1215. They were not strengthened, indicating that the dangers of trustee family intermarriage had passed away.

10. Impotence is an impediment to marriage. (The purpose of marriage is to have children.)

11. Marriage is unbreakable. Only separation from bed and board is permitted, resting upon previous decisions of the church.

Every decision by the church on marriage was based upon a definite point of view and situation. Nowadays, we have so much legislation on marriage that few read it and fewer pay any attention to it. Migratory divorce may be illegal in one state, but no one does anything about it. Jurisdiction rules are so loose that if one cannot get along under the laws of one place, family business is transacted in another. But the church thought about its ordinances going into canon law. Earlier, it has been pointed out that the disorder created by the trustee barbarian families led to the conception of consent by the couple as the only prerequisite to marriage and also the lengthened list of relatives and affinities who could not marry each other. Those regulations were to break up the trustee family. Now we have the royal families in Europe, under the conception of divine rights of kings, stirring up royal family troubles with their use of *lettres de cachet*, requiring their followers to marry within chosen circles.

Such inbreeding aristocracies used marriage to keep the power in the family and led to trouble. Hence, the church action.

The Family Conception at the End of the Sixteenth Century

We have seen that in the later days of the Roman Empire the peoples of Europe had a weakened conception of the family, the atomistic type. The family was a contract, and there could be several types of such contracts, according to whether the persons wanted to unite as man and wife in a *dignitas* family, with husband and wife, parent and child united as one, or whether they wanted a companionate relation, without any conception of family relationship except contractual living together, or *concubinatus*. Any and all of these families could be broken easily, although beginning with Augustus the emperors tried to strengthen the family and the marriage bond by legislation. However, people did not want a strong family, so nothing the emperors could do had an overwhelming effect. Augustus could not keep his own children and grandchildren from committing adultery.

This weakened and contractual form of marriage existed under cover throughout the Middle Ages, in spite of all the church could do. To keep peace and gain the upper hand over the primitive type of trustee family law resorted to by the barbarian chiefs and the feudal barons, the church had to resort to a family conception based solely upon the consent of the persons marrying. This fitted, of course, the idea of individual moral responsibility before God. Consent could be made in a clandestine fashion, and as such could not be regulated, nor could its terms be standardized. Consequently, marriages of a contractual nature and even divorces were obtained by the ruthless few throughout the Middle Ages, through the use of clandestinism. Until the Council of Trent, and in the face of the attacks by all the reformers, the church did not have the power openly to outlaw clandestine marriages. Since the first marriage was considered the only one, those dissatisfied with their marriage could come into the open and claim that the clandestine marriage, allegedly performed earlier, was valid, and that the marriage which they wanted to abandon was not valid.

For the majority, however, up to the thirteenth century and particularly where barbarian law held full sway, the family was primarily of the trustee type. However, the trustee family was beginning to break up then. Certain classes—particularly the masses held under the feudal right of the barbarians in the old empire—had never accepted much of trustee family law, except as they had to in order to live.

We might say that in general by the thirteenth century the dominant family in Western Europe was the domestic type of family. The people were ready for the beginnings of commerce and trade and for the revolutions in all fields which laid the groundwork for our modern period. The inclosure acts would soon be effected, publicly as well as privately; the farms of England would be changed from common tillage to pasture; the former villagers would enter the small domestic factories and make wool into cloth. Society and the family were getting ready for a change, for the fundamental swing towards individualism which gave us the modern times.

If we examine the ideas during the Reformation about this family, we can see that the revolt is well under way. The domestic family had developed so far that people were ready to advocate radical changes in its whole nature and organization. They were ready to grant divorces, so that the family could not engulf the individual for life. They were ready to remove the family from church to civil control, so that it could be the subject of ever-changing legislation. Only in the church were people reluctant to give up the doctrine of marriage as a sacrament. The strong family was vanishing. In the West it had largely vanished as a legal instrument by the thirteenth century. However, there was still need for some form of family guidance. People were ready to recognize rather than oppose consent to marriage and interference by the older families. While the family was exceptionally strong and regulated marriage of its members (even though not legally), there was no need for legislation making parental consent to marriage a necessity long after puberty. Now that family bonds were weaker, society felt the need of its support. The new family could not get along as well by itself as it had under the guidance and support of the older type of familism. Therefore, the church conception of marriage as a sacrament also found its adherents during these times.

Conclusion

Thus from St. Augustine on, the church had been outlining and impressing upon the demoralized peoples of Europe the essence of sacrament in marriage and family life. It was also trying to avoid blood vengeance and the worst phases of barbarian trusteeship as far as possible. It had sought to have the good—the sacrament of the family—accepted; and to avoid the bad—the inbreeding, the building-up of strong willful family strains who, as long as there was no strong central authority to discipline them, would have their own justice, their own vengeance, their own private feuds and wars, resulting in the extermination of whole neighborhoods.

From this can be understood the marriage sacrament, the extreme and far-reaching rules on seven degrees of exogamy, the emphasis upon marriage as requiring the consent of only the spouses-to-be. The barbarian family had in their trustee organization those things which cause interfamily strife. The Romanized families had the secular conception of private contractual marriage. The church sought to convert the Roman idea to that of marriage as a sacrament and to reduce the power of the barbarian family to a livable human organization.

We can also understand now the conceptions of Hegel when he speaks of each set of conditions as having within it its antithesis. Within the family as finally codified in the beginning of the golden age of canon law (the twelfth century) was freedom of consent, clandestine freedom, and the very elements of freedom which, when Roman law and learning were revived, led to the Reformation and its further extension of freedom.

It is possible to understand why Luther, Calvin, Zwingli, Melanchthon, Desiderius Erasmus, Kling, Erasmus Sarcerius, and Basile Monner, among others, would advocate parental interference in marriage, divorce, the secular aspect, as opposed to the sacramental, and civil control of marriage. In the first place, the new era of trade, commerce, civil government, and social change or progress was not possible under the domination of the old family. From the early conception of the dignity of the human personality, instituted by the church, they got the idea of the extension of this dignity, this freedom. The decline of the medieval trustee family made family interference in marriage no longer a danger but, as a matter of fact, a help, a social necessity. Families could no longer endanger society by interfering in marriage. With the coming of travel, movement, and the development of trading towns, the young people could get away from their ancestral families and make marriage and family decisions on their own. They no longer were guided by the rules and regulations, legal or nonlegal, of their families or of local powers under feudal law.

The era of medieval trustee family dominance was over; the domestic family was so well instituted that it was beginning to break up into a far freer family. This was recognized not only by the reformationists but by the bishops of the church at the Council of Trent. They themselves raised the age of free consent to sixteen and eighteen years of age; clandestine marriages were abolished; witnesses were required; parental consent was necessary; the local clergy had to seal the marriage (*proprius parochus*); marriage must be registered and safeguards must be taken to establish semipublic agencies to oversee marriages, since the strong family was breaking up.

The main difference between the reformationists and the Council of Trent was that the reformationists went further than the church would go. Both went in the same direction. Thus, those who contend that the Council of Trent did not move forward in some aspects of family matters are distinctly wrong. The church position is as follows: "La doctrine de l'Église sur l'état de mariage n'a point varié. Ce qui change, ce sont les formes de l'opposition qu'elle recontre" (*Théologie Catholique*, 9, II, 2285). (The doctrine of the church on the state of marriage has never varied. What changes are the forms of opposition it encounters.)

On the main points this is correct. From the time of St. Augustine until today, marriage has been held to be a sacrament. However, adapting rules to social conditions as they exist at given times has brought about certain changes—like that from trusteeship to the domestic family, and from the domestic to the atomistic family. This seems inherent.

Since the time of St. Augustine, *fides, proles,* and *sacramentum* had always been the mainstays of the Catholic doctrine. This order was established in the earlier period. Later, *proles* became the primary value. The Protestants made *proles* increasingly the main stem of the family, keeping *fides,* but losing *sacramentum.* In the early years the church had trouble with the elements of trusteeship. In its later periods, the rise of atomism was to worry it greatly.

7

THE RISE OF MODERN ATOMISM FROM
THE REFORMATION TO THE
NINETEENTH CENTURY

SELDOM IN HISTORY HAS THERE been such a complete and violent change in the attitude toward the family as that which has occurred since the Reformation of the fifteenth and sixteenth centuries in the modern Western world. Such a change took place in Rome from the time of the Twelve Tables through the decadence of the empire and in Greece from the time of Solon through the Hellenic or post-Alexandrian period. Undoubtedly there have been great shifts in the conceptions of the nature of the family bond in Hindu, Confucian, and Buddhist civilizations, as well as among the Jews, Egyptians, Persians, and Muslims. However, these changes generally have been within the trustee and the domestic conceptions of the family bond. Complete atomization of the family has seldom, if ever, gained great headway among these peoples. Among the great masses of Asian populations, social transitions have seldom gone as far as among the common people of the West.

There have also been revolutionary periods, such as the English Revolution of Cromwell, the French Revolution of 1789, and the Russian

Revolution of 1917. During such periods the family, as far as the law was concerned, moved in a few short years from the domestic conception of semisacredness to a purely private agreement of a secular nature. However, as far as their immediate effects were concerned, these three revolutionary attitudes toward the family did not last very long. The Cromwellian reforms lasted from 1653 until they were repealed in 1660. They merely made marriage a civil contract and placed it beneath the jurisdiction of justices of the peace, instead of under the church officials. Divorce was not mentioned since, in spite of the Reformation, people still considered marriage a sacrament.

The French Revolution did not move immediately against family law, regardless of what actually happened in behavior between the sexes. From 1785 on a number of pamphlets and books were written against the family, but it was only in 1791 that Title II, Article 7, was inserted in the constitution. This defined marriage as "only a civil contract." A form for the making of this new civil contract was drawn up in 1792 and the principles of divorce were established. In 1790 in a Catholic country a civil contract could be broken, whereas one hundred and thirty years earlier, in a similar revolution in a Protestant country, it was still sacred, though civil. The law of 1792 made divorce absolute, by mutual consent, for incompatibility of temper, at the request of either spouse and for seven other "reasons." During the year of 1797 there were more divorces than marriages in Paris. In 1798 the people began to react against divorce. A six-month attempt at reconciliation was required before divorce for incompatibility became final. The Code Napoleon reacted against these innovations and made divorce more difficult. It greatly restricted divorce, particularly for incompatibility and by mutual consent. When Napoleon fell, the law of 1816 did away with divorce. It was restored only in 1884.

The philosophy of the family during the French Revolution is very interesting. Of those who witnessed the period, the best exposition is that by André Nougarede (*Histoire des loix sur le mariage et sur le divorce*, Paris, 1803). He had just finished a two-volume history of the family since the earliest Roman days and therefore viewed the changes during the Revolution with broad historical perspective. According to him, the statement by the Assembly that marriage was a civil contract dissolvable by divorce was false, because the Assembly was really trying to put into effect the concepts of the philosophers from Montesquieu through Rousseau, namely, that marriage was a private contract requiring merely civil registration. To prove this Nougarede quotes these philosophers to show that they denied that marriage was a perpetual union of man and wife. Nougarede stated specifically that these philosophers held that birth made the child the property of the parent, not a county. According to Montesquieu, the child had no right to inherit from his parent. If the parent wished to give the child something, that was his own business. In other words, the position taken by St. Augustine that parent and child were one was completely and absolutely denied in the philosophies which motivated the family changes in the Revolution. The Assembly showed this falsity in its actual divorce legislation, which was of three types: action of one party and without determined cause; action by mutual consent; and action with cause. Only divorce with cause, and possibly that of mutual consent, gave the marriage any legal civil contract meaning. Mutual consent divorce put marriage on the level of the Roman *concubinatus* or secondary marriage; one-party divorce without determined cause gave to marriage no more civil consequence than an affair with a prostitute.

After the Revolution of 1917 the family in Russia followed the same meteoric course. For a time, as in France, neither mutual consent nor culpability of one partner was necessary for a divorce. Thus, revolutionary elements of the population carry marriage and family conceptions further than those of legal contract, since to break a contract one party must fail to live up to the agreed terms or both must agree that the contract is unsatisfactory. In Russia, as in France, either party could ask for a divorce. For a while in Russia it was not necessary to notify the other party. The attitude toward marriage in these revolutionary periods became extremely casual. In a French assembly about 1798 Savard made fun of the people for convicting a man and condemning him to penal servitude for bigamy, since all he did was to "neglect a simple formality." To tell the court he wanted a divorce was a simple act of his own volition, a mere "formality."

During the Revolution the family in Russia passed through several stages. The Code of 1918 practically abolished the family as a legal instrument. The individual was made the unit before the state; he was not to be influenced or to have legal responsibility for his relatives or for his spouse. Marriage as a form was kept only as a "concession to political necessity." If one were a female of sixteen or a male of eighteen, an adolescent, sane, unmarried, or divorced, and capable of consent, all that was necessary was to register the marriage with the civil authorities. Divorce was rapid and without control, condition, or delay. Divorce was granted upon registration for mutual consent or the wish of either party. When the couple married they took the same name, but it could be the husband's or the wife's or a combination of both family names. Common residence or common jurisdiction was not necessary. In all legal rights the individual was completely free. Marriage was relieved of every duty which could be taken from it and still allow it to be called marriage. According to the revolutionary doctrine, marriage formed a simple society of equal and free persons who had only their personalities as a common interest. In compliance with this conception of a free union of persons, rights and duties between parents and children were reduced as far as possible. In the Code of 1928 many of these principles were extended in that registration was not necessary for marriage, but registration, once made, was proof of marriage. Even liaisons before adolescence and before proper age could become marriages upon reaching adolescence and the proper age. The only restrictions to marriage were health, sanity, and blood relationship in a direct line, that is, as near as half-brothers and half-sisters. One could not marry parent or grandparent, brother, sister, half-brother or half-sister.

There was the same reaction in Russia as in France. The marriage law of 1936 reverted toward Victorianism. In fact, the laws of 1944 prohibit divorce and reward familism. 1816 in France and 1944 in Russia are almost identical sociological years, as far as the family is concerned. In either case the reverse movement occurred before a counterrevolution took place.

But these are minor fluctuations of the family connected with revolutionary disorganization. Their only importance to us is the influence they have after their times in the gradual spread of disorganization. Thus we have the influence of the Napoleonic Code in Europe after the French Revolution, the influence of the Cromwellian idea upon the secularization of marriage in England, and the popularization and spread of the Marxian antifamilistic conception by its adoption in Russia in the earlier stages of the Revolution. Finally, on the one hand they show in a specific sense the relation between shorter periods of demoralization and family nihilism and on the other the recuperation of society from demoralization and the resurgence of familism. Thus revolutionary periods, with cycles of demoralization and antifamilism, remoralization and profamilism, compress into short periods the longer swings between these two processes, such as that from the Middle Ages to the present, or from early Rome through the empire to the curative periods after the fall of the Western Empire.

Family Conceptions of the Seventeenth Century

After the decisions of the Council of Trent, marriage and family doctrine seemed almost dormant for a century. It was as if the people of northern Europe were ashamed of what they had done and would go no further. England practically fell back on common law, insofar as she had gotten away from it. The same applies to other barbarian law countries. In France in 1579 the Ordinance of Blois had been passed, ordering local officials to keep a copy of the registers of marriages, baptisms, and burials which they were to get from the records of the clergy. These conditions were modified from time to time, particularly because the state interceded between the Protestants and Catholics. A gradual change toward secular control grew up, so that:

> In the last phases of ancient law (before the Revolution of the end of the eighteenth century) the clergy were simple agents of the civil power in the celebration of marriages and for keeping civil registers. In prohibiting the clergy from interfering with civil acts of the state, the temporal power was only using its recognized right of a mandatory power, thus revoking its previous mandates (Translation from Ernest Glasson, *Le mariage civil et le divorce*, Paris, 1880, 247).

Thus we see the growing rights of secular institutions in the family associated with increasing recognition of the secular conception of marriage and the family bond. In our sense of the term, no divorces were permitted until the Revolution. In general, the seventeenth-century family conception is best illustrated by the verse:

> Boire, manger, coucher ensemble
> Est mariage ce me semble.
> (To drink, to eat, to sleep together
> This is marriage, to my mind.)

But after the Ordinance of Blois, to keep it up to date the people added:

> Mais il faut que l'Église y passe.
> (But it is necessary for the church to approve.)

These words indicate that the people considered marriage merely coliving, *copula carnalis*, except that for good form it was necessary to have the church bless the ceremony. This is a long way from the sacramental conception.

The seventeenth century in Germany was one in which secular jurists and lawyers set up their conceptions of the nature of marriage. They differed little from the church theories, but their very presence in this field gave a nonsacramental sanction to marriage and family obligations. As Gierke's studies of the jurisconsults show, from now on the family became a group, one of the numerous groups composing society. It partook of the nature of other social groups except where exceptions were made, as they were by the sixteenth-century school of natural right, which held that the state and family were separated from all other groups, corporations, and associations and were given unique characteristics of their own. In time, however, this uniqueness of character of the family disappeared; by the end of the eighteenth century all groups were considered man-made contracts, not God-made and irrevocable. This was the natural outgrowth of the social contract school, a logical development of their ideas which continued until the general fright given European peoples by the French and American Revolutions.

The first change in Germany in the seventeenth century was the development of the conception that the clergy in registering births, deaths, and marriages, and in celebrating marriages, was acting as an agent of the state rather than as an official of the church. This change is clearly shown by a study of the church records. (Klein Lengden, a typical Nieder-Saxon village just outside of Göttingen, began its registers in 1624 and, like other German villages, acted as agent for the state until the reforms of Bismarck about the end of the nineteenth century.)

The second change was from the conception of marriage beginning with *sponsalia,* or engagement, to the position that *Beischlaf,* or *copula carnalis,* established the union. The medieval church, with its centuries of controversy over *sponsalia de praesenti* versus *sponsalia de futuro,* had held such a sacramental conception of marriage that even the first promise became a part of the contract and could not be broken except for sacramental reasons of an even higher character. It is difficult, of course, to evaluate sacraments, but evidently continence was a higher state than marriage. This enabled the church to define continence as a greater sacrament than marriage, so that during most of the Middle Ages a person who was partner in a marriage *sponsalia per verba de futuro* (promised) but not yet *copula carnalis* (consummated) could put aside marriage to take religious orders. The Germans now adopted an old practice among them of separating engagement and marriage. They held that parties were free to change their minds until *copula carnalis.* This was a further secularization and weakening of the marriage conception, but they held it to be in the interests of good familism. The individual rather than the family was now making the choice; consequently, he was given leeway for errors in original judgment.

During this period a great many seventeenth-century jurists discussed the family more or less incidentally to their theories of law and society. Most outstanding—and typical, because he took a middle-of-the-road policy—was Samuel Pufendorf (1632–94), whose ideas on the family are incidental to his *De jure naturae et gentium,* 1672. He discusses the relation of the state to the sub-bodies (*pecularia corpora civilia subdita*) and finds only the family prior to the state. Consequently the family has kept all rights except those *specifically taken from it by the state.* All other suborganizations of the state have only those rights given them by the state, because they are posterior to and formed by the state. This conception of the family makes it a strong unit, but far from an indissoluble sacrament created and ordained by God.

The seventeenth-century English conception of the family bond may be illustrated by the Cromwell revolution, the results of which were discussed above, and by a few writers like Marc Antoine de Dominis, Archbishop Apostat de Spalato, Milton, Thomas Hobbes, and John Locke. Marc Antoine de Dominis published a two-volume work in London in 1620, *De republica ecclesiastica*. His ideas, half on the side of sacrament and half not, seem to have evoked considerable criticism from the Catholic writers. In volume I he calls marriage a sacrament but leaves a loophole by stating that such a sacrament exists only when the contract is perfect. This permits any marriage to be broken by calling it an imperfect contract. This is an historical repetition of the weakening of the family bond, since the people conceive of more than one type or class of marriage. In volume II, de Dominis goes into Bible history to try to prove that marriage is not a sacrament instituted by Jesus Christ.

The Puritan Philosophy

John Milton, the Puritan poet (1608–74), denied that marriage was either a sacrament or a lower state of living, such as was suggested by the earlier conception of continence as the highest level of life. Milton placed the family on the same level as did Luther. He was as great an advocate of divorce as was Luther and justified it by the same reasons and the same scriptual examples. He emphasized particularly the necessity for maintaining the right of repudiation for the husband.

Milton's arguments are as follows:

Both Old and New Testaments (Moses and Christ) permit divorce for reasons other than adultery.

To prohibit divorce except those that Moses accepted is "against the reason of law."

1. A bad marriage has no purpose, and God had no intention of having marriages without purpose.

2. It is iniquitous to look after the body (separation) and not the mind.

3. Marriage is not a remedy against lust, but the fulfilling of conjugal love, and should be broken if there is no conjugal love.

4. The dissatisfied marriage companion is in greater temptations than before.

5. God wants love and peace in the family and not compulsory marriage performance.

6. Incompatible matrimony is as hard on a Christian as an idolatrous match.

7. Idolatrous heretics ought to be divorced after allowing a reasonable time for conversion.

8. There are greater violations of marriage than adultery, and adultery is permitted as a ground of divorce by Moses and other divines.

9. It is against nature to prohibit divorce when couples are not fitted to each other.

10. At times continuance of marriage will shorten and endanger lives.

11. Many who marry are not fitted for it, and force ought not to be used.

12. Marriage is not a mere carnal coition but a human society, and where sociability cannot be had there is no true matrimony.

Even Hobbes, the most authoritarian of the English thinkers, does not consider the family in any way a sacrament. For him there is only one sacrament, the Leviathan state. There can be as many kinds of marriage as there are civil contracts. Even generation or parenthood gives no unbreakable power to parent-child relations. In disputes over the family, the state has the right of decision under civil law. Consequently marriage is a civil-law contract, and it is implied that the family can be broken. Sacrament, an unbreakable right, is dominion, and the family is a contractual right, not dominion. In the case of Hobbes, however, the differences between the family contract and the state contract are not great.

John Locke published his *Second Treatise of Civil Government* in 1690. He goes the whole way toward considering marriage a purely civil contract. As we Americans ought to know from his effects on our early government and Founding Fathers, his influence, as Pollock said, was "Probably the most important contribution ever made to English constitutional law by an author who was not a lawyer by profession." Locke has a distinctly reverential attitude toward the family. This is characteristic of his time; even the "barebones Parliament" of Cromwell had not dared legislate on divorce. He quotes the Old Testament, "Honor thy father and thy mother," and so forth, at length. But his fundamental analysis is secular in nature.

Law must be a law of "reason"—"the end of law is not to abolish or restrain, but to preserve and enlarge freedom." "The power, then, that parents have over their children arises from that duty which is incumbent upon them, to take care of their offspring during the imperfect state of childhood." Actions must all be within the bounds of law based upon "reason" and "understanding." The fact of the family, and the strength of the marriage bond, depends entirely upon what the members contribute to each other. Begetting gives no power. If it did, what would "become of this paternal power in that part of the world where one woman hath more than one husband at a time? Or in those parts of America where, when husband and wife part, which happens frequently, the children are all left to the mother, follow her and are wholly under her care and provision?"

> Conjugal society is made by a voluntary compact between man and woman, and though it consist chiefly in such a communion and right in one another's bodies as is necessary to its chief end, procreation, yet it draws with it mutual support and assistance, and a communion of interest too, as necessary not only to unite their care and affection, but also necessary to their common offspring, who have a right to be nourished and maintained by them till they are able to provide for themselves.
>
> For the end of conjunction between male and female being not barely procreation, but the continuation of the species, this conjunc-

tion betwixt male and female ought to last, even after procreation, so long as is necessary to the nourishment and support of the young ones, who are to be sustained by those that got them till they are able to shift and provide for themselves.

But though these are ties upon mankind which make the conjugal bonds more firm and lasting in a man than in other species of animals, yet it would give one reason to inquire why this compact, where procreation and education are secured and inheritance taken care for, may not be made determinable either by consent, or at a certain time, or upon certain conditions, as well as any other voluntary compacts, there being no necessity in the nature of the thing, nor to the ends of it, that it should always be for life—I mean, to such as are under no restraint of any positive law which ordains all such contracts to be perpetual.

The ideas and revolts of Puritanism were transplanted to seventeenth-century New England, and with them a fully secular conception of marriage. However, like most post-Reformation Protestants, the Puritans were stricter about formalities than the old church had been. For instance, the marriage ceremony was now secular, but a man could be whipped for kissing his wife in public. Eventually a reaction occurred, but it was not until 1733 that all ministers of the Gospel were permitted to perform the wedding ceremony. Marriages had to be registered in the local towns. Neglect of the legal forms did not invalidate marriage, although the offender might be fined. This is the Reformation doctrine that the true measure of marriage is *copula carnalis*. Nevertheless, here as in England marriage was taken seriously, and if the family did not constitute a sacrament, it was nevertheless considered sacred. Courtship, bundling, precontracts, marriage, adultery, and behavior of children were all subjects of lawmaking. Adulterers were subject to the death penalty if the woman was married or espoused. Later came the "scarlet letter" days of branding for adultery. Incest was also punished by branding. Betrothal, *beweddung*, or *sponsalia de futuro* was revived as a part of the marriage contract. In the colonies where there was no Puritan influence civil marriage came later. This was the case even in the Dutch colonies, which had had civil marriage at home since the sixteenth century. Legislative divorce was established in the New England colonies, but of course it was expensive. Other American colonies used common law separation from bed and board, but we are not too well informed about this.

Thus the seventeenth century saw the revival of common-law custom throughout Europe; the development of common law into written law with regard to the registration of marriages and family affairs; the recognition that states were to regulate the family; and an intellectual challenge by lay thinkers of the inviolability of the marriage contract. This represented the spread of Reformationist dissent in two directions. Luther was influenced in part by the "golden age" of canon law, in part by the residues of tribal or barbarian custom. This same conflict affected the reformers of England and of other north European countries. Luther indicates the existence of the conflict when he tells of the difficulties in explaining to the peasants of northern Europe the meaning of *sponsalia* as interpreted by the church. (There was no such difficulty in explaining this to the trustee family of the aristocracy.) In France, England, Germany, and northern Europe generally, as well as in the North American colonies, the family fell back upon common law. Where there was no common law but only a remembrance of Roman codes, the people adhered more or less to the church conceptions.

A second trend occurring in this century was the growing criticism of the strength of the marriage bond and its breakableness. This movement was to flourish with great profusion and strength in the eighteenth century. Hobbes, Milton, Pufendorf, Marc Antoine de Dominis, the German jurists, the intelligentsia everywhere in changing Europe were setting forth new conceptions of the family bond. When these spread and were accepted there resulted a radical loosening of feeling regarding the sacredness of familism.

The greatest changes were the separation of church from state and the acceptance of nonchurch philosophers as the formulators of state familism. Church historians are right when they say:

> Le début de la grande offensive des régaliens contre les droits exercés
> par l'Église en matière de mariage, on peut en fixer la date au début

du XVII siècle. Alors les juriconsultes commencèrent à tirer de la disjunction du contrat et du sacrement les déductions pratiques dont le couronnement séra la théorie du mariage civil. (*Théologie Catholique*, 9, II, 2262). (The beginning of the grand offensive by the state authorities against the church in the matter of marriage came at the beginning of the seventeenth century. Then the jurists began to draw practical deductions from the distinction between contract and sacrament, and the climax to this was to be the theory of marriage as a civil contract.)

Atomistic Familism of the Eighteenth Century

The eighteenth century was one in which civil marriage and conceptions of state regulation of the family gradually surmounted the former idea of church rule. The eighteenth century was one in which philosophic contempt for the indissolubility of marriage and family bonds completely shattered the sacredness formerly attributed to the family. A premonition of this was given at the end of the seventeenth century when Locke suggested that there was no fundamental reason for a family to hold together after the children were educated and provided for, and implied that limited contractual marriages and families could be created which would terminate after they had accomplished these functions.

French thought regarding the strength of the marriage bond erupted violently in favor of the breakable contract, following the earlier thought of Montaigne and Bodin. Montaigne held that the attempt to strengthen marriage and family bonds by making the union indissoluble and by consistently opposing its dissolution had resulted in the destruction of love and affection as the cohesive agents within the family. In his opinion the Roman family owed its greatness to the freedom of the individual to dissolve the marriage if one of the partners did not fulfill the marriage vows. Bodin held that marriage should be of a dissolvable nature. These philosophers belong to an earlier century but influenced the thinkers of the eighteenth century. Rousseau, who was to the French Revolution what

Tom Paine was to ours, also held that the family contract was dissolvable. Essentially his idea was the same as that of John Locke—that after the children grow up, the family should naturally be dissolved.

Voltaire's *Dictionnaire Philosophique* is, of course, the one complete source for the ideas of the family bond of the French literati of the eighteenth century. The work has been published in many different editions, in many volumes, and includes in its more comprehensive editions a number of papers presented to the Academy of Sciences. A few short quotations will give the essential ideas:

> "Induce your subjects to marry as early as possible."
>
> "The more married men you have, the fewer crimes there will be."
>
> "Let your soldiers marry and they will no longer desert. Bound to their families, they will be bound to their country."
>
> "Marriage is a contract of the law of nations, of which the Roman Catholics have made a sacrament. But contract and sacrament are two very different things; with the one are connected civil effects, with the other the graces of the Church."
>
> "Adultery is an evil only inasmuch as it is a theft; but we do not steal that which is given to us."
>
> "It sometimes happens amongst us that a dissatisfied husband, not choosing to institute a criminal process against his wife for adultery, which would subject him to the imputation of *barbarity*, contents himself with obtaining a separation of person and property (*a mensa et a thoro*)." (Voltaire objects to this practice in favor of absolute divorce.)
>
> "The Justinian code, which we have adopted in several points, authorizes divorce; but the canonical law, which the Catholics have placed before it, does not permit it."
>
> "Divorce is probably of nearly the same date as marriage. I believe, however, that marriage is some weeks more ancient; that is to say, men quarreled with their wives at the end of five days, beat them at the end of a month, and separated from them at the end of six weeks cohabitation."

Thus the French thinkers not only developed the idea that the family was a state phenomenon, but also introduced a skeptical, individualistic, and evolutionary attitude toward marriage. Consequently, marriage becomes a means by which the state gains control over the individual; it will endure as an institution only so long as the state keeps its aims before the people, and so long as the people are willing to subordinate their personal desires to those of the state. The state is to be interested in marriage only to the extent that it gains by such interest—fewer crimes, better soldiers, more virtuous citizens, and so forth. At the same time, marriage is defined as an individualistic contract; the unrestrained individual is given considerable leeway in marriage; he is free to regard family relationships as existing purely for momentary satisfaction. From the intellectual point of view, the fragility of marriage is tremendously increased over its former state. The idea of sacrament, first attacked successfully in the later fourteenth and early fifteenth centuries by the humanists and reformationists, has now been left out of the marriage concept. The stage is being set for the most radical conception of the relation—the idea that the marriage justifies itself only in private, transient, and conscious sensory reactions.

The same movement took place in Germany, although it was not so widespread or so popular as in France. The most antifamilistic writings in Germany in the eighteenth century were anonymous because the northern barbarian states were still more familistic by custom. Most thinkers still had the Lutheran conception of marriage and the family, and while not considered as conferring grace, the family was held the most sacred state of secular man. Laws were widely debated to require church, as opposed to civil, marriage.

David Hume Expresses the Ultimate State View of Modern Familism

The revolution in England was over in the eighteenth century. The people were concerned more with the problems of empire which had fallen into their laps than with marriage. They were still obsessed with the doctrines of common law—their version of the barbarian codes. Dissenters had already gone, or were going rapidly, to the colonies. In the colonies they could set up the type of marriage and family bonds they wished. David Hume was most typical of the philosophers of that century in England. Locke and his tradition of freedom had passed over into France and to the American colonies, where it reappeared again after the French and American Revolutions. Hume was essentially a defender of the family:

> There is a set of men lately sprung up amongst us, who endeavor to distinguish themselves by ridiculing everything, that has hitherto appeared sacred and venerable in the eyes of mankind. Reason, sobriety, honor, friendship, marriage are the perpetual subjects of their insipid raillery; and even public spirit, and a regard to our country, are treated as chimerical and romantic. Were the schemes of these anti-reformers to take place, all the bonds of society must be broken. . . .

Hume here advances beyond the thinking of Locke and emphasizes an idea which becomes popular later in the twentieth century—that familism is essential to the continued purposes of the state and the larger society.

In another essay Hume takes up his theory of marriage, polygamy, and divorce.

> As marriage is an engagement entered into by mutual consent, and has for its end the propagation of the species, it is evident that it must be susceptible of all the variety of conditions which consent established, provided they be not contrary to this end.
>
> A man, in conjoining himself to a woman, is bound to her according to the terms of his engagement: in begetting children, he is bound by all the ties of nature and humanity, to provide for their substance and education. When he has performed these two parts of duty, no one can reproach him with injustice or injury. And as the terms of his engagement, as well as the methods of subsisting his offspring, may be various, it is mere superstition to imagine

that marriage can be entirely uniform, and will admit of only one mode or form. Did not human laws restrain the natural liberty of men, every particular marriage would be as different as contracts or bargains of any other kind of species.

He then discusses alleged cases of polygyny, polyandry, and group marriage:

All regulations, therefore, in this heading, are equally lawful and equally conformable to the principles of nature; though they are not equally convenient, or equally useful to society.

He then rejects polygamy and favors monogamy, and takes up the subject of divorce, particularly divorce by mutual agreement. He says the argument for divorce is based upon cruelty which preserves "by violence, an union which, at first, was made by mutual love, and is now, in effect, dissolved by mutual hatred." Then, freedom of divorce militates against domestic quarrels. Finally, having deprived men of polygamy, why now imprison them from a recurring choice in love?

Against mutual consent divorce he sets up three arguments: what will become of the children ("shall we [put] it in the power of parents, upon every caprice, to render their posterity miserable?"); friendship, the heart of marriage, "thrives under constraint"; and "nothing is more dangerous than to unite two persons so closely in all their interests and concerns, as man and wife, without rendering the union entire and total."

He further notes "when divorces were most frequent among the Romans, marriages were most rare," and concludes, "the exclusion of polygamy and divorces sufficiently recommends our present European practice with regard to marriage."

Thus, the English thinker of the eighteenth century was indecisive. Marriage is a private contract, restrained by the state. There is no necessary uniformity in marriage. Once it has performed its duty by educating the children there is no valid reason why it should not be broken. Even polygamy, polyandry, and polygyny are right in their time and place. However, for public reasons marriage is to be limited to monogamous indissolubility. The empire needs responsible parents, colonists, and soldiers. Furthermore, if persons are forced to stay married, they become used to it and in time come to like it. Both Hume and Voltaire put forth the conception that the state needs the family. This idea again emerged violently in the twentieth century, after marriage had been philosophically dissolved in the nineteenth century.

During this century, England had been having trouble with the old common-law custom of private marriages which, in the urbanization of the country, became badly demoralized and disorganized. The Hardwicke Act was passed in 1753, making all marriages public and requiring them to be preceded by banns. Quakers, Jews, and members of the royal family were excepted. This was an expression of the idea set forth by Hume that the state was to see that marriage and the family adapted themselves to public designs. At that time engagement, either *sponsalia per verba de futuro* or *per verba de praesenti*, was eliminated from its legal connection with marriage.

In the American colonies the people did away with the earlier harsh laws prohibiting church marriages in the New England colonies. Legislative divorce was generally established. The general trend of Protestantism found effective expression in statute and judicial decree. The American legal conception of divorce as pertaining not to the criminal but exclusively to the civil jurisdiction had its birth in the seventeenth century.

Divorce *a mensa et a thoro* was abandoned. The minister and the justice of the peace shared marriage business between them. Legislative divorce was permitted widely and for many "causes." The stage was set for the nineteenth century and the contractualization of the family.

Paine and Anti-institutionalism

Thomas Paine, the Rousseau of our Revolution, did not pay as much attention to the family as did the European rationalists of the eighteenth century. There is a peculiar explanation for this. Paine was a farm boy from the little village of Thetford in England. He was raised in a Quaker background and, as is typical of agrarian revolutionists, although he attacked every other phase of the social order and social institutions, he omitted criticism of the family. Paine did not begin his voluminous political writing until he was past his period of great sexual unrest. He was thirty-seven years of age when he landed in America in mid-January of 1775. Shortly afterward he became the editor of *The Pennsylvania Magazine*. On April 19 of that year the battle of Lexington occurred. From that time on, beginning with *Common Sense* and the *Crisis* papers, to the end of his life, Paine was for the most part involved in revolutionary struggle of a political nature. He was so absorbed in actual revolutionary movements during his stay in America that except for the work of a few months his writing was preponderantly political. When later in France, under sentence of imprisonment and possibly the guillotine, he again had leisure, he was almost sixty years of age. His thoughts turned almost exclusively to religion and this resulted in *The Age of Reason*, his controversial arguments for deism. By that time he was homesick and lonely for the solace of a family. His first wife had been dead for thirty-five years (she died in 1760) and he had been separated from his second wife, Elizabeth Olive, for more than twenty years. (He was imprisoned in 1795, had lived with Elizabeth very little since 1770, and had not seen her since 1774.)

Paine remarks upon this homesickness, in reference to marriage, in a letter from England in 1789:

> Though I appear a sort of wanderer, the married state has not a sincerer friend than I am. It is the harbour of human life, and is, with respect to the things of this world, what the next world is to this. It is *home*; and that one word conveys more than any other word can express. For a few years we may glide along the tide of youthful single life and be wonderfully delighted; but it is a tide that flows but once, and what is still worse, it ebbs faster than it flows and leaves many a hapless voyager aground. I am one, you see, that have experienced the fate I am describing.

To Paine, one institution always remained sacred—the family. This runs through his whole life experience. His consideration of his relations with his second wife as a separation, whereas "common lawyers" whom he had used to get the separation and settlement wanted to consider it an absolute divorce, is one proof. His correspondence with women, almost puritanical in nature, is a second.

However, in the short period when Paine did write freely on non-political or religious subjects, three papers appeared concerning love and marriage—"Cupid and Hymen" (April 1775), "Reflections on Unhappy Marriages" (June 1775), and "An Occasional Letter to the Female Sex" (August 1775). We shall never know whether these would have continued to be autobiographical of his own failure in marriage, as he indicates in "Cupid and Hymen," or whether they would have developed into an advocacy of mutual consent divorce, on the grounds that it would perfect marriage, as occurred with Montaigne. In "Cupid and Hymen" the old man and the young girl have a dream marriage for seven years and then decide not to consummate their real marriage. In *Reflections*, the Indian contrasts the marriages of aborigines and Christians and claims that since Christians cannot separate from their wives:

> as soon as ever you meet you long to part; and not having this relief in your power, by way of revenge, double each other's misery; Whereas in ours, which have no other ceremony than mutual affection, and last no longer than they bestow mutual pleasure, we make it our business to oblige the heart we are afraid to lose. . . .

In eighteenth-century America, however, the people were primarily interested in matters other than divorce and the weakening of the marriage bond. Paine understood this and kept his separation from Elizabeth Olive a secret, because the "Tories would have used it" to break the influence of his patriotic writings. In America the eighteenth century was one of struggle for political freedom. The nineteenth century was to be a struggle for freedom of the individual from the family.

Overall, the philosophers of the eighteenth century secularized the conception of marriage and alienated the people from former religious conceptions of family duty and loyalty. But they also separated the state as a family power from the church and joined forces with the state for the regulation of the family. Earlier, when the Greeks from Solon on, and Augustus through his *Leges Juliae,* sought to regulate marriage, it took a long time before the Greeks and Romans accepted the idea of state control of the family, and it was several centuries before any great amount of attention was paid to public, as opposed to family and religious, regulation of the family. From the point of view of the secularization of the family, the eighteenth-century philosophers effected the Reformation and completed the transition from church to state control of the family. Under the philosophers the state stepped into the quarrels between the Catholics, Lutherans, and Calvinists and assumed control, as earlier the church had assumed control over the waning trustee familism of the Middle Ages. Thus another authoritarian agency, the state philosopher, emerges as the eventual regulator of the family.

The Anglo-Saxon Family

Since our culture is so flavored by descent from the Anglo-Saxon cultural stem, its history concerns us greatly. It is all the more important because Maine, Howard, Westermarck, and others who write within the Anglo-Saxon tradition do not seem to have the slightest conception of the existence of any English family type prior to the late domestic, discussed in Blackstone's *Commentaries on Common Law.*

The early English family was of the trustee variety. We do not know what influence Roman civilization had upon the country, but all evidence seems to indicate that before the country was abandoned to the inroads of the newer barbarians, the trend was toward the domestic type of family. Cities grew up, trade developed, and life in general became more comfortable.

In Harwell, in Berkshire where I studied in detail, the graves of the Roman period have many more adult skeletons and fewer with evidences of death by physical violence than did those of the period after it ceased to be a part of the Roman Empire. Furthermore, the utensils and ornaments (pottery and other evidences of civilization) in the graves of the Roman period are much more developed and efficient than the succeeding ones.

However, the domestic family type never developed very far in England. Among the "unreconstructed" people of the island—the Welsh, Scottish, and isolated hill groups—trustee familism was preserved. Nevertheless, there was a considerable movement toward eliminating blood vengeance and establishing the conception of public justice. Such measures were adopted before the invasions of the Saxons, the Angles, the Jutes, and the Danes, who rebarbarianized this culture. This was the same as the inroads made in other cultures by the cruder peoples who invaded all the other sections of the empire. The evidence of the Roman writers is that the English family and civilization were moving in the same path as the Gallo-Roman family.

After the invasion of the newer barbarians, the family reverted to the trustee type. The *Leges Henrici* of 1118 were distinctly trustee family legislation.

The trustee family ruled in England in the Dark Ages. At the beginning of the twelfth century the English family, except for local customs, was very like the early Roman and Greek families, like the north European barbarian family, or like the organization described by Beowulf.

The decline of this system and the rise of the domestic family conception—a movement which made its greatest headway in the twelfth century—had numerous explanations. Some of these were peculiar to England and others were common changes over all of Western Europe. With the Norman invasion and the revival of commerce and trade, numerous foreigners came into the different parts of the kingdom. As these had no family connections, they became vassals of the feudal lords and the king. The great masses of the people were then reduced in status under a law of villeinage, which gave the lords right to most of the property which ordinarily would have been used to pay compositions. With the growth of feudal power, the church became more influential. The Normans as conquerors established the social system and punished major criminals. The church could now enforce a system of atonement for the acts remaining under its control. Roman law became more developed and was in itself a substitute for family control. Finally, there were considerable differences between the customary penalties for interfamily compositions between the old Saxon, the newer Scandinavian, and the newest Frankish or Anglo-

Norman practice. All of this means simply that trustee family regulation was not adapted to a society of strangers and traders, or to one in which government forces were active and capable of social regulation by public law. The king wanted to establish peace. He and his nobles wanted to rule, and they did not want family feuds to interfere with public authority. Thus the three elements which broke the power of trustee familism in early Greece and Rome were again active. The plebs and traders did not favor trustee familism because it was unfair to them; they lost out because in a *themis* or "expedient" conception of law they had no family connections to protect them. The plebs and traders increased in importance in the kingdom, and the government, which depended upon these newer classes more than upon the older families, sided with them against family law in favor of public law between families. The idea that public law should succeed private law developed very quickly among all classes. The total disappearance of trustee familism was a long process, of course, realized only after centuries. Nevertheless, the old system was proving unsatisfactory and agents—the church and the state—were at hand to take over.

Once the English family reached the full domestic period, its movement toward the atomistic type continued for the same reasons and through the same processes found in all Western society. Philosophers like Milton, Hobbes, Locke, Hume, Paine, and others helped eliminate church influence from the family and to substitute an alliance of state and philosopher for its rule and control. In this alliance the most fragile element was, of course, the philosopher and his ideas.

Factors in the Rise of the Atomistic Family

The analysis in this and the preceding chapter has indicated briefly some of the agents and ideas which effected the change from the trustee family, which dominated Europe from the fifth to the twelfth and fourteenth centuries. From the beginning, Christian doctrine had been that all men were neighbors—not classifiable solely as kinsmen and enemies. As time passed, the church learned to handle the trustee family and gradually molded society into the domestic type. As the church gained in experience it clarified its doctrine and increased in power over its adherents. Many influences—trade, commerce, knowledge—made people dissatisfied with the older family rule. The importance of governments was growing. These agents met in a common desire for a domestic family type. New philosophies, dissatisfaction with the old ways, and opportunities for a new way met now to create a new social order.

Now what were the influences, the processes or mechanics by which the atomistic family gained headway? The following is as near a "causal" analysis as we shall make at this time.

In the first place, new philosophies arose. People had moved a long way from the moral decay of the old Roman Empire. They could no longer believe that those things taken so lightly by the decadent Romans—adultery, sodomy, bestiality, homosexuality, and all the filth of the later empire—would again occur. As a result the people were ready for philosophies which would state that men were naturally good, self-regulating, by nature honest, kind, thoughtful, and capable of moral perfection. By the time of Erasmus and his theory that Folly herself promoted the welfare of society, a whole series of philosophies arose and thrived. Each of these popular philosophies had a different name, but all of them had the same fundamental elements—man is naturally and inescapably good and if freed from the restrictions of the social system of the Roman decline and the Dark Ages, the millennium could be reached.

Erasmus's *Praise of Folly* was simply a broad statement that men made the good society possible more or less instinctively, and by performing the most foolish acts. Women forgot the pains of childbirth and had more children; men were enchained to be parents and family men and rear the next generation because of their folly in seeking the satisfactions of the bridal bed. (They were fools to believe that they had to marry for sexual satisfaction.) In other versions this basic philosophy is to be found in Locke's conception of nature, in Rousseau, in the whole rationalist school of Paine, Comte, Hegel, and Marx, in evolutionism, in nineteenth-century *laissez-faire* economics, and in twentieth-century evolutionary cultural determinism. Contrary philosophies appeared from time to time but did not leave any lasting mark. Slowly but surely the Christian / late-Roman conception of moral restraint and of individual moral ability to judge and be responsible for acts began to give way before this elaborate and variously-stated "Praise of Folly" philosophy. One of the most important philosophical agents in the modern period was cultural determinism. Different systems of cultural determinism have succeeded each other since humanism was introduced.

Along with this change in the philosophical conception of man, new and powerful agents appeared to influence the family. The older agents—the church and the state—began to split apart and disagree. These newer agents were the intellectual and the philosopher, who were to replace the priest, the bishop, and the canon law doctor as the leaders. The state was to become jealous of the joint control it exercised with the church over the family and social systems. Slowly and surely the state broke this alliance in favor of a new unity with the intellectual and reasoning type of man, as opposed to the traditionalist with his emphasis upon the former system of values. This new hybrid, a cross between the questioning intellectual and the growing state, was to make rapid and continuous alterations in the social organization prior to its becoming itself involved in serious difficulties.

The process was further favored by the fact that the union between the state and the intellectual was not achieved simultaneously in all states.

As a result of this combination, new achievements in science and in production would increase the world's supplies of the necessities of life. These achievements would filter back into the traditional states, where the motives to marry and have children were the same as those of the people in the classroom of Folly, pictured by Erasmus. A new source of population was to be found in the rural districts, in the backwoods, and in the traditional and isolated European countries. As the "laws of Folly" began to be abrogated in the cities, in progressive regions, in countries, and so on, the process of family atomism could continue as it had in Greece and Rome, without immediate consequences, because there were European immigrants to fill up the vacuums in the social system—roles similar to those played by the captives, slaves, and "good" barbarians who sustained the population of the Roman Empire. These immigrants into the imperial system kept it alive several centuries after that culture would have fallen into a profound crisis had it been isolated.

As a result of this change in the agents dominating family philosophy, the whole medieval system of familism could be attacked and overturned. The two opposite systems came into sharpest conflict in the time of Thomas Aquinas and Desiderius Erasmus. One was the great "Summa" philosopher of domestic familism; the other was the great optimistic initiator of atomistic family philosophy. The atomistic family was achieved by a process of separation of the church-state hegemony in family rule and the union of the state with the Erasmus-type man. The new philosopher of the family was in a different situation from the old. He was a subject solely of the state and not "married to the realm of God." He was far more subject and responsible to state discipline than was the former religious leader. He could continue to function as long as his actions worked to the benefit of the state. Once his ideas failed to promote state interests, he was subject to replacement. He had stayed in state good-will to date because the difficulties of atomistic familism in one region or country had been compensated for by the strong domestic familism in other regions or countries. As long as there was a substitute source of people with strong moral motivations, no one cared much what happened to familism. During this period an alternate source of population was to be found on the farms, in the hills, in the provincial districts, and in the countries still practicing domestic familism. These filled up the gaps left in the social system by atomistic familism.

Outline of the Change in Family Conceptions in the West

These changes may be outlined briefly as follows for modern Western society: (see next page)

The Rise of Modern Atomism

Period	Conception of the Family	Chief Sources of the Idea
12th–14th centuries	A sacrament conferring grace. Husband and wife, parent and child unbreakably united. Man and woman united for life, parent and child until maturity or marriage. Only religious sanction needed. Marriage begins with engagement (the *sponsalia* controversy).	Church officials; canon law authorities; almost total absence of criticism of family doctrine and no one suggested civil law on marriage.
15th–16th centuries	Family bond strongest union made by man but is not a sacrament and was not specifically created by God as divine authority. Like all man-made things, marriage bond can be broken under extreme conditions. *Sponsalia* as beginning of marriage criticized. Basis for institution: Multiply and replenish the earth.	Luther, Calvin, Reformation writers, Humanists, certain canon law professors and a minority at the council of Trent. Criticism greatest in old barbarian law states.

Period	Conception of the Family	Chief Sources of the Idea
17th century	Family bond still sacred but not a sacrament. Dissenting churches wanted to rule family, almost like Catholic Church, except that family influence was brought in and marriage considered to begin with *copula carnalis* rather than *sponsalia*. Religious act tends to become a civil act also. State "contract" dominates "family contract," at least in certain fields and times, but ordinarily family law in church and state re-affirm each other. Registration of marriage begins in both church and state offices. The familistic elements come into control of family doctrine.	German and north European jurists. Period of Cromwellian Revolution in England. In France, ordinance of Blois and other laws joined civil and religious jurisdiction of the family. In American colonies civil marriage required, but any infraction of marriage punished severely.
18th century	Family a public contract; clergy present as guests and not as officials. Clergy themselves quarrel over contract-sacrament except in most orthodox circles. Concept of family weakened. French Revolution made divorce history, whereas English Revolution, previous century, did not allow divorces. Rise of conception of family as an exclusively civil contract. General acceptance of legislative divorce idea. Divorce in non-Catholic circles *absolute*. Familistic elements are weakening in their control of family doctrine.	French Rationalists, Rousseau . . . Rise of Gallican theory of marriage after debate over marriage of Gaston of Orleans with Margaret of Lorraine. Montaigne, Rousseau; rise of feminist movement against family. "Les philosophes due XVIIIme. siecle ont secularise la conception du mariage. . . ." Most prominent philosophers of Germany and England. American colonial families return to church weddings, but limitation of size of family sets in, so future population comes largely from immigrants, beginning with Scotch-Irish and Palatinate Germans, in that century.

The Rise of Modern Atomism

Period	Conception of the Family	Chief Sources of the Idea
19th century	Rise of weakest possible conception of family. Secular idea and absolute divorce spread everywhere with Napoleonic Code and Industrial Revolution. American laws make family private contract (omnibus divorce). *Feme sole* conception frees persons from family domination. Everything moves from status to contract. Age not of familism but of golden individualism. The individualistic elements gain control of family doctrine. Public control of familism is badly disrupted.	Laws of all European countries. American family law. Rise of Marxian antifamily conception. Evolutionary theory of family nihilism gains domestic acceptance. Rise of overpopulation fears. General acceptance of childlessness and successive polygamy, as in later days of Rome and Greece.

FAMILY AND CIVILIZATION

Period	Conception of the Family	Chief Sources of the Idea
20th century	Weakened family, almost private contract continues *de facto*. Russian Revolution breaks up eastern European family mores. Fright over depopulation and wars. Dictatorial states try to force familism (Germany, Russia, Italy) others try to buy it by family grants (France, England, America, Sweden). General collapse of family values. Some literati become frightened at their own antifamilistic doctrines. Prominent logicians and mathematicians write against marriage and family. *Concubinatus* and secondary forms of marriage proposed by public men. Afraid of the moral controversy of so violent a break, the marriage of *dignitas* prostituted in the press, radio, divorce-mills, and smart circles. The individualistic and statist groups control family doctrine. Attempts to revive public control of familism inherent in the situation.	Laws and propaganda in various countries. Russia gives up her experiment. Nazis and fascists make familism and citizenship related. Sweden gives up "middle way." Blood loss of World War I almost causes a crisis. Population and family congresses spring up among the lay population as frequently and as verbose as Church Councils, from Pierre Lombard and Gratien to the Council of Trent. American family law covers six volumes, and most of it is unsatisfactory, according to the "codifiers." Rise of underpopulation fears. Family breaking begins violently after World War II and this incites countermovement. Polarization of family values widespread as in St. Basil's time.

122

8

PHILOSOPHY AND FAMILISM IN
THE NINETEENTH CENTURY

P HILOSOPHIES OF HUMAN LIFE ALWAYS include directly or indirectly
a conception of the family or of a society in which the family role
is delineated. Furthermore, a particularly dominant philosophy often
precedes the rise of the particular social organization pictured by the
philosopher. The *Praise of Folly* by Erasmus preceded the great period
of blind breeding, colonial expansion, and population development
in Europe from the seventeenth to the nineteenth centuries. Marxian
philosophy, which by indirection pictured an all-powerful state, beyond
ethics, preceded the rise of totalitarian states which has plagued the
twentieth century.

The plan in this chapter is to examine the dominant philosophies
and movements of the nineteenth century to find what their fundamental
implications for the family were. We have already indicated briefly the
ideas of the preceding centuries and the destruction of the historical roots
of culture through the domination of the ideals of Hegel and Comte. Now
this analysis will be carried further. It is particularly important because
scarcely a book on the mentality of the Middle Ages or on modern development mentions contemporary thinking on the family. One would

think from reading the contemporary philosophers that after Aristotle and Plato the family did not exist. A study of the actual documents of the late Middle Ages, however, shows that throughout these centuries society was as concerned with the organization of the family as with any other problem confronting it. In fact, interest in the family was higher than in most other subjects.

The nineteenth century was to see the rise of a number of movements. We shall comment only on those few that directly or indirectly produced a specific family sociology. In the field of economics, the theory of the free and unrestrained individual arose. This individual was to challenge every value in relation to his profit, loss, and gain in material consumption. Deification of the state arose in Hamiltonianism, Hegelianism, Marxism, and social-reformism. These movements all led to the weakening of the family, to the use of state power to weaken the family. These movements were associated with the evolutionary conceptions of history and the rise of ideas of constant linear progress.

The nineteenth-century idea of evolution, with its vision of unending goal-destined progress, had two very important effects upon the family. In the first place, the philosophy destroyed the concept of historical tradition for the nineteenth century. All any college student learned of social science and sociology from the nineteenth century to World War I was a theory of social relativism, the linear "evolution" of society through the nineteenth century, the need for challenging all social institutions including the family, and the possibility of continued improvement through the destruction of accepted values. Every important social movement accepted by the nineteenth century—from classical economics to liberalism and superficial family legislation—had, regardless of its purpose, one result: the destruction of the strength of the family and of its historical traditions.

Consequently, it is not surprising to find what had been ancient Gaul—the most central, the most important, and the last of the great Roman provinces—leading in antifamily tradition during the nineteenth century. This was but a logical sequence to the interior demoralization that occurred during the French Revolution. France, by adhering to the decadent Roman traditions rather than progressing through adoption of the moralistic northern barbarian cultures, in two centuries lost her position as the leading power in Europe. She became a minor state, overrun by former minor European powers, and consequently suffered an almost total political eclipse in the twentieth century. Other powers had rising birth rates up until the last quarter of the nineteenth century. That of France remained static in the modern period. First the neighboring powers followed the trend of diminished population with its devastating social changes, then the United States, and finally Russia. The last to become concerned were the Eastern or Byzantine remnants of the Roman Empire. The results of this family decay came as a shock to the twentieth century. A century of comparative peace and well-being had intervened since the Napoleonic Wars. Now, once again, the structure of society was destroyed, its value systems broken, and the way made ready for constant and increasingly costly wars. No one Western society found itself rich enough in blood to be able to afford the human price of these wars.

The Economic Individual Cult and Familism

Economic individualism emerged during the Middle Ages. Its first intellectual sign was the theory that interest-taking was a normal human activity and not, as in the past, a usurious sin. This idea became dominant after the fall of the Roman Empire. The canonical theory of interest (and associated business practices) was that money was barren and produced nothing; that time could not be sold, and that no one should take interest because it was the same as stealing.

> The dark days which preceded and followed the break-up of the Roman Empire had brought a reaction in economical matters, which, in its turn, had the natural result of strengthening the old hostile feeling against interest. . . . The Christian Church lent its arm. Step by step it managed to introduce the prohibition into legislation. First the taking of interest was forbidden by the Church, but to the clergy only. Then it was forbidden the laity also, but still the prohibition

only came from the Church. At last even the temporal legislation succumbed to the Church's influence, and gave its severe statutes the sanction of Roman law.... Thus Gonzalez Tellez: "for the creditor who makes a profit out of a thing belonging to another person enriches himself at the hurt of another." And still more sharply, Vaconius Vacuna: "Therefore he who gets fruit from that money, whether it be pieces of money or anything else, gets it from a thing which does not belong to him, and it is accordingly all the same as if he were to steal it." (For this, see Eugen von Böhm-Bawerk, *Capital and Interest*, William A. Smart, ed., Brentano's, New York, 1922, chs. I–III. Quotations from 18 and 23)

However, with the revival of trade in Southern Europe in the twelfth century, antagonism to this conception grew up among the learned people, so that the growth of practices taking interest under fictional names increased. *Damnum emergens et lucrum cessans:* one cannot take interest, but one can pay the lender for the damage accruing to him or for the profits he loses. Through the centuries the idea of the economically motivated man gradually emerged.

By the seventeenth century these ideas had emerged so far that men wrote books and advocated programs related to the connection between the activities of the individual and his standard of living. During this and the succeeding century, the idea was thoroughly developed in such writings as B. Mandeville's *Fable of the Bees* and the "Political Arithmeticks" of such men as William Petty, Gregory King, Richard Dunning, Daniel Defoe, Joseph Massie, Arthur Young, David Davies, Sir F. M. Eden, A. Lavoisier, and J. L. LaGrange. It became established that consumption was the major goal of man and that by trying to get more to consume the individual would produce more. Thus all of society would benefit, as Mandeville earlier argued in his *Fable. The Fable of the Bees* was an economic version of Erasmus's *Praise of Folly*; it had the same central idea of cultural determinism—that is, the automatic-internal-control conception of society.

At the same time, the standard of living of the laborer was not always as high as it had been at previous times. This standard fell during the seventeenth century; it reached a very low point during the period of the English Revolution. From that time on it climbed, reaching a period of comparative plenty about the middle of the eighteenth century. Then it fell again and was very low during the American and French Revolutions and the Napoleonic dynasty. After that time, economists (of what is known as the classical school) became increasingly interested in the problem of conquering the misery of the masses by increased production and consumption of economic goods. The primary emphasis was on production at first. Adam Smith, David Ricardo, and the Mills all held fundamentally to the idea that the individual should increase production. At about the same time, the theory of T. R. Malthus gained popularity. Essentially he held that the standard of living was closely related to population and also to family size. Man could either breed himself into the poorhouse and die from misery or marry late, abstain from having too many children, and live comfortably.

Malthus himself was almost puritanical. He had no idea that his theory eventually would be expanded to complete abstention from childbearing. Neo-Malthusianists took up the suggestion and introduced birth control into the family on a large scale. They argued that marriage prevented sexual promiscuity and that birth control would mean that these limited families could live in a greater degree of comfort than the previous unlimited families. One income divided among a small family meant more per individual than the same income divided among many. And from the individual point of view they are, with some exceptions, fundamentally right. From this developed the idea that no children were better than a few.

This theory, tantalizing as it seems, and valid as it is if not carried too far, pervaded the economics and sociology of the nineteenth century in the same manner that we have seen the discoveries of sulfa drugs and penicillin sweep the medical practice during the past decade. It involved breaking up social mores regarding the family and substituting for them individualistic mores. The sentiments of familism were difficult to uproot. No such attempt had been made since the first four centuries of our era, but little by little it was achieved. Excessive birth control was accepted as a family practice in almost all Western countries by the end of the nineteenth century. It spread rapidly from the upper to the lower classes and from city to country.

The rapidity of this movement, once it gained headway, may be illustrated by the decline of the birth rate in Sweden, a more or less isolated northern country. Knut Wicksell introduced the idea in 1880 in a lecture on "The Causes of Human Misery." It fell like a bombshell and had repercussions in every class of the provincial society of that country. The press, the pulpit, and the public raged. Yet the birth rate of about 30 per thousand per year in 1880 fell to about 26 per thousand from 1901 to 1910, to less than 15 per thousand per year by 1930. The net reproduction rate alone fell from about 96 percent of enough to reproduce the population in 1925 to about 75 percent by 1937. The momentum gained by this movement was enormous.

What began as a reform to prevent physical misery became a mania to avoid social duty, particularly the economic burdens and social tasks involved in having and rearing children. The movement went so far that supposedly learned men devoted great attention to the theory that the only way of holding the family together was to find so perfect a form of sexual adjustment that there would never be the least cause for the childless or small-family couple to separate. Such perfection, such a basis for the union, was deemed necessary since there were insufficient children in most marriages to hold the family together. Germany developed its Institut für Sexualwissenschaft. We did the same repeatedly, but on a larger scale; however, in typical American fashion, our institutes were given more roseate titles.

The Ruling Groups of the Family

As we have shown, historically the smaller, or household, family has had three types of ruling or governing bodies. One of these has been the large family itself, which held responsibility and authority over the actions of the family, including those of members against the family, attacks against other families, and individual or collective attacks by members of other families. The very essence of trustee familism is the sovereign power it holds over the family.

Fustel de Coulanges and G. Glotz, among other writers, clearly describe this period for the ancient commonwealths of Greece and Rome. Glotz devotes the first part of his work to an analysis of the early period of Greece when the family was sovereign. Here we have what we know today as government functioning through the family group. What we know as civil law is undertaken by the family.

The same family sovereignty existed after the decline of the ancient Roman Empire, during the medieval period:

> When we speak of the "kindreds" of earlier times, we imply, by the mere use of that comprehensive term, something more than this. We imply that not only do individual kinsmen act on occasion so as to further a kinsman's prospects or shield him from a penalty, but that this kinsman becomes the center of a united group of kindred, who act on his behalf, partly because they have his prospects at heart, but mainly because public opinion, the law, and their own view of life, make them guilty with him, and almost equally liable to penalty; or, in the event of his death by violence, throw the responsibility for vengeance or satisfaction upon the whole group, not only a few near kinsmen. . . .
>
> . . . the cohesive kindred would rally round a member threatened with a lawsuit, and that it probably performed the functions of an insurance society, besides keeping a jealous watch on the inherited land belonging to its members. (Bertha S. Philpotts, *Kindred and Clan in the Middle Ages and After,* Cambridge University Press, 1913, 3, 247, *et passim*)

The second type of ruling group has been a religious dynasty or church. This is most clearly illustrated by canon law in the Middle Ages. At all times religion played a considerable role in family rule. Even today, with the tremendous growth of state power and its laws regarding the family, the most influential factors in familism are still the religious, or extramundane beliefs. Call it what you may—religion, mores, belief in right or wrong—it is still the same thing. However, in the Middle Ages, beginning with St. Augustine and up until the golden age of canon law, the church became more and more the dominating power over the family.

Religion has always been a very important ruling factor in the family. In the trustee type it is essentially a family religion. The organization of the Greek *phratria* and the Roman *curia* or familistic super-families larger than the trustee families was also associated with religious developments patterned after the family religion, but still not domestic. The early Western states, Greece and Rome, were founded upon definite religions of the state, the something which integrated the tribes and sub-units. As Fustel de Coulanges says, "What is certain is, that the bond of the new association was still a religion," even though the state be formed voluntarily, through the superior force of one tribe or the domination of one man (*The Ancient City*). The unusual domination of the family alone by the Church in the Middle Ages was an historical accident due to the failure of state power, but the principle is as old as is the family and religion itself.

The national state constitutes the third ruling group. This may be illustrated by the Greek city-states at the height of their development, by the numerous family laws of imperial Rome, and by the many modern states which, since the sixteenth and seventeenth centuries, have claimed the right—and now, almost the exclusive authority—to govern the family. During such periods any other authority—such as that of churches, either Catholic or Protestant, which formerly dominated the families—is permitted only to the extent that it does not interfere with the absolute power of the state. Marriage is no longer, as Montaigne said, "a religious and devout bond." Rather, marriage is a secular and civil bond made with the consent and under the guidance and regulation of the sovereign state.

The Rise of Statism and the Family

As shown in the preceding chapters, the modern movement toward secularization of the family and the feeling that it should be under state control started early and was part and parcel of the whole humanist movement. The Protestant Reformation, eighteenth-century rationalism, and the liberal and reform movement since the Middle Ages were all factors in its development. It is true that opinions differed as to the nature of the state that was to be set up and its absolute and unbreakable powers, but these differences were merely minor variations in the gigantic pattern of the rising national states. From the time when Machiavelli in *The Prince* set forth the idea that the prince or ruler could do no wrong and that expediency rather than moral principle should guide him in establishing state power, all other thinkers, like Hobbes and Locke, held the opinion that the national state should take on more and more of the business of governing. We have passed from the domination of men by local government, familism, and "the moral idea" to domination by statute law, the product of the national state.

Students of Locke, Rousseau, and Thomas Paine and of the whole rationalist school of the eighteenth century may wish to deny this on the grounds that those thinkers were opposed to extreme state power. All of them made a fine distinction between society and the state and ruled that society had the right to withdraw from the state contract if it proved unsatisfactory, and to form another society and make another state contract. This enabled them to distinguish between monarchy and republican forms of government. It also enabled them to oppose the state contract in one sense and to promote it in another. Thus, Condorçet and Paine give the ultimate logic of their position in the Bill of Rights drawn up for the French government after the Revolution and signed by Louis XVI. While the natural rights of everyone are "liberty, equality and resistance to oppression" they are also "security, property and social protection." "The preservation of liberty depends on submission to the Law, which is the expression of the general will" (Declaration of Rights, paragraphs one and three). This "general will" is the earlier doctrine of Rousseau. Locke also has it in his conception that power is given to the community, not to the sovereign. Thus there is no difference between the fundamental position of Filmer and Hobbes on the one hand and Locke, Rousseau, and Paine on the other. For Paine's devious reasoning on this subject, see the first part of his *Rights of Man,* an attack on Edmund Burke because Burke attacked the French Revolution. There you see from Paine's references that he is but staging the general position of the whole rationalist school.

The nineteenth century saw the final development and dominance of the state in all fields. At the beginning of the century America was struggling to set up her central government, after the weakened confederation had failed to function in the colonies. Distinct differences of opinion existed in the United States between the Hamiltonian view of broad interpretation of the Constitution, which gave the federal government powers in addition to those mentioned in the Constitution, and the Jeffersonian view of strict interpretation of the document, reserving to the states and the local communities all powers not expressly specified as central in the Constitution.

The states grew to be the dominant factor. The fact that they were unable to control familism, or that they lacked a specific doctrine of control, is another matter. The first part of the nineteenth century saw the state emerge clearly above the church and the family, but actually it directed the family very little.

France at that time was just recovering from the Revolution and Napoleon was carving out his scheme for ruling Europe. England was over the shock of the loss of her colonies in America and was bracing herself for the internal struggle with her own revolutionary forces and for the external struggle with Napoleon. Revolutionary talk was rife. Thomas Paine, a former Englishman and the author of our *Common Sense,* was in France, afraid to come home to America because English ships were hovering about the harbor and Paine knew he was wanted for imprisonment in England for writing the British revolutionary document *Rights of Man.* Germany was not a national state, but a collection of petty principalities. Russia was still in her Middle Ages and was a relatively small power, having 25 million people in 1789, as compared with the 26 million in France and the 28 million in the various German states. The states were weak. Beyond state duplication in some countries of the church registers on vital statistics and marriages, modern family legislation had hardly begun. The development of the state and of modern-state family legislation was to come in the nineteenth century.

Four main philosophies of the nineteenth century set forth the conception of the national state and finally the inculcation within that state of state rule of the family. In the United States the idea of the Hamiltonians, that government should rule, kept increasing the powers given the central government. The state governments in turn legislated widely on the family. In an earlier chapter we have discussed some of this legislation and the effects it had upon forcing further laws. Omnibus divorce legislation forced laws against omnibus divorce. The Married Women's Acts led to the Lazy Husband laws. The Civil War made the national government paramount.

Second, the idea of socal reforms by law grew at a rapid rate in the United States. Law piled on law, and government agency upon government agency. Beginning slowly, but spurred on by wars and crises, this movement gained headway rapidly at the end. By 1900 the state had become master of the family. The state recognizes the individual; it pulls him from family sovereignty whenever it deems this expedient. It is not a question of morality of the state. When the family rules the family, it does so for religious ends. When the state rules the family, for good or bad, it rules the family for state ends. If it wants the individual freed from the family, as was the case in the nineteenth century in the Western world, it frees him and family demands must take second place. It is the same in the United States as in other Western powers, although here individualism, as opposed to the family and the state, has for the present gained greater sway.

In Europe, Hegelian and Marxian philosophies held the attention of the people, but in spite of this, the trends in Europe have been essentially the same as those in the United States. In countries openly espousing dictatorial forms of government, the expression of these trends has been exaggerated. Hegel's philosophy of the state (by which he is best known, no matter how much more refined are his other arguments) is given in his *Philosophy of History*. There are several different Hegels and also different groups of Hegelianists, according to whether one follows his theories of causation and social change or his ultimate philosophy of history and the deification of the state. This former Protestant minister and excellent logician, who had fallen from favor for the same reason that Thomas Paine finally dropped into disgrace, became the intellectual Beau Brummell of Berlin and the leading contemporary philosopher of the German state, as Martin Luther had been at an earlier date. Hegel's philosophy was that the course of history had been the course of the development of the idea of freedom. This had taken three essential movements. In the early Orient, the *individual* was free; in classical societies, a *few* (the citizens) were free; in future state, *all* were to be free. "The Final Cause of the World" was to "realize its own freedom by Spirit (*Geist*)," and this was to be achieved by perfecting the German state.

The German nations, under the influence of Christianity, were the first to attain the consciousness, that man, as man, is free: that it is the *freedom* of Spirit which constitutes its essence.

We have seen since that the German state, far from freeing people, was the first in the twentieth century to assume absolute control over the family, to organize and supervise it with full intention of using the family for the furtherance of its designs. From marriage to the grave, from birth to senility, the individual was made a slave of the state. He became merely a tool, an instrument for achieving the state's purpose.

Early Marxism, however, made Hegelianism international. It revealed thoroughly the real meaning of the nineteenth-century trend of the state and the family. Marxism (from the first *Communist Manifesto*, written for the Revolution of 1848, down to the last volume of *Das Kapital* and the final writings on the family and its institution by Engels and the other followers of Marx) was anti-institutional as far as the family was concerned; it was pro-institutional for communist state purposes. To use terminology that applies equally to Rousseau, Paine, Hegel, and Marx, all social institutions were to be dissolved in order to "free the individual," so that the purposes of the communistic order could be achieved through the final and absolute state. As we have seen from parallels in earlier chapters and from the Russian Revolution, in the early stages of the revolution this meant the legal dissolution of the family, in the later stages, its re-creation and rigidification for the purposes of the state. The power assumed was as absolute in Russia as in Germany. After each modern revolution—English, French, and Russian—that has partially or totally dissolved the family, there has been a countermovement to recreate the family as an indispensable agency for the social order. There is no substantial difference between the attitudes of Hume regarding the newly created English family, de Bonald regarding the French family after 1816, and of the Communist leaders after the new Russian family law of 1944. The revolutions varied in their treatment of the family and so did the reactions. The family is now truly the agent, the slave, the handmaiden of the state. As the state varies in intention, so will the family.

These four outstanding philosophies of the nineteenth century—Hamiltonianism, social-reformism by law, Hegelianism, and Marxism—led to the increase of statism and to the gradual development of the idea of absorbing the family for purposes of statism. In this sense they were essentially unfamilistic.

The end of the nineteenth century saw the state dominant and the family with little power to resist. The judge who failed to give easy divorces soon lost his position and prestige. In contrast, in the middle of the seventeenth century, the family was so strong that secularization of marriage by civil registration caused more trouble for the Puritans during the English Revolution than anything else they did. John Milton, who wrote on divorce during that time and who was a Puritan leader, was saved from death after the return of the royal family by some "miracle" which is not even yet understood by historians.

Familism and Evolutionary and Linear Progress Cults

In the nineteenth century, in addition to the other challenges to the strength of the family bond, new "scientific" explanations of the family were offered. These completely divorced it from history; they arose from the schools of anthropology and primitive sociology, where the early and later courses of the family were traced through an evolutionary series.

There were numerous attacks upon various doctrines, but fundamentally, the nineteenth century saw the rise and acceptance of the evolutionary conception of the family. Its proponents gave us instead of history, imagination. Instead of the constant struggle between familism and individualism, they gave us various evolutionary pictures. These have been reviewed in chapter one.

The evolutionary cultists were shortly joined by the adherents of the school of linear progress. This is illustrated in outstanding detail by the works of Herbert Spencer. With the exception of a very few thinkers, from that time to the present these dogmas and schools of thought have to a remarkable degree dominated thought on the family. Since then, books on the family (except relatively few by religious writers and conservative clergymen, both Protestant and Catholic) have become works on evolution, the progress and rise of individualism, or adaptations advisable in the family to bring about improvements, rather than works on the family.

Bury has written a most authoritative work on the rise of the idea of progress. He divides it into three stages. The first was one of casual treatment, and lasted until the French Revolution. After the Revolution, as shown in the works of Hegel, Comte, and the positivist writers associated with his analysis, significance was given to the idea of constant forward movement toward a desirable goal. *The Origin of Species*, by attaching Darwinism to progress, as these ideas were fused by Herbert Spencer, established, in Bury's words, "the reign of the idea of progress." It synthesized the movements predicated in evolutionary thinking and combined them with the idea of a desirable goal, which had been inherent in thinking since the Reformation. This gave us the theory of ultimate development, of necessary progress toward perfectibility.

> Thus in the seventies and eighties of the last century the idea of Progress was becoming a general article of faith. . . . Within the last forty years nearly every civilized country has produced a large literature on social science, in which indefinite Progress is generally assumed as an axiom. (J. B. Bury, *The Idea of Progress*, New York, 1932, 346–48)

Two interesting problems are presented in the rise of the school of evolution and linear movement in social phenomena, which thoughts combined to produce the family philosophy of the nineteenth century. These are the causes of its appearance and its results in thinking about the family. We do not know much about the causes of the movement,

136

except perhaps that the world was ready for some such approach to existing problems. Such theories made social change easy by providing a grab bag for any argument needed. The era of peace, comfort, and semiscientific plundering of the remotest parts of the world, which occurred in Europe after Napoleon and in the United States after the Civil War, may have been instrumental. The most important question is the effect of this synthesization upon thinking in regard to family problems. Briefly, it destroyed history as a fundamental study in social science. Historical life experience became only a moment in evolution. The field of study was muddied by the admixture of man's historical struggle with the family and a weighty group of facts from allegedly primitive societies, so that grounds could be found for *any* conclusions about the family. The family was driven toward inevitable change because "evolution in a linear direction never ends"; the individual was made the unit of social study because we (a) never knew primitives very well, and (b) the new "noble savage" was either too good (with no wars, perfect communism, and the ideal individual) to need a family, or was too bad (with wife stealing, patricide, primitive promiscuity, and the slavery of women) to get along with a family. Finally, skepticism and nihilistic attitudes toward the family could become a cult because anyone could see that we were better off in our family life than the savage, either good or bad, and that we were capable of improving still further.

Disappearance of Family "History" as a Frame of Reference

Before the development of the evolutionary-progressive formulas, history played a definite role in the formation and knowledge of family theory. Church discussions of the family always began with the Old Testament, progressed through the New Testament to known practices during the Roman Empire, and continued through the early Church Fathers (St. Augustine and his group), the canon law doctors, and later discussions by the church councils. Similarly if Montesquieu, Voltaire, Milton, or other writers disagreed with certain practices, they had recourse to known historical documents which they quoted in detail in their arguments. If thinking on the problem of the family had continued along the lines established by the beginning of the nineteenth century, adequate interpretations of the family would have developed, based upon its different relations to other cultural aspects during different stages in national history. One can see great evidence of this in the analyses of Hume, Voltaire, the natural-law school, the social-compact school, and especially in that inspiration of so much of modern thinking, Montesquieu's *The Spirit of the Laws*. As he pointed out:

> Laws; in their most general signification, are the necessary relations arising from the nature of things. (*Spirit of the Laws*, vol. I, 1)

But the rise of the nineteenth-century evolutionary-progressive theories put a stop to this trend. Historians of the family began to neglect the time element and to force their ideas into systems. Instead of history, systems of evolution were created, and the facts of history were made to adapt to the family. We see this process working with great exactness in the books by Henry Sumner Maine, where the period from the early Hindu Codes of Manu to the Roman Twelve Tables is rejected as being nonessential to his theory. Later he skips from the Twelve Tables to medieval law and the modern period. Developments within the family during the Roman Empire were to him of no consequence, because he was intent upon establishing the linear theory of development from early status to later contract in human relations.

Thus, history was eliminated from family sociology. As a substitute, we received a miscellaneous body of primitive practices, varied in type, which were often casually studied and generally misinterpreted. When the seventeenth- and eighteenth-century thinkers wanted to advance some doctrine about the state, imaginary states of nature were set up to justify the ideas the scholar wanted to promote. Examples are Hobbes's defense of absolute monarchy and Rousseau's attack upon this and other institutions. Hobbes imagines nature to be a state of war. To avoid this "natural" conflict, man made an unbreakable contract with the monarch and divine state—the leviathan. Rousseau imagined a state of nature of perfect peace and contentment and maintained that social institutions set up since that time had enslaved men. From these divergent states of imagined nature, these philosophers could reach opposite conclusions.

After the beginning of the nineteenth century, different theorists advanced any desired argument for changes in the family from heterogeneous and casual studies of primitivism. Consequently, the nineteenth century was one in which all agreed on developing goals for the family, but no one seemed to agree on what those goals were. It was like the earlier argument over divorce during the Reformation. One authority would quote the Bible to prove that marriage was a sacrament, another to prove that divorce should be allowed for adultery, and a third to prove that divorce should be granted for any marital dissatisfaction. In the nineteenth century, one quoted primitivism to prove that monogamy had always existed; another stated that we had evolved from primitive promiscuity to monogamy; a third, that our change from matriarchy to patriarchy had given us repression of the Oedipus complex; a fourth, that our evolution had been from patriarchy to the freedom of women and children from domination, and so on. Any school of thought could find an antecedent primitivism as an example of what we should try either to achieve or to avoid.

During all this time, the real history of our family and the reason for the various forms it had taken never entered the discussion. Ever since the Reformation the Catholic Church has been roundly berated in many circles for holding to the sacramental theory of marriage. The leaders in this antisacramental argument apparently have not been aware of the moral conception in the Roman Empire, against which the church reacted, nor of the degraded state from which it strove to raise the family. As far as the family was concerned, all values had so decayed that the question of a population sufficient to carry on civilization was no longer a primary concern of the people. The new generation's main concern was not to carry on the race, but to avoid the filthy, loathsome scourges of venereal disease that sapped the whole Western world after the cross-fertilization of germs that occurred from the mixture of populations. People simply wanted some human relation which would last just beyond the moment.

Conclusion

To a large extent unintentionally, but surely and dramatically, the three great philosophical movements of the nineteenth century—individualism, statism, and evolutionary progressivism—drove familism to the farthest extreme of atomism. In most states, the industrial revolution loosened the family from parental control. Its first result was a rapid increase in the birthrate of these industrial countries, followed by a rapid decline. By 1870–80, the birth rates had begun to decline in almost all European countries. Except in the peasant-agrarian countries of Eastern Europe and Southern Italy, they were below reproductive levels by 1930.

Legal backstays of the family—some degree of *manus*, *potestas*, coverture, and mutuality—were destroyed on a large scale, more so in some countries and periods than in others. The individual arose and became the subject and the dependent of the state. Theories of the family as but a nominal group, a private contract to be broken at will, gained ascendancy. The minds of the people were being filled constantly with the idea that "happiness," as defined by individual egotism, was the goal of life. Marriage and family must justify themselves according to this concept of "happiness" or be abandoned. Happiness is a very subjective term, being defined each moment, each day, and in each age by different psychological considerations. Consequently, the family had no understandable objective for its guidance.

Of course, familism has been retained throughout the most disturbed periods by certain ethical, religious, traditional, and other types of people. Depressions have forced familism simply because during an economic catastrophe no other choice was possible. Many other circumstances have affected the situation. Fundamentally, however, this period led us organizationally, philosophically, and factually to an extreme development of antifamilism.

9

THE NINETEENTH-CENTURY
ATOMISTIC FAMILY

THE STRUGGLE THAT TOOK PLACE from the Reformation to the nineteenth century clearly established the principle that the new master power beyond the family was to be the state. Thus the same general process that took place in Greece and Rome has been repeated in Western society. From the laws of Solon (639 B.C.) through the reforms of the sixth and fifth centuries, the state in Greece took over more and more of the social control formerly dominated by familism and religion. Roman history followed the same course. If we view the meaning of its changes, we see that Western society has undergone an almost identical process. In the Dark Ages neither church nor state could control the family. In the terminology of boxing, both had to "roll with the punches" when it came to dealing with the dominant trustee familism. All these agencies could hope to do through internal regulation was to get families to settle quarrels peacefully. In their early legislation they merely tried to regulate the processes of settling family quarrels by transaction rather than by feud.

With the decline of imperial Rome as a state power in Western society, the church assumed an ever-increasing control over family matters. In Rome, from the time of Augustus until the end of the empire, it was the state that decided whether a man could have one or two wives, and all the hundreds of other family matters. It has already been noted that by the time of Gregory of Tours (circa 590 A.D.) the state was more or less helpless in dealing with the family. The famous Sichaire-Ausregisil family feud had to be settled by the church paying half of the composition (or family fine) to one family and half to the other. Even this gracious settlement did not secure a permanent amend of the breach between the two families. Familism was in power. From that time onward the power of the state to regulate the family declined until, between the tenth and the twelfth centuries A.D., the church gained complete ascendancy. After the Augustinian reforms, the state said "no" to polygamy, either a combination of two wives in the higher sense of the term or to a combination of two in the lower sense. The *concubinatus* form of marriage had to be monogamous as well. But in the tenth and twelfth centuries, and from then until the Council of Trent, the positive law of the family was church canon law. The church prohibited polygamy of any type. One of its strongest attacks against Luther occurred because he permitted secret polygamy to a north European German prince. Furthermore, the church rules on adultery and polygamy not only paralleled those of the Roman emperors, they frequently were much stronger and tried to hold familism on an even stricter level. All family issues were decided by the church, as formerly these had been decided by the Roman law codes. Age of marriage, the meaning of engagement (the *sponsalia* controversy), the relation of engagement to marriage, the nullification of marriage, its partial breakability (from bed and board), and its absolute divorce or nullification—all these and many other questions were decided by the various councils of the church.

Whenever neither the state nor the church was in authority over the family, the family ruled itself. This is the essential meaning of trustee familism, regardless of the period or region in which it has appeared. It was the case for early Greece and Rome, during the Dark Ages in Europe; it exists today in the mountain regions of Southeastern Europe, in Ireland, and in our Appalachian-Ozark family groups, concerning whom we Americans know so little.

Whereas under other conditions in the West, the vicissitudes of the church or of the great family determined what kind of rule the smaller family had, now the conception again arose that the state and the family were interdependent. (This is Hume's idea that familism is essential to the state.)

Development of the State-Family Theory

Thus beginning about 1500, society slowly developed the idea that the family constituted a "cell" within the state. Insofar as there was a complete integration of social thought in any one period, the family and state would parallel one another. To show this development from 1500 onward we can take political theory following the early analysis of Otto von Gierke and Ernest Barker and advance from there to the nineteenth century.

Aristotle, who formed the background for much of modern political theory, held two opposing views of the family and the state. In his earlier analysis, particularly controverting Plato, he holds that family theory and political theory are different:

> [T]hose who think that the principles of a political, a regal, a family, and a herile government are the same are mistaken. . . . (Aristotle, *Politics*, 1)

But Aristotle's position changes by the time he reaches Book II in his *Politics*, so that when he begins to discuss the ideal state, he takes up the question of whether the members should have nothing, something, or everything in common, and here he joins family and political theory.

In the sixteenth century, while the church still ruled the family and before family theory developed under the state, the political thinkers took up Aristotle's two conceptions and differentiated sharply between family theory and political theory. They held that while the family was a fundamental element in, and image of, the state, still it was subject to its own jurisdiction. This seems to have been the prevalent opinion among the sixteenth-century students of jurisprudence; at least it was that held by the most prominent thinkers.

However, by the time the social-compact theory of society super-seded the natural-law theory (eighteenth century), the idea of the family changed also. The family, like the state, became a contract and was considered breakable.

> Only in the sphere of Family-life, and only in the shape of the household community was it possible still to trace a survival of naturally developed and necessarily binding obligation. But even in the sphere of the Family itself the admission that there could be a society which was independent of the will of its members was finally limited to the relation between parents and children under age. When once the age of majority had been attained, a contract of partnership was held to be necessary; and the full logic of the conception was particularly, and increasingly, applied to the insti-tution of marriage. (Gierke in Gierke-Barker, *Natural Law and the Theory of Society*, vol. I, iii)

This same gradually developing principle of the correlation between the conception of the state and that of the family can be seen in the English and French Revolutions. The English Revolution was a Puritan one, putting into power a class that viewed the state essentially as a busi-ness agent to aid the mercantilist class. They instituted state domination of marriage, but being essentially "puritanical," they did not legislate to facilitate divorce.

The French Revolution, a century later, was different in that it was a violent overturning of all social forms of the ancient regime, including the family. It was an attempt to destroy all former state authoritarianism. It also tried by legislation to destroy all authoritarianism in the family. Practically every revolution or violent change of which we have a record has attempted certain reforms of the family. Twice in history the concep-tion of family and state has been such that a dissolution of one (the old traditional state) has meant an attempted dissolution of the other (the old traditional family). These have been the French and the Russian Revolutions.

Most of the revolutionary movements in Greek and Roman history, all of which yielded some legislation either during the revolution or when the reformer came into power, effected some change in the family. None of them tried to abolish the family legislatively. They tried to weaken the family and justly so, because the former family law in many cases gave the family so much power that a strong aristocratic group could have material effect upon the course of the state, through family solidarity. As Sorokin has shown in his *Sociology of Revolution,* in all revolutions the people commit sexual excesses. But to abolish the family as a social institution by making it an object of private will through unilateral and non-notifiable negation of family bonds through legislation—that is where these two revolutions were unique. I discuss this merely to show that when an overhead institution dominates the family, the family is subject to the prevailing philosophy of these overhead social institutions.

Apparently the American Revolution did not touch the family. The Americans had had two violent family reforms within a century: the complete public control of marriage as against the church and the establishment of absolute divorce largely by legislative decree. Thomas Paine, the philosopher of the revolution, was not grounded in philosophy as were Rousseau for the French Revolution and Marx for the Russian Revolution. Paine was a Quaker and, as far as can be found in his writings, he did not attack the family. The common people of the revolution (Sons of Liberty in the East and Scotch-Irish frontiersmen in the West) never really came into power. Furthermore, these were rural peoples, interested in land rights and fee simple ownership and antagonistic to feudal land holding, rather than a group interested in any family doctrine. Peasant revolutions, as Sorokin and I have shown elsewhere, generally concern themselves with land rights. (For this see *Systematic Source Book in Rural Sociology,* vol. II, and my earlier researches on land as a factor in the family budget of various classes at the Minnesota Agricultural Experiment Station as discussed in Carle C. Zimmerman, *Consumption and Standards of Living,* New York, 1935, chs. 13 and 14.)

The "spirit" of the American Revolution finally did achieve fruition in extreme antifamilism, in the omnibus divorce clauses, the *feme sole* conception of married women and the early divorce-mills or easy divorce states. But these were driven back by the counterrevolution, our American Civil War, which established the principle that freedom could not be carried to nullification. In the years immediately following the Civil War, omnibus divorce, *feme sole,* and divorce-mill conceptions disappeared. The divorce-mill, or migratory divorce, reappeared in the twentieth century, but for different reasons.

The Nazi and Fascist revolutions were intended to build strong dictatorial states, so they created a rigid familism in order to have soldiers and workers for the omnipotent state. However, they established the new principle: the state will try to mold the family entirely to its aims. If these aims change, changes will also be attempted in the family.

As far as the family was concerned, these changes in society resulted in an almost complete revolution in the conception of the nature of the family. According to canon law, the family was an expression of the will of God, one of the sacraments, and as immune to state control as the act of communion with God. According to trustee family ideas, familism was something no decent man would let anyone outside his own family and kin group interfere with. According to the new conception, the family is but one of the corporate persons of the state and is entirely at the discretion and will of the state.

These changes came about slowly, over centuries, and almost imperceptibly. They were achieved in part by a growth of new ideas, in part by philosophies of family negationism, in part by changed ideas regarding the "original" nature of man, and in part by the social destructions of bloody revolutions. Nevertheless, by the twentieth century the idea had begun to clarify itself. Hume, of all the philosophers of the eighteenth century, was possibly the one who recognized the central idea most clearly. Others have felt it, but no one has expressed it clearly.

The Nineteenth Century

Thus, from the Reformation period on, the whole process has been one of attempting to change the family from an organization that was to guide itself by divine law as interpreted by canon-law doctors to a state-controlled institution guided by interpreters of the philosophy of the state. The nineteenth century apparently was influenced to a considerable extent by the fact that the old order was materially but not completely broken and the new order, while in formation, had no definite philosophy of the family. The power of kinship groups was shattered. All over the Western world there were several hundred millions of people who could and did move to the town, the city, or a new land where kin-control meant nothing.

The same futility existed in the church and in the state attempts to control familism. The standard of established values of the church could be flouted. Neither Protestant ministers nor Catholic priests had close and effective control over members of their congregations. As far as the real power of the state was concerned, literally thousands of laws were passed, but familism was really less regulated at the end of the period than at the beginning.

In the second decade of the nineteenth century America and Britain had settled their controversy and the reaction to the revolution had occurred in France. A remarkable change now took place in the conception of the family. During this century family obligations, from the legal and philosophical points of view, reached the lowest ebb ever attained within a nonrevolutionary period. However, there was no attempt at complete nullification of the family bond, or complete negation such as exists during actual revolutionary periods. Disregarding evaluative conceptions and looking at the matter purely from the sociological point of view—the importance of the family bond as an influence on behavior—this was the century of great atomism in human relations. Such periods had occurred earlier in Greece and Rome, but hardly on the scale seen during this century. During the nineteenth and early part of the twentieth centuries, the conception arose in Western society that the mildest disagreements were cause for absolute separation and breaking of the family bond. Personality must flourish, unthwarted by the family. Family bonds were not taken seriously, especially in smart and sophisticated circles. Private family vengeance for adultery or other crimes against the family was looked upon as an anachronism. To illustrate the contrast between these and trustee family times, it may be noted that during trustee periods one person could be asked to sacrifice himself for the family, as soldiers today are asked to volunteer for especially dangerous missions which mean almost certain death. To refuse a family obligation or to disgrace a family meant infamy.

The following movements were particularly outstanding in the nineteenth-century confusion over the family:

1. The rise and popularization of absolute and "causeless" divorce.

2. The rise of race suicide again in France (Roman Gaul) where the *dignitas* family lost once more its conception that it exists for purposes of reproduction. *Sacramentum* and *fides* had been attacked; now *proles* was rejected.

3. The spread of this idea into cultures derived from barbarian law (England, Sweden, Germany, and the United States) where the *dignitas* family also lost its reproductive conceptions. As *proles* was rejected in France, so it was rejected in the Western world.

4. The rise of "evolutionary" history, with its conceptions of ever-moving, formless society, in place of factual history based upon what is known about man.

5. The American nonrevolutionary experiment in family law nullification.

6. The rise of the earlier Marxian antifamilism in Europe and its spread with the growth of Marxian conceptions of politics and economics.

7. The instruction in nihilism of the family bond among the Slavs through the Russian Revolution. (This time the Eastern Empire gets an antifamilistic philosophy from the West, repaying it for the education in antifamilism received by the West from the East in the code of Solon to the Twelve Tables and in the introduction of later Greek philosophy to Rome.)

8. The development of a "public" which would not permit dual marriage forms, along with the rise of social and intellectual classes who want non-*dignitas* marriage. Not being able to achieve it, especially among those cultures derived from the barbarian, by the use of a *concubinatus* or non-*dignitas* form, they have led the way in breaking up the *dignitas* form.

All of these changes, whether good or bad, are characteristic of the period from the end of the French Revolution to World War I. Absolute and causeless divorce became accepted and popular. For a period in the middle of the century, America nullified the family as a public contract under the control of law. In its formative stages, the Marxian conception of the all-powerful state was extremely antithetical to former conceptions of the family. It is true that Marxism visualized a perfected family, but this was to be achieved by freeing man rather than restricting him by positive laws. (The later Marxism, or all-powerful state conception, has gone in for rather severe family regulation by the state.)

During this same century, a new conception of "history" began to dominate the mind of man. Prior to that time, philosophers of history had noted recurrent stages in history, but now the straight-line evolutionary conception arose. Hegel and Comte set the example for this by reducing all human movement and change from the beginning of time to three succeeding stages of human progress. According to Hegel, in the first stage one individual was free (monarchy), in the second a few were free (aristocracy), and the third stage would occur in the modern state, when all would be free (representative government). Comte conceived of the earliest, or theological, stage as one in which men believed in a personal god. This was followed by a second metaphysical stage, when men believed in God and religion as a force or essence. The last stage was to be a period of positivism, in which men measured and weighed society empirically and were to take conscious control of its direction.

These ideas were hidden beneath a profuse verbiage in the original works of these writers, but no words can cover the fact that they were simply "catchy" beliefs that overturned the philosophy of history which since the beginning of time had dominated Greece, Rome, and Western society. Greek or Roman historians took a period or a great social movement within history and described and analyzed it to arrive logically at their conclusions.

Herodotus wrote about the wars between Asia and Greece. Thucydides dealt with the Peloponnesian War. Polybius described and philosophized about the process by which Rome eventually became master of the Mediterranean world. Livy dealt with facts and ideas of the rise of the Roman Empire from the alleged first migrations from Troy.

After the Renaissance, modern philosophers of history seemed dominated by an idea expressed by Machiavelli in his *Discourses on Titus Livius* and by Montesquieu in his *Spirit of the Laws*. They compared similar movements in classic and modern history and tried to determine the sociological principles involved. But the philosophical historians of the nineteenth century, following Hegel and Comte, fitted historical fact into a preconceived theory. This trend was followed by Maine, Spencer, and all the evolutionary sociologists of the century. They assembled numerous facts, but fitted them into pre-conceived straight-line evolutionary theories.

These successive changes in social thinking were closely paralleled by changes in the attitude toward the family which, for the most part, were questioned only by a few traditionalists. Few sociologists felt impelled to search through history for the real facts that would give meaning and validity to their interpretations.

Nineteenth-Century Divorce

Divorce has had an interesting history. In trustee family times, breaking of marriage is accomplished primarily by family repudiation for childlessness, adultery, or some serious crime against the family. To protect the wife, the cognates, her relatives, are called into the family court or governing body to help decide the matter. Unfairness to the woman has led to some of the most serious of private family wars or feuds. (A man is responsible to his wife's as well as to his own family.)

In domestic family times divorce is generally permitted, but is looked down upon. An indication of this is found in the fact that it was not until after World War I that dramas given in the United States forewent their previous moralizing insinuations regarding the evils of divorce. D. N. Koster, a historian of the American theater, has noted,

> With the shift, after the War, in public attitude on divorce toward a
> position of greater tolerance and a tendency to regard marriage and

> divorce more from the point of view of the individual's happiness and
> less from the social institutional point of view, came a corresponding
> change on the part of the American dramatists. No longer was there
> so much moralizing about divorce; instead there was a noticeable ten-
> dency to the acceptance of it as an integral part of American life, and a
> consequent study of its effect upon individuals. (Koster, *The Theme of
> Divorce in American Drama* 1871–1939, Philadelphia, 1942, 107-108)

In our medieval period divorce was allowed only from bed and
board, or by nullification on the theory that no marriage existed. There
were various devices whereby a person could take church orders and—
since chastity was a higher state than marriage—achieve some voidance
of previous nuptial arrangements. This was particularly true if it could
be shown that marriage, which was sometimes considered to begin with
engagement (*sponsalia*), had not been completed by *copula carnalis*. But
the Reformation and the seventeenth- and eighteenth-century philosophy
(both in jurisprudence and in general theories of society) favored absolute
divorce. The contractual theory of the family as a limited agreement for
a specific purpose gained headway. The nineteenth century was one
in which absolute divorce became not only possible but permissible in
practically all Western countries. Its popularity grew rapidly.

Divorce is a phenomenon which flourishes in certain specific
conditions. These are found in new countries, among mixed populations
upset by revolutions, wars, and other factors destructive to tradition and
family relationships. Naturally, in the Americas (particularly among the
Protestant groups in North America), among the Protestant groups in
Europe, and during the revolutionary and war periods, this idea of divorce
has had its widest influence and popularity.

For instance, France, a Catholic country, had an extreme surge of
divorce in the Revolutionary period of 1789. Dozens of pamphlets were
circulated attacking the family. After the dictatorship of Napoleon, pamphlets of the opposite type began to appear, and the writings of de Bonald
and other Catholic leaders began to gain headway. In 1816, divorce was
abolished. Then after the minor revolution of 1831, pamphlets attacking
the family and advocating the renewal of permissible divorce legislation

gained great circulation. But nothing was really done to permit divorce again until 1884.

This familiar pattern of divorce indicates that it is an aspect of the growth of individualism and "rationalism" in society. Marriage no longer guided by families or carefully supervised from its inception by community and religious leaders (*proprius parochus*) yielded an increasingly greater proportion of failures. The family was breaking violently from its former conception of status and sacrament, under the newer conception of a contractual and secular act. Divorce became a "solution" for families already broken, from families often established without proper foresight in the first place.

Rise of "Causeless" Divorce

At the same time that these other changes came about in divorce, the theory of "cause" in divorce changed from objective to subjective factors, from major to minor reasons, and from what may be called fundamental breach of marriage bonds to purely personal grounds. This may be considered such a radical change in the concept of cause as to speak of it as a change from a cause divorce to a causeless one. Not all divorces now are causeless, but the possibility of securing divorce without fundamental violation of family integrity and purposes has become a potent factor. This is an accompaniment of the purely romantic conception of love, and the theory that marriage exists primarily for the partners and secondarily, if at all, for the bearing of children.

This difference in the conception of divorce is difficult to explain and is associated with no particular type of divorce form. In later Greece when it became the accepted thing for the individual to keep a mistress (or worse) as well as a secluded wife, relations with the extramarital object of love could be purely transitory and dropped without formal reason. This idea began to spread within the household and the real marriage assumed a great deal of this causelessness. (One could dispose of a marriage as one disposed of a mistress.) In Rome, it could be measured by the difference between the breaking up of the *dignitas* marriage as contrasted to the severance of a second-class, or *concubinatus*, marriage. In modern society, both marriage and divorce go through the same public channels—the altar and the courts—but there has been increasing use of causeless divorce.

This point is raised purely to point out the developing conception of the atomistic family. Where the union is strong, petty annoyances are lived down, but major violations generally lead to a separation. Where the union is weak, major factors (disloyalty, nonsupport, absence, childlessness) are often overlooked, but the person has less capacity to endure the petty annoyances inherent in the attempt by two persons to live in as close a relationship as is involved in marriage.

Consequently, a study of the alleged "causes" for divorce no longer has great significance. They are merely forms used to satisfy the public temper. The real inner reason is that families now have to be held together more through the efforts of those personally involved than through the pressure of society. There are no longer numerous children to complicate divorce. Increase in economic opportunities for women has made their situation, in case of a separation, much less difficult from that point of view. Our whole social organization is geared to a situation where causeless divorce is easy and is becoming the modal type.

The old statement that "divorce is merely a remedy for a family situation already broken" is truer in some respects than we have realized. Causeless divorce is common practice in any society where social organization is geared to the individual and to atomistic familism. It is seized upon as a remedy by people whose personalities jar upon each other, when religious belief, legislation, and the pressure of parenthood are not great enough influences to hold the marriage together.

In our society, causeless divorce is most popular among those classes and types of people who would have used the secondary Roman marriage form or who, in Greece, would have used extrafamily relationships for sexual and personal satisfaction. (See Demosthenes, *Against Neaera.*) Its inclusion in the same legal system as the cause-divorce and the *dignitas* marriage in modern society has had considerable influence upon the difficulty of maintaining the *dignitas* marriage, particularly in the United States.

Nullification of Manus and Potestas
in Nineteenth-Century America

As has been pointed out repeatedly, times exist when there is little or no written law on the family. Such was true for early Rome, Greece (and we might add India, Egypt, China, Southeastern Asia), and the Middle Ages of our culture, particularly among the barbarians. This does not mean that there is not some mention of the family in the written or unwritten codes which dominate these times.

The Code of Hammurabi, the Zend-Avesta, the Vedic Hymns, the sagas collected by Confucius, the Ramayana and Mahabharata of Southeastern Asia, the Old Testament, the Talmud, the Koran, and the laws of Solon, the Twelve Tables, the sagas of the Anglo-Saxons, the barbarian codes of the Slavs, Germans, English, the *Iliad* and the *Odyssey*, all mention the family, and some delimit it in detail, not only from birth to the grave but from the birth of the alleged founder of the family to the hypothetical grave of its last survivor. However, these writings are minuscule when contrasted with a Roman law text on the family or the numerous volumes attempting to summarize and categorize our present family law solely in the United States.

But in those times and places where there seems to be no family law, there is an unwritten and minutely detailed law that controls the families. This has been pointed out from time to time in the discussions of family courts or assemblies, transaction, cojuration, composition, amend, *wergild*, and so forth. The point discussed here is the attempt in nineteenth-century America to nullify family law by the adoption of omnibus divorce clauses and *feme sole* conceptions as the American law for families in the nineteenth century. This represents the abolition during nonrevolutionary times and for all families (not only those who adopt a lesser form like *concubinatus*) of *manus* and *patria potestas*. *Manus* (mutual power of husband and wife) and *patria potestas* (mutual power of parent and child) are the key forms of power upon which the entire rights and duties of familism depend. *Manus* and *potestas* are the keystones in the arch of domestic society, the essential nut-locks in the machine which must hold the family together.

Manus and *patria potestas* are fundamentally rights which go together. Mutual right of husband and wife is so intermingled with mutual right of parent and child that a movement toward dissolution of *manus* automatically dissolves *patria potestas*, either in theory or capacity. In a situation where coverture exists to the extent that the domicile of the husband is the domicile of the wife and vice versa, the children, the parents, the husband and wife are in constant companionship and amenable to common periods of consultation, advice, admonition, and help. Where the domicile is different, whatever *patria potestas* exists is impossible to apply because one parent or the other is absent from the children most of the time. The same applies to the conception of the wife as a *feme sole* in relation to her property. *Patria potestas* (or the mutual right and control of the parent over the children and the expectations of the children from the parent) depends largely upon the right of the parent over property. For instance, if a child wants permission from a parent to do something involving an expenditure of money, the power of the parent to facilitate the matter (if it is a wise action) or to hinder it (if unwise) depends upon whether that parent has a positive or a negative right in decisions regarding the family property from which the income must come. If a child wishes to purchase a gun, the father has no restraining power if the child can get the money from the mother, and the mother has no restraining power if it can be purchased from a separate property fund rather than from a family fund. Neither has any facilitation power if the money is controlled by one rather than by both, that is, as mutual family property.

This is a purely hypothetical case, which could be ironed out by agreement between the parents who realize that no matter what the law they must act in unison. The point under discussion here is the decline of *manus* and *potestas* as *family powers* with actions seeking to split or break *manus* as far as property is concerned. Factually, of course, laws abrogating *manus* are passed in periods of growing childlessness and inspired by people who have no intention of having children, so these points do not come into consideration. Furthermore, as pointed out above, no matter what the law, the parent has to do what he or she can to hold the family together and make it function.

Nevertheless, from about 1820 until the reaction after our Civil War, *manus* and *potestas* were destroyed as legal powers in the United States through what are known in law as the "married women's acts," the *feme sole* movement, and the accompanying "omnibus divorce clauses," which were passed in the various divorce-mill states. Our Civil War, which decided that freedom did not mean the right of states to withdraw from the Union, also established psychologically in the United States the conception that freedom in the family did not mean the abolition of *manus* and *potestas*, or the complete abnegation of *baron* and *feme* and coverture.

Now let us see what these specific acts were, which led to the intentional or unintentional inroads into *manus* and *potestas*.

> In 1821 the legislature of Maine had authorized the wife, when deserted by her husband, to sue, make contracts, and convey real estate as if unmarried, prescribing the mode of procedure in such cases. A like law previously existed in Massachusetts. These appear to have been the earliest of the married women's acts, properly so called: the first-fruits of the modern agitation on women's rights. The example was soon followed elsewhere. New Hampshire, Vermont, Tennessee, Kentucky and Michigan all passed important laws of a similar character before 1850. The independence of married women whose husbands were convicts, runaways, and profligates thus became the first point gained in the new system. . . . The right of a married woman to dispose of her property by will was legalized in Illinois, Pennsylvania, Michigan and Connecticut about [1845]. . . . In Connecticut, Ohio, Indiana and Missouri, the first reforms appear to have been directed towards exempting the wife's property from liability for her husband's debts, rather than giving her complete dominion over it. [But] the year 1848 saw a wondrous revolution effected in the foremost states of this Union as to the property rights of married women; and this revolution has since extended to every section of the country. . . . [The New York law of 1848] provided that the real and personal property of any female already married, or who may hereafter marry, which she shall own

at the time of marriage, and the rents, issues, and profits thereof, shall not be subject to the disposal of her husband, nor be liable for his debts, and shall continue her sole and separate property as if she were a single female; and that any married female may lawfully receive and hold property in like manner from any person other than her husband, whether by gift, grant, devise or bequest. This statute, passed at such a time by the foremost State . . . could not fail to make a deep national impression. . . . From this time forth, the revolution became rapid. . . . (James Schouler, *Law of Husband and Wife*, Boston, 1882, 251–55 *et passim*)

The influence of this legislation strikes fundamentally at the powers between husband and wife and parent and child. Disregarding the fact that by then the propertied classes in the United States were childless or had extremely small families, this general change in family doctrine had developed and has expanded since then, as far as legislation is concerned. Lazy Husband laws, penalizing family deserters; the privilege of women to bring civil suits for alienation of affection and for criminal conversation; permission for wives to sue in their own names in the case of torts or civil damages of a noncontractual nature; the abolition of the doctrine that a woman committing a crime in the presence of her husband is supposed to act by his coercion; the proposed system whereby husband and wife can sue each other without breaking up the marriage; permission for husband-wife suits in matters of tort; the proposed system whereby child may sue parent and vice versa; all these and many more acts indicate the steady fragmentation of any legal meaning to *manus* and *patria potestas*.

Justice Thornton, in 1872, recognized this as follows:

The ancient landmarks are gone. The maxims and authorities and adjudications of the past have faded away. The foundations hitherto deemed so essential for the preservation of the nuptial contract and the maintainence of the marriage relation, are crumbling. The unity of husband and wife has been severed. . . . (*Martin v. Robson*)

Vernier, in his *American Family Laws*, holds that the movement was to remove the wife's common-law disabilities and to equalize the rights of husband and wife. Then he gives another reason—to equalize the burdens between spouses. Most of this, like most of life, is merely sentimental rationalization. Under coverture man and woman were in the same boat together. Then the woman was legally freed, so the husband had to be freed; they were again equal, but there was no family left under the law. Most of this hastily conceived family legislation, which few read and fewer still paid attention to, was made for and by people who do not have or do not desire to have families, but merely want a secondary form of marriage, which the honest Romans arranged for in their *concubinatus*.

Nullification of Many Legal Aspects of the Marriage Contract

Not only in the field of *manus* and *potestas* were revolutionary changes in marriage worked out in the nineteenth century. The nature and obligations of the marriage contract were also drastically changed. In America this was more than a matter of making absolute divorce available to the people. Through law and procedure the marriage contract lost most of its legal meaning and fell back for its chief support upon the intentions and the unsupported ability of people to get along together. Legal rules holding the family intact were so relaxed that escape was very easy. Consequently, foresight and precautions concerning entrance to marriage were relaxed; those who married had no particular legal reason to make great sacrifices to make the union a success.

Ordinarily, even in atomistic periods when the individual is comparatively free from family domination, the public—the family, the state, or the church—maintains considerable interest in the continuity of the marriage relation and insists that, if possible, unusual sacrifices be made by the individual to maintain this relation. The major revolution in the family in nineteenth-century America shattered this idea. The movements were of three types—omnibus divorce clauses in the legislation;

development of divorce-mills, or states of quick and easy divorce; and the conception of validity of divorce in jurisdictions different from that of the residence, the property, the children, and the partner being sued. These developments culminated eventually in the official withdrawal of effective public interest in the family, except that exerted through the pressure of public opinion. A fourth change was the development of the idea of marriage removed from the jurisdiction of domicile. Easy divorce and easy marriage go together. At the Council of Trent the church made a great deal of *proprius parochus*. This was the idea that, as far as possible, marriages were to be made in the parish of domicile so that judgment of the families and the local clergy would have some influence upon the marriage. At that time marriage, even among the Protestants, was factually unbreakable. Now that *manus* and *potestas*, as well as the marriage contract, have lost most of their legal sanction, the why and wherefore of entering marriage is naturally given less public consideration.

The omnibus divorce clause and the divorce-mill states have an interesting history. Beginning about 1820 and going out of the legislations about 1880, a series of states passed laws which permitted judicial divorce in the local courts and, after specifying reasons, added statements in intent as follows:

> [And divorce may be granted] for any other reason which the court shall deem necessary.

This was a radical change in legislation regarding the family. As a matter of fact, outside of the divorce by mutual agreement permitted under the French Revolution for a few years after 1792, this was the greatest relaxation of official concern in the marriage bond since the Roman matrons of the higher classes openly registered themselves in the *stuprum* lists in order to escape the economic consequences of loss of property, under the law *Julia de adulteriis*, for adultery.

Actually, this was the most radical change ever to occur in the entire history of barbarian, Anglo-Saxon common law regarding the family. The church had considered marriage a holy sacrament, a heavenly thing. Anglo-Saxon and common law had considered marriage a political and social status, a thing of natural right.

Justice Story in his *Conflict of Laws* held that:

> Marriage is not a mere contract between the parties, subject, as to
> its continuance, dissolution and effects, to their mere pleasure and
> intentions. But it is treated as a civil institution, the most interesting
> and important in its nature of any in society. (Par. 200)

But omnibus divorce clauses, legislated by Indiana, Illinois, Connecticut, Washington, Maine, Utah, Louisiana, and other states, left
discretion in divorce to the judge. He, being an uninformed official in a
divorce-mill state, or region, or court, could and did do just as he chose.
In other words, he satisfied the client who hired the lawyer.

However, these statements must now be qualified. In our country,
following ancient Anglo-Saxon precedent, judges also make laws. The
legislatures pass many resolutions; the judges subject them to discussion
and, through the various court processes, decide whether the matter is
law and, if so, what kind of law. This is a familiar process in the field of
the family. For instance, canon law doctors in the Middle Ages argued
for three hundred years about whether marriage began with the engagement (*verba de futuro*), the wedding ceremony (*verba de praesenti*), or
the honeymoon (*copula carnalis*). So also in the nineteenth century the
judges took up the *meaning* of these omnibus divorce clauses.

Essentially they held that this did not give the judge power to do
as he liked. He must adhere to "legal principles" and these must be "so
blended as to constitute an established course of justice."

However, the only alternative to the misuse of an omnibus divorce
clause was "appeal" by the defendant. Less than 1 percent are ever ap-
pealed since, in atomistic periods, most divorce cases are the results of
collusion or connivance (regardless of what other aspects they may have).
Even with the abolition of these clauses by 1900, the absolute divorce rate
in the United States was higher than the combined absolute divorce rates
in Italy, Austria, England, Scotland, Finland, Bavaria, Belgium, Serbia,
Sweden, Norway, and Holland. Much of our population originated in
these eleven countries.

Consequently, along with this nullification of public interest, the
divorce-mill business grew up, probably beginning in Connecticut but

moving westward with the frontier. As public sentiment waxed and waned, the movement had its ups and downs. At present three or four such states exist, all of which combine business, false and easily acquired jurisdiction, short residence (from six weeks to three months), and the conception that divorce is merely the breaking of a private contract. Several states are now competing for the business, and one may make a choice as to where a divorce vacation may be spent. The affluent may go to one or two foreign countries where the same business flourishes. Occasionally one of the divorces is overthrown by the courts on grounds of jurisdiction, particularly when children are involved, but most of them stand, even if contested.

Finally, bona fide jurisdiction gave way to jurisdiction for divorce. When the state first took control of marriage after the Reformation, the original idea was that the state would be severer than the Catholic Church in matters of marriage purity. This was one of the arguments of both Luther and Calvin. This appeared to be true for a while after the English Revolution and in the seventeenth-century American colonies. The church countered this formal aspect of strictness with the idea of *propius parochus*, instituted after the Council of Trent. Now bona fide jurisdiction of the court of the domicile over the husband, wife, children, and property, as a unit, has given way to the conception of jurisdiction for divorce alone. Migratory divorce state jurisdiction is obviously for one purpose alone, and divorce is granted, although the real domicile of both parties, the children, and the property of the family may be elsewhere and under another jurisdiction. At first, the courts in the real jurisdiction states would overthrow the specially acquired jurisdictional divorces, but lately the tendency has been to say that if people want divorces, they should have them. The law is not to "reform" but to "serve." Although this is contested in legal theory, it is in fact true.

By a five to four vote, a recent Supreme Court decision has questioned spurious jurisdiction for divorce purposes alone, but the case was closely contested (*North Carolina* v. *Williams*, U.S.S. Court, May 21, 1945). The couple went to Nevada for six weeks and immediately after divorcing their North Carolina spouses, married and returned to North Carolina. The point at issue was whether the bona fide domicile was

Nevada. The Supreme Court decided that it was not, and that Nevada did not have jurisdiction.

The contrasting opinions in this case indicate clearly that as far as law is concerned, public control over marriage and familism in the United States has practically ceased to operate. Unless the case is a flagrant one, and there are funds for legal contests, major issues of familism are decided by the individuals themselves. In the case of *North Carolina* v. *Williams* the governor pardoned the couple after conviction.

Thus the nineteenth century (and its aftermath in the twentieth) has nullified at least temporarily the greater part of real state control over marriage. *Manus, potestas,* the public contractual nature of marriage, bona fide jurisdiction, good intent, and the conception of injured and culpable parties have disappeared from public regulation of marriage and the family. What is left is a tangled and contradictory mass of legislation, most of it dealing with individuals and not the family, most of it ineffective except when well-intentioned people or an occasional public-minded jurist stands against the tides of dissolution battering marriage and the family.

Nevada, The Pioneer State

Nevada, one of the states to go into the divorce-mill business, started the process about 1909, when a lawyer advertised in the East to get divorce business. A reaction occurred and the lawyer was disbarred. The law was then strengthened by making jurisdiction apply only to those living in Nevada for one year. This was in 1913. In 1915 the time was reduced to six months; in 1927, to three months; in 1931, to six weeks. The later changes were to meet competition from other states. Nevada merchants would have preferred to have persons seeking divorce live there longer and spend more money. In Nevada (at least in 1935) county jurisdiction was not specified separately from state jurisdiction, so if a judge in one county tried to be too scrupulous, "counsel" took his client into another county where he felt less apprehensive of embarrassment, permitted his client to gain a residence in that county by sitting in the automobile while the papers were being filed, and immediately after that, had the case heard and disposed of. This weapon has been a most potent one to discipline those judges who endeavor to be conscientious. To shun a judge's court under local conditions is not only to insult him subtly, but also to break his spirit and schedule him for retirement. Usually, he capitulates rather than be looked upon as a "destroyer of business." Idaho, Florida, and Arkansas were soon competing for the business with Nevada.

10

DISRUPTION OF PUBLIC
CONTROL OF FAMILISM

T HESE DEVELOPMENTS OF THE NINETEENTH century occurred when
the church (Protestant and Catholic alike) had receded in its domination over the family and the state had failed to demonstrate its ability
to control the issues involved. In the late nineteenth century and first
half of the twentieth, we were to see the almost complete disruption of
social control over the family, particularly in America. In America, the
disruption was facilitated by the fact that we have a very mobile, changing, democratic society. Family jurisdiction and rule are vested in state
legislatures, and the actions of one legislature can annul those of another.
(This is true in fact if not in law.) But fundamentally familism moved in
the same direction in all Western countries, because the chief facilitating
agent was an extreme concept of the freedom of the individual. While in
other countries the individual could not be so blatant in his disregard of
public control over familism, the differences between these countries and
America is largely one of degree only—and not a great degree at that.

The rise of this process of individualization is examined in this
chapter, and the methods by which social control of familism has, to a
large extent, broken down in America are described.

The Atomistic Concept in the Nineteenth Century

A peculiar attitude of the public toward the destruction of the family was one of the phases of the change that took place in the nineteenth century. This attitude was divided. There was, on the one hand, the citizen who wanted a *dignitas* marriage and who had no intention that the Protestant Reformation's secularization of society should go beyond the development of political and economic institutions favoring material development and a high standard of living. On the other hand, this material development created classes not interested in *dignitas* marriages. As in third- and fourth-century Greece and in imperial Rome, this class favored comfortable, semipermanent sex relations, unencumbered by the need for reproduction, a common life (*manus*), parental duties (*potestas*), or binding relations within the family.

Under trustee conditions, breaking of the family (i.e., those matters which lead to divorce) is handled primarily by the kin group. Stealing from the family, giving a thief access to family possessions, adultery, and other severe antifamily crimes lead to repudiation of the guilty individual. Essentially, this is not divorce, but the casting out of the person by the family for intense disloyalty.

Under domestic conditions divorce becomes a civil matter. It is adjudicated before the public by a guiltless and a guilty party. If both are guilty, the matter is theoretically refused on the legal grounds of recrimination.

In atomistic times, the family gives way and disintegrates in favor of the individual. Marriage becomes a highly private matter. Obviously, this disintegration can go only so far without resulting in the negation of the whole of social life. Therefore, an acute antagonism arises between those who want the religious or public control of a *dignitas* marriage and those who want no social interference whatsoever in their quickly made and often quickly broken sexual unions. The two classes may be divided into those who live for the future and those who live for the moment.

The argument between those who want the *dignitas* marriage and those who feel that public interference is a restriction upon the individual has been carried on throughout history. Until the atomistic family was established there was very little—one might say there was no—argument on this subject in either Greece or Rome. After the decline of Rome, and until the sixth century, there was some argument between the bishops of the church and the secularized Roman Gauls. Most of the differences of opinion occurred between the bishops and the ruling families, who carried barbarian law of the trustee family to extremes. The ruling barbarian families did offer some opposition to the monogamic principles set forth by the church, but it was more in the nature of an argument of the "king can do no wrong" theory than an attack upon the family sacrament.

The reformationists reopened the argument in the late fifteenth and sixteenth centuries, particularly the humanist Erasmus, the Protestants Luther and Calvin, and the intellectual Jean Bodin. Their essential idea, however, was to build up secular power. As shown repeatedly in this work, beyond Luther's compromise with one German prince on the matter of polygyny, none of these writers had any idea other than that under secular control the family would be strengthened. All of them discussed the matter merely incidentally to their basic underlying drive for secularism, and the development of what has now become the modern state.

The French Revolution gave great impetus to the argument. However, the writers still used seemingly ethical motives in their pursuit of the relaxation of the public control of the family. In his *Lettres persanes* (no. 117), Montesquieu held that divorce and marriage of the clergy ought to be permitted to remedy the problem of depopulation of the Christian countries. He held that the only difficulty would lie in the solution of the problem of children, in the case of divorce. Diderot, in *Complement au voyage de Bougainville*, wanted relaxation of family control because tyrannous men make property of women. Rousseau, in his *Confessions*, and Madame d'Epinay, in her *Memoirs*, were ostensibly puritanical in the outward reasons advanced for advocating the decline of marriage control, no matter what may have been their inner feelings. During the revolutionary period the argument was between certain Catholic officials, or other high Catholic philosophers such as de Bonald, and the revolutionary legislators. The legislators gave highly honorable reasons for weakening marriage control, such as Cailly's *Griefs et plaintes des femmes mariées*.

Control of Marriage in the United States in the Nineteenth Century

This argument on public control of marriage went on as before in the United States during the nineteenth century, both sides using the same reasons as before. Most outstanding, and yet typical of the thousands of arguments used, was the series of letters between Horace Greeley and Robert Dale Owen, published in the *New York Tribune* in 1860.

A few brief excerpts from these letters will illustrate the differences and will lead to the discussion of the development of that class in our modern population which seeks further relaxation of public control of marriage and the decrease of all the other paraphernalia of domestic familism.

Greeley in writing against elaboration and relaxation of the divorce laws in New York State in 1860 held:

> The paradise of free-lovers is the State of Indiana, where the lax principles of Robert Dale Owen, and the utter want of principles of John Pettit [leading revisers of the laws] combined to establish, some years since, a state of law which enables men or women to get unmarried nearly at pleasure. A legal friend in that state recently remarked to us, that, at one County Court, he obtained eleven divorces one day before dinner; "and it wasn't a good day for divorces either." In one case within his knowledge, a prominent citizen of an Eastern manufacturing city, came to Indiana, went through the usual routine, and obtained his divorce about dinner-time, and in the course of the evening was married to his new inamorata, who had come on for the purpose, and was staying at the same hotel with him. They soon started home, having no more use for the State of Indiana; and, on arriving, he introduced his new wife to her astonished predecessor, whom he notified that she must pack up and go, as there was no room for her in that house any longer. And she went.
>
> ... we know of an instance in which a woman long since departed from her worthless husband, and trying hard to earn a meager living

for their children, was disabled and crippled by a railroad accident; yet the law gives her no right of action against the culpable company; her broken ankles are legally her runaway husband's, not her own; and he would probably sell them outright for a gallon of good brandy, and let the company finish the breaking of them at its own convenience. We heartily approve of such changes in our laws as would make this deserted wife the legal owner of her own ankles; but we would not dissolve the marriage obligation to constancy for any other cause than that recognized as sufficient by Jesus Christ.

To this polemic, Owen replied approximately as follows:

1. The Indiana law on divorce is largely as I found it thirty-four years ago. To its numerous provisions, I added only one—habitual drunkenness as a cause of divorce.

2. The Indiana law now requires a year's residence for divorce jurisdiction.

3. The Indiana family is all right. The real center of free love is New York and New England, where reasonable divorce is refused.

4. The New York law permits divorce for adultery alone. Indiana law permits divorce also for abandonment, cruelty, habitual drunkenness, and for any other cause for which the court may deem it proper that a divorce should be granted. These are not lax principles according to the Christian rule, "By their fruits ye shall know them." [In addition, the Indiana law actually permitted divorce for impotency, and conviction of one partner of an infamous crime.]

5. "God forgive you, Horace Greeley, the inhuman sentiment [that he would require a virtuous wife to live with and not divorce a drunken wretch]."

6. Marriage was made for man, not man for marriage. "It fulfills God's intentions as long as the domestic home is the abode of purity, of noble sentiment, of loving kindness, or, at least, of mutual forebearance."

7. "The question remains, whether it be more pleasing in the sight of God and more conducive to virtue in man, to part decently in peace, or to live in shameful discord."

In answering, Greeley introduced an old English term, *bantling*. "Why should not they who have devised something better than old fashioned marriage give their bantling a distinctive *name*, and not appropriate ours?" The argument went on and on, involving the Scriptures, Hebrew and Roman law, etc. The Greeley faction represented the arguments of the group resisting change since the days of Luther; the Owen faction represented the arguments of the extremists. There was no substantial difference between the arguments of Erasmus, Jean Bodin, and Owen, and no substantial difference between the arguments of the Catholic bishops and Greeley, except of course in minor details, such as the permission of divorce in a limited number of cases for adultery. Separation from bed and board, and not absolute divorce, was the chief form of divorce permitted in New York.

Owen quotes the same scripture and uses the same arguments as did John Milton, and Milton did the same as Hugo Grotius and Paulus Fagius. Every advocate of divorce between the rise of the Humanists and the nineteenth century does the same. The most used quotation is Deut. 24:1: "When a man hath taken a wife, and married her, and it comes to pass that she find no favor in his eyes, because he hath found some uncleanliness in her: then let him write her a bill of divorcement, and give *it* to her hand, and send her out of his house." To which Deuteronomy adds, verse 2: "And when she is departed out of the house, she may go and be another man's wife."

This argument introduces the three social classes concerned in changes in the marriage bond—the opponents of change (like Greeley), or those holding the social structure and the family bond to be a permanent union; the prochange group (like Owen), who feel that society can be improved by a wise relaxation of public conceptions of the permanent unity of the strong marriage bond; and the third group of in-betweens, who want a non-*manus*, non-*potestas*, easily dissolvable marriage, but who fear public criticism should they step out of order, in a formal sense, in the marriage relation. This latter group is represented by the business man discussed by Greeley, who used the weakness in the family law of Indiana to achieve an alteration in the marriage bond, which could not be endorsed by either of the two groups represented by Greeley and Owen.

Struggle against Public Restrictions on Familism

Thus in modern society there are developing groups of people who do not want the higher or *dignitas* marriage form, with its *manus, potestas,* common life, and so on. It is this group and their relation to the moral sentiments of both the "Greeley" and "Owen" groups which gives the unique character to marriage and marriage laws in the United States of America. It applies also in a lesser degree to the *haut monde* of Europe and seems to be spreading not only here but in Europe from the *haut monde* (particularly among the literati) to the common masses. This social class sprang from the new *bourgeoisie* and literati of the nineteenth century. At first their familistic attitudes were kept more or less secret (one went to Indiana or the Dakotas for a divorce), but since the change in moral ideas occurring after World War I, it is no longer necessary to be secretive. Here, as earlier in Rome, we have again reached the stage where women are known not for the number of their years, but for the number of their husbands.

There is, however, one difference worth reporting between Roman and Greek times and ours, and that is that in the modern world the circulation of ideas and customs is far more rapid than it was in Greece and Rome, because of the vastly expanded means of communication. Also, the world today consists of not one but many empires, which leads to great wars between the sovereign states. During these wars, different customs, modes of thought, and so forth are spread among the great masses of common people who form the bulk of our civilian-manned armies. (Our wars now are like those between the Western and Eastern Roman Empires.)

The above is true in the same sense that the debauchery and other forms of behavior in Rome excelled those in Greece. The tremendous upswing of all forms of venereal diseases in Rome after it had absorbed the mixture of strains in the then-known Western world must have been awful, although little is known about it. The *Asiatic lust,* as Augustine calls it in his *City of God,* left new strains of syphilis and all venereal diseases in the empire. Since little was known of how to cure these evils, they flourished more or less unchecked. Things were as bad then as they were after the Renaissance in Europe, when new diseases and invigorated strains caused so much trouble. Greece had to send as many physicians to Rome as courtesans. From the time of Nero on (emperor 54–68 A.D.), public physicians or archiaters had to be created to combat this evil.

As to the influence of wars, Willard Waller remarks:

> Soldiers and civilians alike participate in the relaxation of the sexual morality in time of war. . . . Children are neglected. . . . After a war, women do not easily give up their new found freedom. . . . The disorganized man wants a woman. Almost any woman will do. . . . The veteran who does not marry has an unusually good opportunity for cultivating dalliance relationships. . . . We must think . . . of millions of blasted lives. (Waller, *The Family, A Dynamic Interpretation,* New York, 1938, 84 and 130 ff. *et passim*)

The whole postwar problem is reduced to this. Society, as we know it, develops demoralized social classes—products of many ill-advised war marriages, veterans shocked by war, a new set of social climbers, literati, public entertainers and newly rich—who do not care for a confining marriage, a marriage of children, of *manus* and *potestas.* They look about for escapes, loopholes which will permit them to live as they want and yet not bring them into public disrepute. Out of this comes a reduction in the meaning of marriage in law. The people who do need support in their *dignitas* marriages find little or no effective public backing, at least in law, for the multitudinous trials and tribulations in the very exasperating job of having and rearing a family. In many respects the modern parent has become an unfortunate "victim of circumstances"; the real "forgotten man" today is the parent.

Comparison of the Social Control of the Family

The whole problem might be summarized as follows. In Greece in the fourth century B.C., in Rome after the first century A.D., and in the Western world during the nineteenth century, the same social situation arose. The family decayed; divorce, adultery, sex license, childlessness, and other such forms of behavior increased to astronomical proportions. In Greece the *dignitas* family became childless and was more or less the private property of a decadent male group who wished to have nonfamily public affairs. The family failed to function as a social force.

In Rome, essentially two types of families were created, but still the actual *dignitas* form degenerated, and this degeneration went beyond mere childlessness. Adultery and *stuprum* entered the *dignitas* family and the public and the legislators were unable to cope with it. Again the family failed to function.

In modern life everyone marries, but the whole marriage system is impenetrated with conceptions which in Greece were reserved for nonfamily life and in Rome were distributed impartially through *concubinatus*, nonfamily life, and the *dignitas* marriage. Those who do want children and a marriage of *dignitas* in the modern world do not even have the domestic sanctity privilege of the Greeks, nor the support of the differentiating character of Roman law.

We are one of the most marrying societies. We are, at the same time, the most divorced. Certain classes, of increasing significance, take neither marriage nor divorce seriously. The very philosophy of marriage has changed. Scores of books are written on marriage and the family. Almost without exception they view marriage and the family as a private affair. "If your wife or husband does not suit you . . . find one who does." Marriage is taken more lightly in our society than the purchase of an animal. If one purchases an animal, he comes under the supervision of the town dogcatcher, the Society for the Prevention of Cruelty to Animals, an agricultural agency, or some public health agency interested in tuberculosis, animal diseases, fever tick eradication, or undulant fever. In the family, however, the steady movement is toward the inviolability of private right and private agreement.

It is true that we have many family laws, volumes of them. Some of them try to mold the family into the semblance of a public institution. But all of society, from the writers of family books on down, have ideas which · fundamentally place the individual rampantly above the family and are openly skeptical, even derisive, of any suggestion of familism.

The fact is now well known, and associated with these changes, that the Western world has entered a period of demoralization comparable to the periods when both Greece and Rome turned from growth to decay. Divorce, premarital sex experience, sex promiscuity, homosexuality, versatility in sex, birth control carried to excess, spread of birth control to every segment of the population, positive antagonism to parenthood, clandestine marriage, migratory divorce, marriage for sex alone, contempt for familism, even in the so-called educated circles—all are increasing rapidly. In spite of our virtuous words, and without even the intellectual honesty of the Greeks and Romans, we have gone as far as they, and it would appear that we are going even father. The family crisis of the nineteenth and twentieth centuries is like that in Greece and Rome, except that we do not recognize it and are intellectually dishonest with ourselves on this subject.

The important differences in the modern family are the way the facts are hidden and the way we try to cover the *dignitas* and the lesser family with the same shade of respectability. In Greece there was no denial of the double standard for men, nor of the division of women into three social classes. From the time Socrates complimented the public woman on the fact that a group of "friends" was economically more productive than an estate or a herd of cattle, down to the essay on "Love" delivered by Plutarch in Rome about 90 A.D.—a period of five hundred years—the Greeks, while maintaining a little delicacy, made their fundamental sex disunity a matter of public record. The Romans struggled somewhat harder to keep the facts hidden. The literature, from Tacitus and Suetonius to Procopius—a period of five hundred years also—repeatedly mentions severe persecutions of violators of family and marriage bonds. Adultery could be and was used as a charge for persecution of political opponents. Public men could not "laugh the thing off," as Demosthenes is claimed to have tried to do in Greece in the case against Senator Timarchus by

Aeschines. In the modern family there is an attempt to cover and hide all.

We are not sure just why this is the case or what it means. It is possible that the evolution of a moral code of universal mores like that seen in the rise of Christian ethics has become a permanent influence in society and although out of fashion right now will resurge in a wave of public condemnation of antifamilism. Finally, it might mean that morals and antifamilism have nonidentical cycles. Morals can be fairly good while the family is decaying and vice versa.

This last hypothesis is doubtful. Morals are generally closely correlated with familism, because they constitute the essence of much of familism and vice versa. Then again, all objective evidence points to the fact that we have developed as far toward atomism as had the Greeks and Romans in the centuries of great atomism already mentioned. The probable explanation of the difference is found in the prevalence of the Christian moral code.

The main question, from the standpoint of both morals and familism and the trends they take, is whether this presence of Christian codes is merely a hangover from the past or a permanent force which has the chance of recuperating and expressing itself as a puritanical force, either in the form of suasion or through compulsory legislation of the Justinian type.

Right now it is clear that the social control of the family, either by Christianity or the state, is at a low ebb. What moral virtue and familism remains is largely a product of the individual ideals and the encouragement and example set by the minority of unsupported *dignitas* families.

The Model of the Domestic Family

When Pericles in his funeral oration for the unknown soldier, delivered about 430 B.C., deals with the circumstances leading up to the Peloponnesian War, he gives a clear picture of a society that has grown great because it had a staunch social basis in the domestic family and had also the location, human resources, and opportunity to develop trade, commerce, the arts, and a great civilization. Pericles was talking to people who still held family values of the domestic type paramount. What Pericles said and implied about the Athenian family in 430 B.C. was to be repeated in slightly different words 175 years later, but now with reference to the Romans. Polybius tries to explain why Carthage and Greece had been mastered by Rome in the struggle for the domination of the Mediterranean. In this explanation he points out that the Greeks no longer possessed the familistic traits pictured for Athens by Pericles, whereas the Romans did. The complaints implicit in Polybius were not that civilization was going to fall. Not that; by this time Polybius had become psychologically identified with the new mistress of civilization—Rome. The meaning of Polybius is that the Greeks, bearers of the beacon of civilization 200 years before, had failed miserably as contributors to cultural continuity. Polybius did not, like Plato or Demosthenes, spill any useless tears or needlessly endanger his life over the lost cause of the Greeks. They were too far gone for that. It is true he used his influence with the Romans to mitigate the punishment and destruction in Greece. Nevertheless, he welcomed the new masters of the world because he saw that they then had the moral and psychological strength to hold it together.

In all the discussions of the domestic family, from the time of Pericles and Polybius to this day, the same fundamental appraisal of its meaning-values is reiterated in different words and in changed situations. It makes no difference whether it is Augustus, St. Augustine, St. Isidore, St. Thomas Aquinas, Desiderius Erasmus, Martin Luther, or David Hume who is appraising the family, or whether he is attacking or affirming it—the evaluation in terms of meaning is more or less identical.

The Model of the Atomistic Family

The same may be said of the atomistic family, either in its first golden age of development or in its iron age of rust and dissolution. Aeschines developed the theory when he told the Athenian court that the money involved in a certain lawsuit was not important—family preservation and the social gains from this were paramount. Tacitus understood it when he spoke of "adultery reigning without control" and "virtue a crime that led to certain ruin." In the same passage, he spoke of domestic examples of "truth and honor" and of relations standing forth in the causes of their "unhappy kindred." But these phrases are used to contrast a minority of the "old Romans" with the decadent great majority. The later Roman writers, either such proponents of familism as the Christians and Stoics, or the sneerers, like Aulus Gellius, gave the same meaning-evaluations to the atomistic type. Modern writers follow the same pattern. They speak of the atomistic family as an isolated cultural unit in the sense of its possessing freedom from most of the meaning-values of local civilization. They may admire or despise it as a form, but from Erasmus and Bacon through Rousseau to Bertrand Russell, we find the same general scale of meaning-values attached to the atomistic type.

The Extreme Cases of Western Society

The characteristic differences between family systems in Western society and other civilized and primitive groups show that the physical facts of family systems and changes, the meaning-values, and the complete expression of the causal-vehicular agents influencing the family have reached their most acute and violent expressions in the past three or four thousand years of Western society. Insofar as human history is helpful in drawing sociological generalizations, Western society is the great family laboratory. Western society has shown us the widest possible variations in the family. It gives us the Homeric, Beowulfian, early Greek, Roman, and Dark Ages trustee type. It repeatedly gives us the domestic middle type, from the days of Hesiod to Pericles, Cato to Augustus, and St. Thomas to Rousseau. Finally, it also has its repeated expressions of the atomistic type of family in both its good and bad forms. Each development in Western society has had its variations within each larger form, such as a fairly stable atomistic type and the fragmented family of the Jazz Age. The absolute maximums of these expressions can be found in the attitudes of two writers of about 100 A.D., Plutarch and Tacitus. Plutarch, viewing decadent Greek society, justified adultery as a delicate tribute to the married partner; Tacitus, contemporaneously viewing north European barbarian society, pointed out that their punishment for adultery was being buried alive in a swamp. The change from the family of Homer to that of the "vile heterogeneous mass" which Tacitus finds in Greece in the first century A.D. represents the absolute extreme swings of the family.

11

THE WESTERN FAMILY AND
THE PURPOSES OF FAMILY SOCIOLOGY

IN CHAPTER ONE THE STATEMENT was made that "cause and law" are the primary differences between a "record of social events concerning the family and the existence of a science of sociology." In this chapter it is necessary to elaborate this statement to show what it means for family sociology and to prepare the ground for the development in the following chapters of cause and law theories.

In the logical sense, the purpose of the preceding chapters was to prepare for the elaboration of this section. We have taken existing knowledge of the family in Western society from Greek civilization to the major family decision of our own Supreme Court at the end of World War II (*North Carolina* v. *Williams*) and put it into logical order. This has told us the story of the Greek family, which set a pattern of development from the trustee through the domestic to the atomistic type, along with the other changes in Greek civilization. Then, from Demosthenes through Plutarch, we saw the decay of the Greek atomistic family and the breaking-up and nullification of the social importance of the great Greek civilization.

At that period our attention shifted to the Roman family, since this culture or civilization then took the lead in world events. The formative Roman family had also been of the trustee type and the various stages of development in the Roman family followed identically the Greek sequence: trustee, domestic, and atomistic. Rome's historical greatness coincided with the atomistic family organization. The Greek cycle and the Roman cycle were the same; both were seemingly an inevitable and logical human experience. Eventually the Roman atomistic family, like the Greek, began to break up. Roman society, in a slight variation of the Greek experience, attempted a wholesale reform and preservation of the family, based on the hypothesis that the society could not retain its strength and historical continuity unless atomistic family mores were purified and a stronger unit preserved and reinforced. That struggle in Rome, the intellectual elements of which are to be found in germinal form in Greek Socratic thought (in Xenophon and Plato, and partially in Aristotle and Polybius) occupied the last five centuries of the empire. Late Roman intellectual endeavor at social control (from Augustus, the first emperor, through Justinian) had as its major or primary thesis the elements of family reform. The different upsurges or expressions of this movement were recorded in the Augustan reforms; in the moral philosophies of the pagan stoics, best illustrated by Marcus Aurelius; in the Christian philosophy, as crystalized by St. Augustine; and in the repressive secular law codes of the Christian Emperors (Constantine through Justinian). All of these movements had one common meaning in the sense that they were, among other things, attempts to control society by familistic reorganization and family preservation. Xenophon and Plato had been unwilling to accept the thesis of the Athenian tyrants that Socrates was responsible for family decay in Greece. However, they recognized Greek family decay in their attempts to clear Socrates of the blame and infamy heaped upon him. All the Roman movements listed above took as basic the idea that family decay was a major facilitating factor in the breaking-up of the greatness and continuity of that civilization.

Thus, Roman civilization differed from the Greek in that it attempted to preserve historical continuity and the level of culture by remedies applied to the intimate human relations crystallized about the family. Rome underwent five centuries of historical experience of this type, as contrasted with the relatively feeble reforms inculcated in Greek life between the adulthood of Socrates and the suicide of Demosthenes (440 to 322 B.C.).

As has been shown, at the end of the Roman experience the historical continuity was sadly broken and the level of culture in Western society fell to that of the Western barbarians. The reorganization of social processes after 410 A.D., when Rome was sacked by the barbarians, eventually resulted in the dominance of trustee familism in all Western society.

If the main characters of Homer had come to life again in the ages of Pericles, Cicero, or Plutarch, they would have been killed as pirates or brigands after due process of public trial. Had they lived in the European Dark Ages, they would have been the companions of Beowulf, sipped wine with Gregory of Tours, or gotten into trouble with Pope Nicholas I. This Pope finally forced Lothaire to give up his Waldrade—the medieval Helen of Troy. The trustee family and its type of society was in power again during the Dark Ages.

The analysis which follows this trustee period of the Dark Ages shows that Western society again had the same fundamental cyclical relations between family and civilization that were noted earlier for the Greek and Roman forerunners of modern society. In the ninth and tenth centuries the same disfranchised and ambitious classes who fought the trustee family of the Homeric type in the early Roman kingdom preceding the Republic, turned against barbarian trustee family domination of Europe. Here again, as in the early Graeco-Roman days recorded by Fustel de Coulanges, religion became an agent or vehicle in bringing about the change. The church of the Middle Ages was the power above all others which led the way to modernization of the trustee family into the domestic type, in opposition to the antihuman excesses of the medieval Homeric-Beowulfian trustee characters.

One difference, however, should be noted in the change from the trustee to the domestic family in the Middle Ages. In the early Greek and Roman changes, religion operated more as a limited vehicle of the change and less as a fundamental directive cause. Prior to the modern Dark Ages, the earliest universal religions (within the purview of the periods and places covered by this work) had no previous historical records or dogmas to use as standards for the change. Consequently, the developing Greek and Roman religions, described by Fustel, pushed out into the dark more as simple vehicular agencies in the change than as causal forces. But in medieval times religion had a standard of performance always before it—the synthesis of Christian doctrine into a family sociology, achieved in the systematizations by Basil, Jerome, Augustine, and the other early Church Fathers. The church leaders who brought about the family change of the early Middle Ages always had before them as a guide the theories of St. Augustine and other early intellectual church leaders, redigested and set up as dogmatic beacon lights by the mission of St. Isidore.

In spite of this growth in the understanding by the religious agencies which broke the trustee control of modern society between the ninth and the fifteenth centuries, the general social process was the same in modern Western society as it had been earlier in Greece and Rome. The breaking of localism and familism freed the secular forces which eventually matured into strong nations and statehood. The church made state development possible by freeing early medieval society from its localism and brutal trustee control. The state, in its turn, became jealous of the secular control in the hands of the church and turned savagely against this vehicle, which had been the causal agent or sociological midwife of its birth.

All of this antireligious philosophy is inherent in the *Praise of Folly* (not the praise of God by St. Thomas, nor the praise of Good by Plato and Aristotle) by Erasmus. From the point of view of Erasmus, man no longer needed a *Summa Theologica* as a guide or causal agent for his actions. Folly made him inherently good and from there he could proceed ever onward. Folly was to Erasmus what the "good savage" was to Rousseau and the "economic man" to the thinkers of the nineteenth century.

Thus the elements and philosophical thinking leading to the atomism of personality and the family seemed more or less inherent in the processes set in motion by the domestication of the trustee family. Before the backlands of Europe had lost their trustee familism, the sophisticated circles of Western Europe had prepared the way for the atomistic family. Again, as in Greece and Rome, centuries of enlightenment and of intellectual challenge of all the older values of society prepared for the change to the atomistic family. Speaking from the standpoint of fundamental sociology, and recognizing the differences in the stage, the time, the actors, and the scenery, modern Western society has followed the Graeco-Roman path. Formally speaking, history has thus far repeated itself.

The real purpose (or purposes) of family sociology is to examine this process as outlined here and to seek its meaning in terms of the past, present, and future. It seeks the causes of family-civilization change, if there are such. It examines the agents of the change from the standpoint of their aims, their reasons for being, and their present vitality and virility. Is this sociological repetition of family history accidental or inevitable? It might be argued that the rise of the Greek atomistic family was essential to the growth of Greek greatness, and that the aftermath was an historical accident. As evidence of this, it might be cited that the greatness of Rome lasted many more centuries than did the greatness of Greece after the onset of the atomistic family. It might also be noted that agents which in Greece and Rome were only vehicles, in early modern society showed signs of being more permanent and purposive causal-agents.

12

THE DYNAMICS OF FAMILISM

AMILISM IS A SYSTEM OF life which must be built largely from within. It is a product of the most elementary and most violent emotions of the human character—love, hate, sex, food, sacrifice, punishment, loneliness, and extrasensory faith. From birth through death there is nothing mild about the family or its training, mating, supporting, procreating, directing, and dying activities. The physical, ascetic, aesthetic, and other emotional pains and pleasures of family life are never colored by mild grayish psychological tones. Familism, when it is other than prosaic cohabitation, is either violently red, dazzlingly white, or midnight black. The pains of men dying for national ideals on the battlefield are brief compared to the long mental suffering of the parents who, as in many cases nowadays, have lost an only son. Seldom do mothers, even of many sons (and despite the smugness of the dissipated Pericles who recommended such stoicism), remember a lost son without tears. Thus it is evident at the start of this discussion that most of family sociology constructed in Western society, whether valid or not, is the work of amateurs. To them familism is something they see, but whose inner meaning they seldom comprehend.

The statement that familism is a closed social-value system has definite meaning and implications. Familism is a series of conscious and unconscious acts and influences which, once experienced, cannot be avoided, dismissed, or erased. On the other hand, these acts bear definite relations to the life cycle of the individual, from the cradle to the grave. If the meanings are deliberately or accidentally avoided, that system of life experience is no longer attainable to the individual. Finally, experiencing those meanings is the only way to an understanding of them, although experience in itself is no guarantee of understanding.

This raises a question much debated among sociologists as to whether childhood or immaturity in a family is sufficient experience for one to say that the person understands familism. The position taken by some is that having been raised in families, most persons readily understand the family from an experiential point of view. Others, with whom I agree, hold that the great and revealing experiences of familism come primarily after adulthood. The child has gone through most of the basic experiences of familism before he has even a faint idea of their real meaning. He understands only the pleasurable and receiving aspects of the family system and few or none of the sacrificial (pleasurable in a different sense) and giving aspects of the family. In this analysis and later it is assumed that the fundamental aspects of understanding familism come only through experience on an adult level.

Social Consequences of Familism

The fact that familism is a system of behavior that must be experienced to be understood and that once experienced in totality molds character types has many direct and indirect social consequences. First of all is the fact already mentioned that nonfamilistic persons cannot understand family behavior in any deep sense because its methods of control, its systems of rewards and punishments, and its outlook upon life are distinctly different from the world of direct individual and nonfamily experience. The family gives more and requires more of the individual than do other social organizations. For long periods of youth, it gives everything without recompense, as if life itself brought with it certain inherent rights of birth in no way dependent upon the innate goodness or ability of the parents. Then for long periods it takes from the individual without direct accountable physical recompense. The person, as his role changes from family dependent to family head (parent) is demoted from king to slave, thus upsetting the usual nonfamily experience of growth from less freedom and responsibility to greater. The psychology of this is interesting. Familism has to be motivated by the acceptance of ideals of behavior based upon a *way of life* and not upon the usual system of rewards and punishments in nonfamily society. As a result, it is easy for persons to escape the demotion of social freedom by a conscious avoidance of the family. Consequently when familistic ideals are broken among the masses, we find whole peoples turning away from familism and extremely violent eruptions against this system.

This may be explained and illustrated in part as follows. First, we have to consider Europe as a continent with enormous population reproduction capacity as late as three generations (or seventy-five years) ago. At that time, Europe was industrializing itself, building up cities, increasing in population, and sending countless millions of people to the new world. Between 1820 and 1920 alone, the United States of America received approximately forty million adult immigrants from Europe. All at once the situation began to change. Fifty years ago net reproduction rates of Western Europe were about 210, based upon 100 as the ability of a people to reproduce its numbers. By 1933, the net reproduction rate had dropped to about 90, or a minus ten percent of reproduction. Since then the situation has grown much worse. Even excluding the influence of World War II, which must be enormous, European populations, with a few exceptions for the Catholic, rural, and Slavic regions, are all struggling against broken family systems which promise that a reduction in numbers of people will set in before another generation passes by.

Thus we see mass movements against the family impenetrating whole cultures in a relatively short time once the people begin to think of themselves as their own arbiters of population policy, as contrasted to an earlier time when a different conception held natural or moral law to be a social force prescribing a familistic way of life. In the nineteenth century the common people of Europe held that natural or moral law, as distinct from individual ideas, was a social force external from the individual and constraining him to a way of life. We must not forget the violent shock given Western society when the revolutionary government of England during Cromwell's time attempted to remove the family from "natural" and "moral" law influences and to place marriage under the justices of the peace.

The extinction of faith in the familistic system in Europe in the last two generations is identical with the movements in Greece during the century following the Peloponnesian Wars and in Rome from about 150 A.D. to 250 A.D. In each case the change in the faith and belief in family systems was associated with rapid adoption of negative reproductive rates, increased acceptance of perverted forms of sex behavior, and with enormous crises in the very civilizations themselves.

Thus the chief social consequence of familism becoming a semi-closed value system is that when the controlling agents of these values in a given society lose their familism, there is no group of "educators" or leaders who understand the significance of the system. The controlling group no longer understands familism; no other agency has the prestige or ability to impress its ideals upon the masses. When the ruling groups—those with prestige—abandon familism, there is simply no agency which can understand the situation or do anything to remedy it. The writers in Greece and Rome in the periods when the upper-class families had become increasingly atomized had no clear-cut picture of the meaning of this nor its consequences to the whole culture. Isaeus would refer to the family decline in order to win a lawsuit; Demosthenes would use it to justify the immoral behavior of his colleague Timarchus; and Polybius discussed the matter in an attempt to illustrate different views on social causation. No one in the society, particularly no great influential group, had any basic comprehension of the matter.

The same situation occurred when the Roman family began to decline. A Roman patrician came before the Senate and asked for help. He brought his children with him and, pointing to them, said these were the children Augustus "forced him to have." After Augustus, the Roman upper classes never retained any real understanding of family values. Plutarch reveals this change in moral values in his sneer at the Romans who had children in order to have heirs; to him it seemed easier to adopt an heir. Apparently Aulus Gellius was unconcerned that the stories he was collecting for his children were of a great civilization already crumbling about him. There were some moralists who seemed startled at the lack of *fides* among the people, but no one seemed to have a thoughtful understanding of the total disjuncture of the whole social system. In other words, the family system disintegrated first among the literate and influential classes. When this was achieved they still had the authority to control the family system, but no longer had the capacity to understand its full meaning. New recruits to the ruling class took over their old ideas of conduct.

Specific Application to the United States

Let us now interpret the meaning of this in the development of family sociology in the United States of America. It must be recognized first of all that the familistic experience of our upper and prestige-controlling classes was badly shattered long before the American Revolution. Jaffee has studied the problem of differential fertility in early America seriously. In 1800 he found that if the reproduction rate in the rural districts were taken as 100, that of cities under 10,000 people was 70; that of cities of 25,000 was 57; and that of larger cities, 64. He then showed from numerous studies for the different regions and states of the union that everywhere the reproduction rates for families of the wealthier groups (those with more than $3,000 taxable property) were between two-thirds and three-quarters the size of those of the masses; that the rate of the middle groups (those paying taxes on less than $3,000 property) was only about four-fifths that of the nontaxpayers. On the Eastern seaboard and in the longer settled and wealthier districts, people had very small families. In the middle states they were larger, and on the frontiers, still larger. He concludes:

> [T]hese differentials have already existed for a long time. . . . [I]t is likely that fertility differentials were as large at the beginning of the

nineteenth century as they are today. . . . [I]t may well be assumed that they had been in existence since the beginning of the eighteenth century, if not earlier, for a culture would take some time—at least three or four generations—to develop such differentials. (A. Jaffee in *Eugenical News*, September, 1940. Here he is reporting on a number of studies made from early census records for the National Resources Committee)

By the beginning of the eighteenth century, the family system of the "influential" people in the cities, the literate and wealthy classes, and those along the Eastern seaboard had already become the type found among those very classes today. After 1700 America grew primarily not from the loins of its first pioneers but through the influx of immigrants and the numerous progeny that they had before they rose to wealth, individualization, and literacy. The Scotch-Irish and Germans in the middle colonies, those who left the seaboard and went west into the hills and down into the Shenandoah Valley, were the first new immigrant groups. They came in here before the Revolution during the eighteenth century. Finding land and opportunity already absorbed in the cities and along the coast, they "went west" and became, in the words of Frederick Jackson Turner, the "first frontier peoples." After that it was not the first settlers but the Huguenots and others who contributed the mass of people who were to become the great American union. In the early nineteenth century America grew primarily because of the immigration of the English, Scotch, Irish, and others. They came either to go to the frontier or to become wage earners, the "undeserving poor" of the industrializing East and New England.

In the early eighteenth century this situation was observed by Benjamin Franklin, who always seemed to understand things long before anyone else. He wrote a curious little lampoon of the situation in his bagatelle "The Strange Case of Polly Baker." His story dealt with a young woman who was brought before a judge in Roxbury (a section of Boston) and charged with having given birth to four fatherless children. In defense of herself she made an impassioned speech concerning the lack of marriage ideals among the people of Boston (representing the wealthy city groups of that time) and defended herself as a good mother, one who was furnishing children to help build up America. According to Franklin the judge declared the woman not guilty of any crime, married her, moved out to the frontier, and raised a large brood of children by her.

Franklin's writings on the subject of population indicate clearly that this process of expansion on the borders and among the rural and new peoples was primary to the peopling of the colonies. He notes that population was doubling every twenty-five years, but attributes it to the cheap and plentiful lands, low age of marriage among the pioneer rural families, and the simplicity of life. The cities, the artisans, the cultured people, the slaves, and the slave-owning families he specifically mentions as not contributing to the rapid increase. He mentions the frugal, the agrarian, the Scotch, and the "Palatine Boor" types of people as increasing.

During the whole nineteenth century and up to the First World War the peopling of this country was accomplished primarily by these early Appalachian-Ozark people, the forty million immigrants from Europe, and the familistic attitudes of these Catholic and Lutheran immigrants—which they retained for one or two generations. The intellectual tradition, the idea of what was "truly American," was preserved in the minds, culture, and institutions of the well-to-do, the seaboard colonists, and the urban peoples, but familism as a value system did not function actively among these groups.

When the doors of immigration were closed (first by war, later by law, and finally by the disruption of familistic attitudes in the European sources themselves) the antifamilism of the old cultured classes—and of their new recruits from recent immigrants—finally began to have effect. First, the more recent immigrants and then the hillbillies began to adopt the psychology and sociology of the Gilded Age. The transition was achieved very rapidly among the common people. Since there was not a great cultivated class that really understood familism, there was no one with sufficient prestige and influence to evaluate and help preserve familism among the common people. This has been the course of familism in the United States and, to a considerable extent, in Greece and Rome during comparable sociological periods.

The importance of this is that within the same generation America became a world power and lost her fundamental familistic capacity. Europeans ceased coming here in important numbers and in the same generation the masses quickly adopted the "American family pattern." Nor have we shown the capacity to develop an influential "ruling class" with any great experiential or intellectual conception of the basic need and role of familism.

Cultural Integration and Familism

Since familism is a very closely integrated system having distinct biosocial influences upon its members, it follows that the total society is profoundly influenced by the amount and type of familism present at any particular time. Familism is so closely related to all other basic acts of man that it tends to color the entire culture. When familism is ascendant, it is a factor so integrated with all the other cultural elements that they take on a family character themselves. On the other hand, when familism is distinctly weak in a society, all the cultural elements take on an antifamily tinge.

This process has already been partially described for highly familistic times such as those in early Greece and Rome and the Middle Ages. In those periods ideals of good or bad were highly colored by conceptions of kin duty. The administration of justice, property and inheritance systems, religious belief, local organization, and all other phases of life become allied with the familistic ideas and ideals of clan and *fidelitas*. In its extreme forms, it is difficult for the stranger to exist unless he is able to persuade some family to adopt him, protect him, and give him the semblance of family membership (clientship).

In atomistic periods most of this disappears. The family seems unimportant and the whole culture takes on an individualistic coloration. The advertisements, the radio, the movies, housing construction, leasing of apartments, jobs—everything is individualized. For instance, when a family situation is pictured in the advertisements of our modern newspapers, seldom are more than one or two children included in the picture. The advertisers depict and appeal to the fashionably small family. "Child" has been substituted for "children"; the large family has again, as in the time of Gellius, become amusing. Radio characters are portrayed as having one or two children. In the motion pictures, the family seems to be motivated by little more than self-love. Houses are built for the small, almost childless couple and can hardly be expanded for increased families. Landlords do not want to take tenants with children and refuse to do so unless circumstances force it. Dining rooms are reduced in size and more and more of the space is taken up by living rooms, where the differences in age, sex, and interests of the family members soon conflict with each other. Children's clothing, theoretically cheaper to produce than adults', becomes more expensive than adult clothing. Children's toys are cheaply made; they seldom last through the interest period of one child, much less several. A civilization that can make automobiles to stand the test of being driven over cliffs does not produce a child's tricycle that can be properly oiled. The childless couple, or the couple with at the most one or two children, can migrate freely from job to job. The woman is freed from many domestic duties. She can either enter outside work or seek to advance the interests of her husband by playing an important role in business or bureaucratic politics. Baby carriages cost more than lawn mowers. The whole system is unfamilistic.

Nevertheless, through all these periods certain general aspects of familism affect all cultures, because these seem the inescapable results of even a minimum of familism. The attachment between husband and wife, parent and child, kin and kin seems to be greater and on the whole more emotionally stirring than relations between other human beings. Thousands of human relations are broken daily, some with greater and some with less social and personal consequences. But the striking ones, those causing the greater emotional upsets and the most profound reactions, are still those of familism. Returning soldiers still shoot erring wives. Women still hide their dead babies to bring their husbands home from the armed forces.

As Waller suggests, "the young die good." Loss of children, whether one of many or an only child, is a devastating social experience. Even in a cynical "love in the machine age" period, divorce seems far more devastating than the breaking of other relations. When the various totalitarian governments of present and recent years tried to disrupt family allegiances completely in favor of the state, they still kept the old principle of "family hostages." "You may travel to the United States, but your relatives must remain with us as hostages." This was the system used by the ancient Romans to keep the barbarians from fresh uprisings against Roman rule. Family vengeance is still the world's greatest and most common motive for crime (the unwritten law). Family crimes are still considered the world's most despicable acts. Family hatreds, the obverse of family loyalty, are still the strongest passions. In view of the strong emotional impact of these acts, ordinary deaths, breakings of other human relationships, crimes, and hatreds pale into insignificance.

Thus we are led to conclude that familism is the greatest single factor in cultural integration. The family contribution is a basic one. It exists in part because of its own internal powers and in part because of the existence of a functioning society itself. The basic habits and fundamental beliefs in a value system exist simply because the family exists, and are directed around familism. Thus cultures are fairly well integrated about a system of values to the extent that familism is present.

This neither reflects upon the other integrating forces in cultures nor does it tend to set up a theory that familistic integration is sufficient in itself. It merely makes family traits basic and universal. It merely indicates that when familism, which creates these values by its existence, is handicapped or destroyed by the physical and psychological resistances of an antifamily system of behavior, even these basic family agreements reach a low level in cultural integration.

Thus we see how decayed familism, a result of many other changes in a social system, becomes a "cause," or at least a vehicular agent, of further decay. This explains many phases of the "totalitarian" decay in late Greece and Rome, and also points out the extreme difficulties with which our present Western society is beset. It indicates also how this same familistic remnant becomes an influence or vehicular agent in the reappearance of familism. This happened in Western society in the Dark Ages, in both the Greek and Roman sectors (Eastern and Western Europe). When the decay had gone so far that only remnants of familism were left, these remnants became the motivating agents of a new dominant culture. When conditions got so bad that the world had no room for and could no longer support the Plutarchian-Gellian-deipnosophistic culture and philosophy, about all that society had left to integrate the culture were a few basic family values. These mixed with the preserved yeast of the barbarian law codes gave us the main integration of Western society almost from the time of the death of Justinian to the Norman conquest.

Childbearing Fundamental to Familism

This leads us to a consideration of what constitutes the fundamental factor or influence upon whose existence the total of family values is built and integrated. What are the main elements of the family or of family functions?

The canon law doctors and philosophers of the Christian church held that there were three bases or functions of familism. These were first stated as fidelity, childbearing, and indissoluble unity—*fides, proles,* and *sacramentum*. Later the order was changed to childbearing, fidelity, and unity—*proles, fides,* and *sacramentum*. This change of order indicates that even in these three essentials a certain greater causal—or meaning—significance was given to childbearing as the first and determining step.

Such a change in priority of emphasis as this is understandable because the fully formed family does not exist until children enter the picture. The family is the meeting place of three systems of values—those existing between husband and wife, between parent and child, and between these personalities and the more distant relatives. Only when the bloodstreams are mixed in a child does the joint personality of parent and child exist. The main systems of value between the household and kin arise only after the child is born. An almost irrevocable status right of the child in that of the kin is created by the legitimate birth of the offspring. Consequently, *proles,* or the intent of such, is paramount to the full development of *fides* and *sacramentum*.

The parent who prevents a baby from swallowing a safety pin, keeps him from high places, warns a child daily about crossing the street, and inspects the evacuation functions of a child during the first years of its life does more protecting of a family member than the whole police force of the United States does altogether for the child in its entire preadult life. The great fire hazards for a child are scalding water, matches, electrical circuits, stoves (wood, gas, and electric), and fireplaces. The family members and only the family members are the ones who take care of these dangers—not the fire departments. The religious and moral attitudes and behavior of the parents still have ten times more influence upon the value behavior of the young than all the other "moral" agencies put together. The parents' system of moral attitudes is still the most important influence upon the child.

This is true of all the functions which William Ogburn and others claim have left the family. In its real meaning, where children exist, all the functions enumerated by Ogburn remain primarily within the family. The only real decline in primary familistic functions in the different sociological experiences of the family occurred when clan and private law and protection gave way to the state, something which began to happen in Western Europe about the twelfth century. The industrial revolution and the development of cities have added a great deal of embellishment to our social system, but still have not destroyed the real meaning of family functions in the parent-child unit.

All of this is to show that *proles*, or childbearing, is and remains the fundamental independent variable about which the other family functions evolve and upon which they are inescapably dependent. If there are children in the family, the other major functions are inescapable. In societies where reproduction is expected of the people, these familistic values of *fides* and *sacramentum* become part of the general social values, nor can they be escaped by the accepted legitimate liaisons between other couples, even if these do not have children. On the other hand, the decay of *fides* and *sacramentum* values among the rest of society is bound to affect the acceptance of these values by the units with children or those formed on the assumption that children were to be produced.

This is illustrated by the similar periods in Greece and Rome, when these cultures experimented with the *hetaerae* and *concubinatus* or lesser, secondary, and childless liaisons for some of the people and expected the *dignitas* and other more serious forms of marriage to furnish children and to be unities of "faith" and "for eternity." *Fides* and *sacramentum* were not retained in these societies simply because the "smart people," who were supposed to be the leaders, did not have such values and the masses refused to live by the old standards. Soon after the *hetaera* problem arose in Greece, we see a great increase in the divorce rate and an equally great decrease in the childbirths. This happened in Rome after the *concubinatus*. Value systems cannot be broken for a few without being broken for all.

Where the value systems are broken and families must exist largely through the individual's desire (and not because of any compelling moral, religious, or legal code) we see more clearly the role of *proles* or childbearing as the main stem of the family. The childless couples are most frequently divorced. Part of this is due to the fact that divorces occur most frequently in the earlier years of marriage and part to the fact that, inevitably, certain types of persons never want to have children or to remain married. On the other hand, there is the inescapable fact that childbearing creates resistances to the breaking-up of the marriage. Children are uniting family factors, both internally and externally. The couple must pause and consider a divorce more seriously when children are involved. Outsiders also take a much more serious view of divorce when there are children.

We are thus driven to the conclusion that the basis of familism is the birth rate. Societies that have numerous children have to have familism. Other societies (those with few children) do not have it. Moreover, the system of religious values is essentially family ethics. *Fides* and *sacramentum* are value-systems inherent in *proles*. Those classes with few children seldom take other familistic values very seriously, unless they are forced to a surface adherence by "public opinion" (meaning by this, the family mores still preserved by the masses of the people). The periods when childlessness becomes the mode are those in which the intellectuals openly challenge the validity of marriage faith and marriage sacrament. In other periods the intellectual does not dare challenge family values.

If we take Ogburn's theory and rephrase it, the decay of family functions is associated with a decay in the family. His statistics simply prove that allegiance to family values and processes disappears as more and more of the people have few or no children. Since the functions of the family depend upon having a family, a decrease in those functions does not mean a new type of family, but that fewer and fewer of the people become immersed in a full familistic system of values. The residual third or two-ninths of the population who have three or more children still have to carry on the functions always inherent in familism. They procreate, protect, educate, socialize, and guide the next generation, and with a minimum of social recognition. They do this to the extent that another generation appears. Under the present negative fertility rates in Western society, few new generations will appear after the excess of mothers from the previous generation of higher and sustaining birth rates has died off.

In other words, children are the fundamental basis of familism. A decay in familism is a decay in the social system of biological reproduction. Consequently those societies in which familism has decayed are those that are themselves decaying—and very rapidly. The decay of the family becomes a fundamental "cause" or vehicular agent for the further decay of the society.

This is exactly what happened in Greece and Rome in the later periods, and this is exactly what is happening in our Western society today. No amount of hemming and hawing, or hiding our heads like ostriches, can disguise this fact.

The Process of Family Decay

In order to outline the steps whereby this decay becomes established, it is necessary to keep before us two fundamental facts. The first is that reproduction, even in the most virile times of a society, is limited to a small segment of the living population. The second is that the breaking of a familistic system can go through approximately two generations before the results are immediately noticeable to the populations involved. When there is a constant supply of immigrants related by ideas and ideals to the older population, this process of family decay can continue for many more generations without great biological effect.

Not all the children born marry and have children.

> Of the individuals who die out, from two-fifths to two-thirds, according to the period and country, are unmarried; of those who have married, one-third to one-seventh die without descendants. The generation which survives does not therefore, descend from the whole of the generation which disappears, but from only a fraction thereof which varies, roughly speaking, from a maximum of one-half to a minimum of two-ninths. (C. Gini, *Population, Harris Foundation Lectures*, Chicago, IL, 1929, 17)

In other words, in the most familistic of times the biosocial introduction to familism is only experienced by a bare half of the population. At other periods the ratio is much smaller. We may illustrate this for the American white population in 1920 and 1930. About 90 percent of our population now lives to the age of twenty-five, at which time they are in the middle of their most fertile age. A great many do not marry at these ages; some never marry. According to the reproductive system existing in the United States, in 1920 12 percent of the wives had no children and 38 percent had only one or two. In 1920 the remaining 50 percent had what may be called functioning families—those of three or more children. They produced about 83 percent of the next generation. Thus more than four-fifths of the new generation came from one half of the last generation, after that previous generation had already lost 10–15 percent through death before maturity or nonmarriage. Only a third of the generation born in the latter part of the nineteenth century became the parents of the youths who fought World War II.

By 1930 the situation was still more startling. Of those who were born ten years later than the 1920 group of parents, and who survived to the age of marriage and married, almost a quarter (23.1 percent) had no children and 40 percent had only one or two. In 1930, one-third of the wives were producing more than three-fourths of the children (33–35 percent were producing 76.5 percent). Here we have a case where effectual familism impenetrated as a biosocial influence only about two-ninths or less of the actual previous generation. By 1940 the situation was even worse.

Thus the process of family decay is somewhat as follows. For reasons that we cannot go into here, the main system of values begins to lose control. This may be illustrated by the anti-institutional line of reasoning dominating Western society for some time past. When this system of anti-institutionalism finally reaches the family, it is well advanced. The intellectual currents of the time become antifamilistic. Other changes in houses, factory methods, urbanization, and so on are merely facilitating influences—not formal causes in the Aristotelian sense, but efficient or moving causes. The formal cause lies back in the main system of values and the process whereby this is broken. The leaders of the people begin to adopt antifamilism. This group includes the educators, the wealthy, and the governing classes. Since they follow these practices, they have no possible understanding of familism. They do not immediately get into trouble with the social system because the masses are still ignorant (as Erasmus noted in *Praise of Folly*), or religious or traditional or immersed in self-renewing family systems. The situation moves on and on because the backward, rural, mountainous, isolated, and distant regions, populations, or countries still have to be drained of their surplus population and familistic values.

These familistic groups enter the social pyramid of the unfamilistic peoples at the bottom and keep it alive falsely or mechanically until their offspring are absorbed and until they too become immersed in this unfamilistic system of values. By this time a crisis is imminent but the intellectual cannot see or understand it simply because he is a non-participant in the family system. Finally the society reaches a period in which the human springs of the progressive societies have dried up. At that time within this society less than a third of the families reproduce themselves and a small surplus. They understand a system of values entirely different from that of the dominant rulers. However, they are a minority and they cannot compete with the other classes who challenge even their value systems. This process can go on to an actual decay of a society, as happened in Greece and Rome. By this time family decay has changed from a low order of cause to a high one. The family decay changes from an effect to a cause. Prior to this time it decayed as a result of the general value system decay; now the general value system decays because there is no familism to stop it.

Only a general revival of intelligence and sound social thinking can stop this process from reaching its ultimate maximum. Western society has not previously demonstrated that it can easily stop this process.

13

THE TRUSTEE FAMILY SYSTEM—
CAUSAL ANALYSIS

Now that these basic family ideas are before us, let us turn to the trustee family system and give it a "causal" analysis. What causes it to appear and how far does it become a causal system in itself for its continuance or its decay? This is one of the initial problems which we have to consider.

It has already been shown that the family is a unit varying in social power according to the significance of three separate types of social bonds—those binding husband and wife, those between parent and child, and those of the household and the clan, the *gens*, or outer group of relatives. We might call these three the *manus*, *potestas*, and *genos* powers, thereby naming the power of the *gens* over the household according to the Greek term for *gens* or clan. The trustee family is the name given to the family system when the powers of *manus*, *potestas*, and *genos* tend to reach their maximums. Here the relatives are very influential in all the key problems of the small family. Practically, they have control of the relations between the small family, or household, and the outer world.

It will be recalled also that when the trustee family is the dominant type certain purely familistic legal forms and practices rule the society. We have already mentioned such terms as transaction, composition, amend, repudiation, cojuration, *wergild*, feud, private law, family council, and others for the conditions of trustee times.

Finally, the trustee family system has been shown as the dominant type in certain times and conditions of Western society. It was the main type in Homeric Greece, in Rome prior to and including the Twelve Tables epoch, and in modern society in nearly all its phases from the sixth to the tenth and twelfth centuries. It continued in Eastern and northern Europe many centuries later, generally not disappearing in many of those countries before the fifteenth century. In isolated pockets of European society it has even endured almost until the present. In the hilly districts of Wales, Scotland, and Ireland it lasted longer than in the cultivated and low country where the influence of the Norman invasion very quickly ended it. In the Balkans even today it has to be taken into consideration.

Further, we have the clearly authenticated historical reemergence of the trustee family system among our own Southern highlanders, the Jacksonian type of people who went through the Shenandoah Gap of the Valley of Virginia and settled in the rougher regions of Kentucky, Tennessee, Arkansas, and Southern Missouri. This limited redevelopment of the trustee family from the domestic type has occurred numerous times in the history of civilization.

One of the best evidences of the trustee family is widespread, private vengeance involving wars between the dominant family groups and their retainers.

All these feuds had relatively the same social meaning. The family members, friends, retainers, and clients were closely bound together by strong sentiments of solidarity. An offense against one member of the family reflected upon the honor of the family. The jurists coined an expression for these troubles, using the word *décoloré*, which meant that the family of the injured felt stained or discolored by the injury. Relative helped relative. Actual outbreaks were infrequent, but family hatreds smoldered on. It took a long time for religious leaders and state intervention to suppress entirely this private family vengeance.

The Appalachian-Ozark Trustee Family System

It is not necessary for us to go back to the Middle Ages or to isolated districts of Europe to find the trustee family system. A great rebirth occurred among the Scotch-Irish, English, and other settlers who gave us our second frontier in the Appalachian-Ozark regions. These peoples came into the Shenandoah Valley of Virginia and poured through the Cumberland Gap into the mountainous districts of the Western and Southern states. The system is most outstandingly preserved today in the region where Kentucky, Virginia, and West Virginia meet. It is the dominant system even today in the nineteen counties of the Southeastern area of Kentucky, but, in one form or another, its practices have spread through all the mountain districts dominated by these Jacksonian frontiersmen. In the disillusionments at the end of the Civil War, family feuds flared violently in the isolated regions of Texas and also throughout the whole area of the Missouri and Arkansas Ozarks. Even in the west, in the vigilante days before law and order were completely established, it involved the federal government—President Hayes tried vainly to stop what was known as "the Lincoln County war" in New Mexico. In a similar manner, the Pleasant Valley vendetta between the Grahams and the Tewksburys in Arizona burned itself out with the killing of all but a single survivor on one side. This was in spite of the attempts of all the public forces of Arizona to stop it. However, these were merely sporadic developments outside of the mountain regions. The trustee family as it exists, even today in America, was a redevelopment by the Jacksonian peoples settled in the mountainous regions by the postrevolutionary migrants.

We have then in the Appalachian-Ozark region a case study which repeats, to a limited extent, the movement of the family system in the whole of Western society from the fifth and sixth centuries of our era. There were several important differences, however, that should always be kept in mind. In the earlier experience of Western society, the peoples had the barbarian law codes to furnish a framework of law into which the new system could fit. Furthermore, in the late Roman days there were no operative outside influences of great importance to hinder the rise of the trustee family. In the United States the people had to break new ground. Since there was no settled system of transaction, composition, and amend existing in our society, they had to form their own codes more or less blindly.

This same process is to be found in all the great mountain feuds which have ravaged much of our Southern Appalachian-Ozark region for the past century and a half. Over and above these groups was a legal system adapted to the individual or to the domestic and atomistic family conceptions. We had no room or provisions allowing for private interfamily justice. Consequently the Southern Appalachian-Ozark trustee family system had to develop as a lawless and undercover method of settling disputes. When we see it from that point of view and make allowances for the outside pressures against the system, we can see in it a repetition of the earlier historical experience in which the trustee family rose to be the fundamental system after the decay of the Roman Empire.

The change in the fifth and sixth centuries was from the Roman atomistic family to the trustee organization of the Dark Ages, and this was a more violent reversal than that which occurred in the Southern Appalachians.

Type Reversal among the Appalachian-Ozark Families

It must be pointed out that the families that formed this group of Jacksonian peoples did not have the trustee system when they first congregated in America. They were primarily lowland families from Scotland and North England who had been settled in North Ireland to "civilize" the Irish. The British government had its hands full dealing with the Scottish highland clans and the turbulent trustee-organized South Irish. Ulster was resettled to break up this combination of Irish private law and local justice typical of trustee family conditions. Furthermore, when these Scotch-Irish peoples came to America they were fairly well educated. Ford shows that they were the group instrumental in forming Princeton University, our first "American college," in 1754. The standards of scholarship in the Presbyterian ministry had always been high, even in Ulster. The Scotch-Irish

Presbyterians surrounded the Valley of Virginia, its entrances, and all the Southern avenues through the Cumberland Gap—the first approach to the interior and to the west. They took the intellectual standards of the Presbyterian Church with them into Kentucky and the West before the Revolution. Other groups entering these Western streams of migration had an equally high intellectual tradition. The counties in the Southern Appalachians, where the trustee family arose and still flowers, had Presbyterian and other intellectual leaders before the Revolution. What took place in the formation of the trustee family was a quick reversion in family organization, achieved early and long preserved because of a series of conditioning environmental factors. These, with the exceptions already noted, are identical to those which caused its development in Western society during the early Dark Ages.

One of the marks of the decay of the Presbyterian tradition was the development of the camp meeting. The first camp meeting is said to have taken place in Logan County, Kentucky, in July 1800. The camp meeting was an attempt to revive religion and to substitute annual meetings of Christians for the inadequate local weekly meetings of the organized churches. By this time it is clear that organized Presbyterian and other institutional religions had reached a low ebb among these people and that they were trying to find some substitute. The decline of the former domestic type of religions was one of the necessary steps toward the development of the trustee family in the mountains.

When the Scotch-Irish and others poured through the Cumberland Gap to the Western side of the Appalachians they had a well-organized system of public justice and a domestic family organization. A quick and enduring reversal to private justice and trustee family organization—preserved largely intact in the more isolated counties even today—occurred after they had settled on the other side of the gap.

The existence of this system of public justice is well authenticated. In 1738, all Virginia west of the Blue Ridge was laid out into two counties, Frederick and Augusta, the more Western of which was Augusta. In 1742 the first court was established in Augusta, and it held meetings from 1745 on. We have records of the court and grand jury acts from that period on. By 1752 the development of private conceptions of justice was already indicated when the constables began to report inability to execute sheriff's returns because of "an axe," "a gun," "the defendant outrode me," or "heel play." These early signs of unwillingness to accept public justice were multiplied during the Indian wars and soon the local people were settling their troubles with the Indians by organizing volunteer companies of relatives and friends to rid the country of the enemy.

Kentucky (Trustee Family) Feuds

The specific details of all the Kentucky feuds and the significance of private justice in the Southern Appalachians is not well known to us because, until the assassination of Governor Goebel on January 30, 1900, few outsiders knew of the situation or paid much attention to it. Since then numerous journalists have dealt with the "feuds" but largely in a purely descriptive manner.

The newspaper writers tend to confuse the Scotch-Irish and English names of the people with the Southern (Catholic) Irish people and to blame the feuds on the "fighting Irish." As a matter of fact, the people who form these groups and who are connected with these family wars are of Scotch-Irish, English, and German origin, in the order mentioned. Furthermore, the newswriters tend to find the "causes" of the family wars in the incidents which led to the first bloodshed—such as the pigs of the Hatfield-McCoys, or the possession of the slave-girl in Garrard county in 1826. None of them see that these feuds are simply the breaking-out into actual war of jurisdictions of families which have always placed themselves above public agencies as law-making and regulating organisms for their members. The feuds are merely spectacular outbreaks of trustee familism. The feudist is an outlaw only from the standpoint of the central government—not from the point of view of his clan or kinsmen.

Interesting as they are, we will not give the histories of any of these feuds. They all show the same characteristics. The families have developed a conception of autonomy for groups of kinsmen. The stronger and more militant families take the lead and the others join sides as clients and colleagues for protection. The families try to control local politics so that if a member is captured by the "law" he can be freed on very flimsy evidence, perjured testimony (cojuration), or by frank recognition that the victim either was killed or killed someone in a legitimate interfamily war. The opposite side either has its own justice of the peace try its members or, failing that, keeps the killers hidden, or even gets them away from the toils of public law by threats or abduction from custody.

If the different phases of the trustee family are considered one by one, it is found that certain phases are more developed among these people than others. *Lex talionis* and feud are more developed than the controlling and peace-making aspects of the trustee family.

> I shall never forget the first feud-battle which I witnessed. It was election day. The noble Feud Leaders were extremely busy keeping certain angry men apart, keeping them from discussing politics or drinking whiskey. I never saw more earnest effort. . . . That lad caught sight of the man who years before had slain his father. . . . A feud was started which raged for three years and, in which, a hundred and fifty noble men lost their lives. . . . The battles were never pitched. They were always purely incidental, brought on unexpectedly. Some reckless boy, or some irresponsible drunken man would start the trouble. Then, of course, the others would join in. (J. A. Burns, *The Crucible, A Tale of the Kentucky Feuds*, Oneida, KY, 1928, 36–41)

The absence of any system for settling interfamily disputes other than that of pacification by clan elders, actual warfare, or the flight of the persons immediately involved (or even the whole family on one side) is evident in the histories of all these numerous disputes. The original Garrard-White feud, which raged in Clay County, Kentucky, for nearly a century, was brought to a truce in 1901 after the killing of Governor Goebel in January 1900. A real treaty of peace was drawn up at the instance of third parties and the truce was entered into in 1901. This lasted until 1904 when fighting again broke out, resulting in numerous casualties. The affair was brought to an end only by the ultimate outside intervention of the state of Kentucky. The families themselves had not worked out any system (short of private war) to settle disputes.

Thus the trustee family system in the Appalachian-Ozark region was essentially of a crude and unstable type which could not last because it had all the disadvantages of the trustee system and none of its developments or refinements. It either had to revert back to the domestic system through the forcible intervention of outside agencies, or develop of itself into a "league of families" or units of extremely strong clan families that would enforce public interest against the undisciplined private family vendettas. In this case both forces were at work. Some men from the clans themselves were working inwardly "to learn how to solve the problem of the feuds." They were bringing the feud leaders into alliance. On the other hand, outraged public opinion was clamoring for force.

> When the law shall arise in the majesty that is its attribute and administer stern, inexorable justice, taking no account of family connections or blood vengeance, but only of crimes committed; when public opinion shall make it impossible for a chief magistrate to blacken his soul by pardoning a cowardly assassin for selfish political ends, then, and only then, will the Frankenstein of the Kentucky Mountains receive its death thrust, and the Land of the Feuds cease to be a blot on the map of the United States. (This is the peroration which ends the investigation of those feuds by Davis and Smith, *Munsey's Magazine*, November 1903, inspired by the assassination of the governor of Kentucky)

The Trustee System — Causal Analysis

Thus the trustee family is the elevation of family and familism from a system that rules part of or all the internal life of the household until it becomes the regulatory system for all or most of the society. It is achieved through the mechanisms of making the *genos* right, or the law of kin, the ruling principle in extradomestic relations. Much of the total social processes of the society comes under extended family jurisdiction. When the system reaches its greatest development, public law and state or national social processes are exceedingly limited. "Barbarian" codes, the name given the legal systems when the trustee system is paramount, are simple and limited in nature. Most of the processes of social regulation are left to the families themselves.

In the Kentucky highlands, where this system developed, the trustee regulation had to exist beside what was ostensibly a public and nonfamily system of law and order. To maintain their control, the families had to have their men elected as the sheriffs, judges, justices of the peace, and other public officials. It was only by this method that they could be sure the principles of family regulation and family justice would be carried out according to their family views. That was why many Kentucky feuds allegedly started over "politics." One of the methods of "warfare" and also "control" in family strife was to elect members of the opposing families to public office. Then the family in power could enforce its jurisdiction upon the others by the prestige of public law. Many of the first killings in the Kentucky feuds included sheriffs and judges from the opposing family officials, so that "justice" according to the lights of another kin-group could be imposed.

This is the picture we have of trustee society, whether it is one given by a reporter in the Kentucky highlands or that found in Homer, Beowulf, Gregory of Tours, or medieval Europe. The Greek heroes of Homer would have been discussed in *Munsey's Magazine* if they had lived in early-twentieth-century America. Henry Watterson of the *Louisville Courier-Journal*, who spent a good deal of printer's ink declaiming against feud conditions in the Kentucky mountains, would have enjoyed many pleasant evenings if he could have chatted with Gregory of Tours about conditions in sixth- and seventh-century France. Beowulf would feel sympathetic with the reformers from the Kentucky clans, because he, like them, went on a long pilgrimage to try to prevent his kin from exterminating themselves in useless strife.

From this point of view, we may speak of the primitive form of trustee society as fundamentally an unbalanced and unstable condition of society. The family system is given responsibilities for which it is essentially not suited and which it is incapable of carrying out properly. The family has to carry on the functions of government—make wars, rule commerce, incorporate strangers, inflict the death penalty, regulate matters between families, distribute justice, and perform many other acts for which it is in no way fitted. Family loyalties are too violent to insure impartial justice for members and strangers alike. A survey of the historical periods of the trustee family shows how unwillingly family members are punished. At most they are banished and continue to be an ever-present threat to the law and security of other peoples and regions. In dealings with strangers, punishment can be based not upon justice but upon revenge. The essential and necessary philosophy of the primitive form of the trustee family organization is, "Let us wipe out the whole clan and then there will be peace."

It may be said then that no great civilization is possible under purely trustee family conditions. That is what we find from an historical survey, whether of Europe or the Orient, of ancient, modern, or tribal life. The higher civilization depends essentially upon the functioning of several agents—a system of faith or religious belief that all men are entitled to equal consideration and a system of government or governments to enforce that faith—as well as a familistic system. Consequently we find that the "rebellions" against trustee familism are always dominated by a combination of religious faith (a new religion, to quote Fustel de Coulanges) and public law. *Dike* or absolute justice, as opposed to *themis* or the expedient conception of law, arises with the idea that "vengeance is the Lord's" (and not the family's).

Thus the "causal" agent in the trustee family is the nonfunctioning of "world" religious conceptions and governments. Whatever makes these two great aspects of the social mind weak or incapable of functioning, raises the causal nexus for the trustee family. It makes no difference whether we are describing fifth-century Europe or eighteenth-century Kentucky. In the one case, the government of the Roman Empire decayed and the Christian forces allied with it in its later days seemed incapable, at that time, of functioning alone. When the Scotch-Irish and others went through the Cumberland Gap they lost connection with the central government of the United States, and the Presbyterian culture and discipline could not function without the backing of some public law. In each case, the ruder form of the trustee family system became dominant over all other types of rule.

"Pure" trustee family society is essentially unstable. One of the first steps it takes, where there is intelligence, hope, and knowledge of better things, is to regulate and meliorate these conditions. If there is no possibility of these changes, there is no civilization. It is no accident that world religions and decent strong governments are the handmaidens of great civilizations. The world's great civilizations have been those where first religion and then government has controlled the trustee family, taken over its nonfamily functions, and given the domestic family and the free individual a chance to develop.

Some of the first steps to remedy this instability are taken by the codification and melioration of trustee family law itself. In Japan, this has been achieved partly by the development of "house" law, where the practices of one house are imposed upon a region. That country actually made the transition to a strong central government several times by accepting *one* house law as the national law. This is the principle of the Kamakura and Tokugawa shogunates.

One of the first evidences of this development in Western history is the rise of customary use and then the prescribed use of transaction, composition, and amend to settle disputes between families. A system of payments is developed so that families feel that the settlement of disputes by peaceful means, according to this schedule, is "right." Public law, backed by religion, becomes recognized as a social force in itself. The taking of blood-money may be awkward; it generally is accepted purely as a matter of expediency. Many law students who do not understand this system are amused at it. They cannot understand why the killing of a "low" person can be excused for a small amount, whereas another death costs more. They cannot understand the extreme payments required for homicide in some "composition" schedules. But the important thing is not the blood-money. You can never pay the blood-money and then kill a person. It is not the "price of human life," as some legalists have called it. It is essentially that in this society, experience has taught the people that if anyone is killed, it is better to insist upon a peaceful settlement by economic penalty than to let unbridled private vengeance take sway. The blood price is always an expression of "hope" for a peaceful settlement. It is based upon what the people feel will satisfy the "honor" or remove the "stain" from the relatives of the injured. Consequently, it varies greatly from class to class and society to society.

The first step above a formal or customary schedule of compositions occurs when the religious leader works among the people to get them to settle difficulties this way rather than by resorting to violence. After that comes the second step, when the ruler, king, leading family head, or someone with power and ambition tries to force the people to settle difficulties peacefully. Semblances of "king's courts" are set up to stimulate these organizations and a part of the composition or blood-money is eventually paid to the court or ruling family. This is where the *fredum* system arises. The public agency makes money by enforcing peace; for this it receives a part of the composition. To avoid this, more and more families take up transaction, composition, and amend out of court and blood vengeance is driven further from the realm of accepted social behavior. These *fredum* payments are the rudimentary elements of our modern system of public fines for transgressors. From that to the pure conception that the public, and the public alone, punishes the transgressor is but a logical forward step. The intelligent clan leaders who are opposed to wild and unregulated bloodshed find their prestige and power strengthened on every side.

The Trustee System—Meaning Analysis

The meaning of the trustee family system is clear. It is the simplest form of organized society, and even in highly organized societies it is the ever-present reserve element. Even today in the United States, where "kin," "clan," and "relatives" exist, we have our "nepotisms" in business, finance, politics, and, in some cases unfortunately, in mixtures of the three. The developed trustee system is basically strong. It is founded upon some of the most fundamental passions, beliefs, and attachments of life. In the Middle Ages, particularly after the tenth century, the church found it extremely difficult to control its milder forms among the ruling families of Europe. Papal decisions could hardly be enforced in regard to interfamily alliances unless it could be shown that not only the *rule* but also political and social *expediency* were both against familistic domination of certain problems. Gregory of Tours, Nicholas I, and Gregory IX made great contributions to the development of medieval civilization by their use of the wise principle of expediency in dealing with the rampant trustee family system of their times.

The explanation of this is as follows. Trustee familism is dangerous only when it is unchecked by more powerful forces. Under a wise system of regulation and public control it makes great contributions toward easing the governing of the mechanisms of society. The trustee family should not fall into disrepute as a form of social organization simply because our records of it come from the most unorganized and bitter conditions of its existence, as found in the Homeric poems, Beowulfian times, and Tacitean descriptions, or accounts of the Kentucky highlanders. The great aristocratic and ruling families that have carried the burdens of social control over centuries use this principle. (See *Anna Karenina* for Tolstoy's description of this in nineteenth-century Russia.)

Families are disciplinary agencies. Furthermore, they have ways and means of knowing human character and of handling it that are not available to the general public. A family member can often be asked to do things for the sake of family loyalty that can be asked of no other person for no other reason. Practically all the descriptions of "altruistic suicide" given by Durkheim deal with situations where self-immolation for family reasons is thought to be required of the individuals concerned. Where trustee familism is limited to those things which the family can do expeditiously and where it is subject to judicious public control, its presence adds greatly to the solidarity and strength of society.

The trustee family must also be looked at from the point of view that it is a partial causal system for the creation of its antithetical and supporting elements—the religious institution and the central state. Inter-family strife leads to a widening conception of religious faith and control. Widening religious faith in the idea that all men outside the family "are brothers"—as St. Augustine expressed it—leads to the development of public law agencies to enforce this "interfamily" principle. As Fustel de Coulanges shows in his *Ancient City*, the state and the public can evolve only through a religious change introduced with other changes in the old family law.

The first antithetical elements—developed law, religion, or state—must of course move slowly with the family. The first reforms must be closely related to the psychology of the family. The state and the church have to steal gradually from the family those things which the family can do least well or which it is in disrepute for attempting. The state fails if it and the church come directly to the family with highly involved ways of doing things, foreign to the old family system. This principle of gradually adapting highly public systems of control to former familistic peoples is the crux of successful colonial law.

This can be seen in the development of church control in Western society in the Middle Ages. The church stood for *proles, fides,* and *sacramentum* in the family. This three-dimensional conception of human relations was closely modeled after that of the trustee family. The church merely reinforced the *proles, fides,* and *sacramentum* of the family. The breaking of complete family control came about only gradually. The greatest breach came when permission for will-making was permitted the family head. At first he could do this only if he made a will leaving a little of the property to the church. Individualism does not develop at one fell swoop from a familistically integrated society.

Verification Based upon the Family System of Western Europe

For purposes of verification, let us turn to the modifications of the trustee family in Western Europe. Among these people the first organized system of justice was that of family vengeance. Fourteen hundred years after Tacitus, regions in the low countries still had family quarrels, feuds, and composition with amend or reconciliation similar to those mentioned by him. At the time of Tacitus the *wergild* or composition amount (in cattle) for various crimes between families was fixed (*certo numero*), and a part of this composition went as a *fredum* or *regi vel civitati* to the ruling powers or "state." This was taken from the *wergild* paid by the family of the guilty party. The history of this whole period was that of struggle between the public and the trustee families as to whether crimes were to be punished privately by the families or openly as acts "against the public interest."

The struggles between the Homeric versus the civilized versions of the trustee family are well illustrated by the works cited. Public forces in the Merovingian and Carolingian epochs were able to limit considerably these *querelles de sang* (blood feuds). However, during the anarchical conditions of the tenth and eleventh centuries, public forces gave way and blood feuds between families gained greater sway.

The songs and the chronicles of the eleventh century describe a situation in which the solidarity of relatives of the leading families is one of the principal elements of cohesion in the social life. The feuds arising from a homicide or an injury forced whole families into wars with each other that were often long and atrocious. To terminate these, it was necessary to have actual treaties of peace between whole families. The efforts of the church to reduce the exercise of the law of vengeance by recourse to the "peace and truce of God" were generally in vain. During this time when public justice was uncertain or nonexistent, the common people had to join in with this system of familism in order to get any protection at all.

The situation began to improve after the eleventh century. The cities began to impose peace within their walls; the outbreaks occurring were those between cities. "Family" feuds had now grown up, enlarged, or—in Kentucky parlance—been limited to "county" feuds. Trade and industry began to prosper within these peaceful cities. Wise leaders began to find ways of limiting and restraining blood quarrels. In the twelfth century numerous documents show how the magistrates aided in bringing about peaceful truces. The next step was to enforce severe punishment upon those who violated these truces. The rest of the story is similar to that described for Kentucky. Public forces (religious and secular) gradually gained control over the Homeric variety of trustee familism and finally completely broke it up in favor of a domestic family with interfamily justice administered by public courts and officials.

Conclusion

This chapter has shown that the trustee family system, previously described as a historical phenomenon, exists in the contemporary United
States, particularly in the Southern Appalachian-Ozark highland regions.
Here the trustee system can be studied as a living thing, unimpeded by
the fogs and difficulties of historical reconstruction. In this historical
example we find a people, who in 1750 had a domestic type of family
organization, placed in a position where their relation to central law-
enforcing agencies and to a strong version of historical Christianity was
decisively weakened. The trustee family arose to meet this situation
without anyone "planning it." Since the highland people themselves
had no strong cultural ties with, or remembrance of, a previous system
of trustee family organization, they had to retrace many of the earlier
steps of the relation between the family system and civilization. The first
development was of the crudest Homeric type of trustee family, with its
associated mores of blood vengeance and local family vendettas. These
continued unabated in the mountains for more than a century. Gradually it developed into a more "civilized" state where the opposing family
systems integrated themselves into larger units, limiting warfare within
each group and channeling this into the disputes of the more dominant
groups, those of the Hills vs. the Evans, the Hatfields vs. the McCoys, the
Howards vs. the Turners, the Logans vs. the Tollivers, the Hargisses vs.
the Cockrills, the Frenches vs. the Eversoles, and others. Finally, as the
original families either perished or a greater number of people became
involved, the private wars became known by the counties of location,
such as the feuds of Bell, Clay, or Breathitt Counties.

Within this crude system of social control, strong movements of
resistance against the inhuman bloodshed arose. The leaders became
motivated by a conception that private vengeance against a clan or group
was sinful, irreligious, and wrong.

> This was especially true of the men who were spoken of as "Feud
> Leaders." Many people think that feud leaders are men who spend
> their lives laying schemes to get their enemies killed. Just the reverse

is true. They are peacemakers. . . . They used [their] strength of character and influence to bring about reconciliation and to avert bloodshed. (*The Crucible*, 45–6)

Along with the development of this feeling, the professional religious leader becomes a feud peacemaker, a role similar to that taken by the bishops in the early Middle Ages. As Burns tells us:

A short time after this I met Rev. H. L. McMurry, a Baptist preacher from Kansas. He encouraged me greatly. His vision for the mountains was the same as mine, his faith in God the same.

Together we went to Oneida, my father's boyhood home, and the center of the "Baker-Howard Feud" which was raging there at that time. Together we planned the beginning of Oneida Institute. (*The Crucible*, 61)

The religious leader works to develop the trustee family of the cruder variety into a unit that can settle disputes, both within and between families, by a peaceful process of justice in which the attempt is made to punish the offender directly through transaction. If the family cannot discipline the individual by peaceful composition and amend, they repudiate him or drive him away. However, religion alone can only mitigate, and not prohibit, this full trustee family process. The absolute forbidding power of public law is needed and was used not only in the Middle Ages but in Kentucky. First Henry Watterson and then the editors of *Munsey's Magazine* pointed the finger of public outrage against this unregulated system of private warfare. The next step undertaken was to bring in public law and enforce it stringently. The trustee family became "civilized" again.

This gives us in miniature the "causal" processes as far as we care to pursue them in this study. Those conditions which lead to the weakening or breaking-up of the higher agencies of civilization—the churches promulgating universal religious beliefs and agencies capable of making effective the enforcement of public law—are the primary causal agents of trustee familism. The lack of these creates the series of facilitating conditions in which the trustee family has to take over. The "formal" or "first" cause lies, of course, in society itself. On the other hand, the unnecessary brutalities of the trustee system, its unrestricted penalizing of innocent and guilty alike, become the "causes" of reactions against this type of familism. The first phases of this process are to "humanize" the trustee family, to move it from its Homeric brutality toward a limited system of peaceful settlement of internal and external disputes.

Once the trustee family is humanized in this respect, it becomes a very stable institution, and if there are no other strong civilizing forces available to carry the development further, it apparently can remain almost eternally at this stage of development. In many sections of medieval Europe society remained primarily at this stage for periods of as long as six centuries in the more exposed districts, and for as long as nine or more centuries in the isolated regions. Primitive societies (those never developing high civilizations) seem to carry on this social system more or less in perpetuity, the "social" peace being broken from time to time by "upheavals," "reversions," and "calamities." Under given situations a return to Homeric trusteeism seems inevitable when the otherwise fairly peaceful arrangements of primitive society are disturbed.

But if there is a "trend" in the general culture toward a more complicated civilization (one of the processes described by Sorokin for Western society in terms of movements from an ideational toward a sensate culture), this eventually influences the mitigated trustee family to move more and more away from "home-rule" conditions. These steps involve the almost complete demolition of *genos* power as an active force with *right* and *duty* to control the household unit. When this movement gains headway and further "reforms" the family, the next step is a unit that we have described here as the "domestic" family.

14

THE DOMESTIC FAMILY SYSTEM—
CAUSAL ANALYSIS

W E NOW COME TO THE domestic family system, the basic type of all developed civilization. Here *genos* or clan power is subordinated to public and universal agencies—the church and the state. Private law gives way to public law. Of the three basic powers that link family members together—*manus*, *potestas*, and *genos*—the last loses its "right" and "official duty" within the domestic institution. Relatives outside the household limits may still gossip, advise, quarrel with, aid, abet, or interfere informally in the domestic institution, but fundamentally the members of the household are largely free from outside influences as long as they keep within the bounds of accepted public behavior. The family council now becomes purely informal. Most matters have to be patched up by agreements and conciliations between husband and wife or between husband, wife, and children. The influence of the children must not be disregarded, no matter what the state of public law or outside conditions. Children are definite personalities and generally have more sustained vigor than parents. From the first crying spell when the child is cuddled to sleep until the last final quarrel over which heir takes the family rugs and which takes the silverware, they are an informal ruling force in the family, and one usually neglected in treatises on family sociology written most often by celibates or by members of companionate, sterile, or unhappy marriages.

Domestic Familism and Civilized Man

The domestic family institution is the most pervasive of all the social aggregates of man. Even within trustee conditions it is the basic local unit of the clan. The clan or *genos* group does not interefere with it except in cases of extreme necessity. When Homer's Achilles, in league with his "blood brothers," the aggregates of Achaean clans united under the leadership of Agamemnon, faces the Trojans, it is the killing of Patroclus, a member of the *domestic* family of Achilles, that leads to the dramatic changes whereby "the anger of the son of Peleus (Achilles' father)" can be sufficiently mollified so that Homer can bring his epic to a logical end. Patroclus, adopted brother and companion of Achilles, is killed by Hector (of Priam's Trojan clan) in the field of battle. Achilles, angry with Agamemnon for depriving him of his war booty, Briseis, has withdrawn from the Achaean ranks and is preparing to return home. Without his moral and material aid the European Greeks cannot overcome the Trojans united under the clan leadership of Priam. When Patroclus, of Achilles' domestic unit, is killed by a Trojan, Achilles overlooks his quarrel with Agamemnon and returns to the battle.

Homer successfully outlined the basic sentiments of the domestic family. The greatest general motivation for complete self-sacrifice and immolation lies always within the system of infinite beliefs that are found in the domestic family. The clan thrives only because it upholds the strong domestic family units.

This is true in all accounts that we have of trustee family times. The domestic relations between husband and wife and parent and child are *the* fundamental traits even when the clan, as a governing agency, stands guard as the agent or vehicle between that unit and the other peoples known as "the world at large."

Furthermore, three times in Western world history—or during that period of the last few thousand years known as the "period of civilization"—the domestic family type has become almost exclusively the system of society. These have been the middle periods of Greek, Roman, and modern cultures. Between the periods when the clans give way to religious and civil forces and those when societies reach the peaks of nihilism and antifamilism, the domestic family rules. Largely for discussion purposes, this period has been marked off in Greece by the advent of the conditions described by Hesiod down to the Peloponnesian Wars. In Rome it occurred largely between the time of the promulgation of the first written law code (the Twelve Tables) and the first century A.D. In modern times, the domestic institution was certainly paramount after canon law reached its greatest development and before the destructive influence of eighteenth-century rational anti-institutionalism began to dominate the masses of the people.

This does not mean that, at any one historical time, one family system completely extinguished all others. Blood vengeance and trustee familism never seem to dominate life completely, nor do they ever completely disappear. While the family quarrels of the "feudal" age were considerably broken up by the church and the Renaissance, they still continued.

Finally, even in days of the external dominance of atomism, we have to recognize the domestic family institutions and relations as the basic system. Even when the legal and social systems give way in favor of the individual as opposed to the family, those domestic units with children, who reproduce the society, are the fundamental mainstay. For instance, in 1920 approximately half the American families (those with three or more children) were of this domestic variety. In 1930, this had dropped to less than 38 percent. Nevertheless, insofar as there is any stable society left, these domestic unities have to set the patterns of accepted social behavior. The few domestic unities left are the ones which transmit the culture of the past to the future. They have to mold the society of the future in its basic human and subcultural systems of values. They have to determine and preserve the basic value systems of society. In this, as will be shown, they are considerably handicapped both personally and in a social sense by the atomistic units which dominate the culture. The people in domestic units cannot move from job to job, purchase new automobiles every year, live in the fashionable sections of their communities, or do a thousand things the others can do, simply because their energy is largely absorbed in the rearing and training of the next generation. They cannot be the "smart" people, because they have responsibilities of a more serious nature.

> He that hath a wife and children hath given hostages to fortune; for they are impediments to great enterprises, either of virtue or mischief. (Francis Bacon, *Of Marriage and Single Life*)

Thus we see that, in all stages and levels of civilization, the domestic family institution is basic to society. No civilization can proceed without it. No *great* civilization has endured for any length of time without paying considerable attention to the organization, promulgation, and protection of the domestic family.

Generalization of Domestic Family Traits

We must think of the domestic unit as representing the most typical aspects of familism, largely undiluted by the extraneous characteristics which involve the trustee and atomistic systems. In it, all family forces are concentrated in the relation between husband and wife and parent and child. In its purest condition it is not an integral part of a ruling system, such as is to be found in the governing system outside the home in the trustee type of society. Neither does it make the home a hotel or meeting place of strangers and adults in the "sensate" way of life. It is founded on the conception that the primary function of the household unit is to work out the almost undiluted social relations of *manus* and *potestas*. *Genos* or clan interference is at a minimum. Public courts, religions, and other moral or law-enforcing agencies exist outside the home for the purpose of controlling public, nonfamilistic adult behavior. While public law or religion may set up "norms," or ideals of behavior, for the inner members of the family, these seldom have any great impact upon the intimate members of the family, so long as they are able to get along without making a public fuss or asking for outside interference. The law may rule that the male parent is the head of the household, but that does not make him so. The law may also rule that the married woman is a *feme sole*, entitled to the legal rights of a single woman even though married, but that does not make her so.

The head of the household may be the "powerful patriarch" of a "despotic type," according to the legal characterization and the claims of the reformers, but this does not always have to be so. When several persons live together in the same house the problem of getting along becomes the paramount issue. It is a personal one that depends entirely upon the ability to give and take. There can be no universal answers to domination in the domestic institution. Even within family units it changes from day to day, time to time, and unit to unit. The universal and eternally recognizable characterizations of certain types of family personalities, all of them enacting time and again the same basic roles, testify to this. The "mother-in-law" joke, the "nagging wife," the "henpecked husband," the "ungovernable adolescent," the "dominating child" are universal and timeless characterizations. We find them in religious literature, in the Bible, in the Greek plays, in Erasmus, in literature of the Renaissance and Reformation, and in all earlier or later records of human behavior.

> And Adam called his wife's name Eve; because she was the mother of all living. Unto Adam also and to his wife did the Lord God make coats of skins, and clothed them. And the Lord God said, Behold, the man is become as one of us, To know good and evil. (Genesis 3:20–2)

"To know good and evil" in this biblical quotation has a double significance. One is, of course, the biblical story of the fall of mankind from its primitive godly state. The other is that within the domestic family institution all things are possible. Man and woman were united as husband and wife, and the young united as parents and children; from now on they must face the endless human task of trying to get along with each other. They must settle their own personal problems as best they can, according to the changing nature of their personalities and not according to any externally established universal laws or norms of human behavior.

The fact that, regardless of law and dictate or other public norms, the domestic family has to overcome its problems according to the variety and changing nature of the personalities within the group, is illustrated by folklore, truisms, and family sayings. On any particular problem, and regardless of time, place, or modal type of family, we find opposing answers to every question as to what the family should do. We can illustrate this matter with reference to dominant attitudes between children and parents. Should parents be strict, lenient, both, or neither in regard to children? Should the same principles apply to male and female children alike? Do the same principles apply when there are many children as when there are only one or two? There are multitudinous and conflicting answers to these numerous questions. In general, folklore indicates that the problem is primarily one of judgment, depending upon the persons, the circumstances, and the abilities of parents and children.

We see that regardless of outside norms, to the extent that the domestic family functions as a unity of husband and wife, parent and child, it has to rule itself. Furthermore, there is never one certain and decisive answer to any single question as to what to do about a family problem. While the outside norm may affect the internal situation in a number of ways, as long as this norm holds or helps hold the family together, the internal problem must be settled by it according to its ability and according to the circumstances.

Thus the domestic family is a traditional system of varying rules of human behavior whereby husband and wife, parent and child—elements in the major system of relations which carries on the subcultural social processes—adjust themselves to each other. The system varies according to personalities rather than according to time and place. Changes in the outer social system affect the presence or absence of the domestic family *but not its primary system of internal regulation.* At times the domestic family is primarily responsible to the clan, at others to the church, and at others to the state. Regardless of these outer conditions, the domestic family, to the extent that it exists, has its own variant internal system.

Domestic Family—General Causal Analysis

Thus when we turn to the *causes* of the domestic family we have two grave problems to consider—what is the fundamental cause of the system itself and what causes or conditions make the system more dominant at some times than at others? What is it that makes people within the domestic unit act according to expediency regardless of the norms set up by clans, religions, laws, psychologists, sociologists, and moralists? Once that matter is settled, there is the further problem of why the domestic family is most prevalent in the middle stages of civilization, existing then as the prevailing modal unit, and is least prevalent in the early and late phases of society. What are the principles and rules whereby the domestic family arises as the modal type from trustee or atomistic conditions? Why and how does it give way from time to time to engulfment in the trustee and atomistic conditions? These are fundamental questions of family sociology, the answers to which have never before been systematically sought.

The answer to the first question is fairly simple. Here again we can do something seldom possible in an analysis of social causation. We can immediately embrace the whole hierarchy of causation and speak of the final and absolute cause. The domestic family exists in the independent system described above because of the variations in human nature and personality. Of all social agencies in human society, the domestic family is the one institution that can never, for one moment, escape the vagaries of and changes in human nature. This statement also may be illustrated by references to family folklore which universally sustain the principle that family life is a deep experience wherein human relations become the paramount value system.

> Call not that man wretched, who, whatever ills he suffers, has a child he loves.
>
> He knows not what love is that hath no children.
>
> The heart of the childless is empty; and so is the heart of him that hath no wife.
>
> Who has not children knows not why he lives.

These four proverbs from different cultures illustrate the psychological effects of the family upon the individual. Essentially they indicate a feeling that in itself the coexistence of man and wife, parent and child becomes a law and experience incapable of being understood by those who have not experienced it. Other systems of values dwindle in importance before the all-embracing problems presented by the coexistence within the family of the personalities involved.

In a similar way there are other bits of folklore that reveal the variability of human nature and the adaptation of the family to such a variation. It is interesting to note that folklore tells us that good children can seldom be expected. The family must make the best of whatever appears.

- He whom the gods love dies young.
- Wise children don't live long.
- So wise, so young, they say, do ne'er live long.
- Bad children make the father good.
- Happy is he that is happy in his children.
- Many a good father has a bad son.
- Youth is a blunder; manhood a struggle; old age a regret.

To counter the difficulties of control within family organization, the strongest moral strictures are imposed upon the disobedient family member:

> Honor thy father and thy mother, as the Lord thy God hath commanded thee; that thy days may be prolonged, and that it may go well with thee, in the land which the Lord thy God giveth to thee.
>
> Thou shalt not kill, commit adultery, steal, bear false witness, nor desire thy neighbor's wife. (Deuteronomy 5:16–21)

Other codes of behavior are of a somewhat similar familistically controlled nature.

Thus we reach the conclusion that the domestic family is of one essential variant type simply because it inevitably encounters an almost identical group of problems. Good women sometimes marry good men and sometimes bad ones. Strong-minded women sometimes dominate the family and are sometimes themselves dominated. Good children may spring from bad families as well as from good families. Some children are not difficult to make behave; others raise serious problems. Good children sometimes have to make their parents good and sometimes even good parents cannot raise good children.

Within all these possible and realizable combinations of human nature, there are naturally certain modal principles. Generally, parents are more experienced than their children, and the community or public expects them to assume leadership in making good citizens of the next generation. Ordinarily, the law will strictly discipline erring parents but will remove the children from the parents only as a last resort. Older children are supposed to be more responsible and steadier than younger ones. The responsibility given older children casts them in a role that is character-forming. Men are supposed to be better equipped than women to meet the external demands of earning an income and providing from the economic market. Women are supposed to have a more intimate knowledge of and to be better equipped emotionally to deal with the internal problems of family control and discipline. Consequently we have more or less standardized roles in the family, such as father, mother, parent, older son, older daughter, favored younger son, favored younger daughter, or favored most beautiful daughter. However, there are a thousand variations within all these standard procedures. These lead to multiple ways for the family to handle any given situation. This shows that there is a universal domestic family variant that is connected directly with the fact that the family is the one institution which, above any other, has to conform directly to the changes and vagaries of human nature. The primary "cause" of the domestic family procedure itself is human nature, and its variations between age, sex, and experience groups.

Whether as the modal type in middle periods of civilization or as one dependent upon either trustee or outer public control, this universal domestic family type is always to be found in society. Even today, when domestic familism is almost at its lowest ebb, this same variant universal domestic familism exists.

Domestic Family—Modal Causal Analysis

Now let us take the domestic family and study the causes and associated conditions whereby it becomes the modal system for a society. The three main periods in which it became the dominant type in Western society have already been outlined. In middle Greece, middle Rome, and in our modern society it became the dominant type and embraced the whole culture in these three societies. From then on, it passed into the atomistic type. On the other hand, we have repeated cases in which the domestic type apparently started to develop, and from those semideveloped conditions returned to the more primitive and localistic kind of family. Illustrations of these partial trends are to be found in the Russian family after the ninth century; in the Italian conditions of the fifteenth century; in the Japanese society during the fourteenth and fifteenth centuries; and for the Ulster Scotch-Irish in America. In Russia, in the earlier period, the influence of the Greek Orthodox Church and of the more civilized economic conditions in Byzantium seemed to promote a steady growth of domestic conditions in the Slavic regions to the north. However, these were overthrown by the unsettled conditions and the trustee family system brought in by invading Mongols. In Italy in the fifteenth century we seem to get a picture in which the trustee family, which had been considerably humanized toward the modal domestic type, broke forth again in all of its "ferocious brutality." In the same manner, the Japanese trustee family seems to have been integrated almost to the modal domestic type under something similar to a central government (house law of one house) before the difficulties of the fourteenth and fifteenth centuries, at which time it reverted to local clan rule and private civil war. Finally the lowland Scotch, English, and Irish who formed the "Ulster Plantation" must have been almost completely domesticized before reverting to "feud" conditions again as they passed from the Valley of Virginia to the more isolated hilly regions of Kentucky, West Virginia, and Tennessee.

In each of these cases we notice some of the same common denominators affecting the domestic family. Strong governments do not want local anarchy. Religious views of the "world brotherhood type" are opposed to local anarchy. The conception that even outside the family "all men are neighbors" is opposed to local conditions in which, under trustee organization, "so many of the Children of God are sacrificed needlessly." Here the conception of interfamily relations of St. Augustine is coupled with the plea of Gregory of Tours when he tried to settle the Sichaire-Austregisil feud by a transaction, composition, and amend to stop the bloodshed in Gregory's section of France.

In England the new central government introduced by William the Conqueror was opposed to local trustee familistic regulation by the native "clans" and feudatories operating under the former barbarian code of *leges henrici*. The barbarian code was amended and abolished; from that time on the constant struggle in England was to establish the domestic family as the modal type throughout the British Isles. This was not completely achieved in the remote and hilly districts of Scotland and Ireland for some centuries. Nevertheless, the efforts of the government to "civilize" the people were constant.

This is shown in detail by a study of the reign of Henry II (1133–89). This man, in spite of his faults, believed in justice by courts and the rule of the country by the central government. He established the system of enforcing legal decrees by a form of semitraveling courts, which soon brought into the hinterland (Western and northern England, Wales, Scotland, Ireland) "the fundamental privilege of trial by jury," "uniform jurisprudence," and other movements "to check the influence of feudality and clanship, to make the inhabitants of distant counties better acquainted with the capital city and more accustomed to the course of government, and to impair the spirit of provincial patriotism and animosity."

In the case of the partial reversion of the Italian family to trustee conditions, similar to the change that occurred among the Scotch-Irish in America, we have a reversal of these conditions. In each case a religious and social system that upheld traditions leading to the domestic family was temporarily broken up. In Kentucky, the people were isolated from Presbyterian social influences and from control by a central government, through its courts and law enforcement agencies. In the Italian Renaissance, the fundamental motivation for the upsurge of blood vengeance and the primitive trustee family organization as opposed to the more peaceful domestic type was this very breaking-up of government (sack of Rome, 1527) and a decline in the strength of the religious agents.

In speaking here of religion, we are referring of course to those types of religious philosophy that are called "world religions." They think of families as being strongly integrated within themselves but above the household; their concept is one of equality of the individuals before the law. They have a universal moral code that they think should be extended to all men and they seek the application of what Le Play has called "universal decalogues."

The domestic family is seemingly caused or facilitated by the rise and dominance of the trustee-familistic antithetical agencies or state and national religions, psychologies, and political phenomena of this nature. They make the trustee family give up those functions that compete with them, thereby isolating the domestic family from clan domination. Under the trustee family, trade, commerce, and the great society are not capable of much development. Glotz shows this in his study of the Greek family when he indicates that the very persons thrown out of the Greek trustee family by the processes of banishment were forced by circumstances to go into trade. In many cases this trade developed from piracy, which was first forced upon them by their circumstances. Then, having become wealthy, either they or their successors were interested in a form of family life in Greece that would permit trade and also keep their fortunes free from the domination of the paternal stem families. New reforms permitting each domestic unit to run its own affairs were forced by them and by other dissatisfied groups.

Conditions within the trustee family also prepare the ground for the rise of the domestic family. As repeatedly pointed out, the trustee family exaggerates its control over the domestic unit under certain circumstances and instead of using the great family solidarity to protect the domestic unit, it exhausts it by incessant warfare and interfamily feuds. The smaller unit cannot find humane conditions of existence because, instead of functioning as a family, it becomes merely a corporal's squad in the external wars created by trustee family organization. These "bad" conditions lead to attempts to control the trustee family, to destroy its power of arbitrary violence, and to substitute ethical and juridical rules for blood-solidarity in the world above the domestic family. Thus we may think of the disciplining of the clan system as one of the first moves toward the eventual domination of the domestic family as a modal type. A well-regulated and working system of transaction, composition, and amend, associated with other developments of belief, practice, and public interest in disputes between families, is a close approach to the domestic family type. As a matter of fact, when the public holds a moral belief that violators of peaceful settlements of intrafamily disputes should be punished by court action, the religious beliefs antithetical to the trustee family have gained great ground. And when a ruler steps in and demands settlement before public courts, with a part of the composition as a *fredum* tax to be paid to the public servants, domestic family conditions or the complete dominance of the family system by domestic practices is almost at hand.

We must also reckon with the fact that the domestic family system has within itself some of its own "causative" powers or forces. Relatives living in different households do not necessarily like each other. One of the great Kentucky feuds was one within branches of the same family. The leaders of one faction of the family were opposed by the leaders of the other and the different branches took sides until the internal family warfare was as bitter and bloody as the feuds between families. Consequently, the domestic unit has within itself systems of loyalty that transcend those between branches of the same clan-family. At times they feel relieved to see religious leaders and public agencies come forth and to settle matters by arbitration, God's will, or public force. In *The Crucible*, Burns noted this. When he first started his work among the feuding people:

> Young people flocked to my schools. Boys would walk by my side
> and ask questions while they held my hands. I scattered my work all
> over the country, seeking the most needy localities. . . . The work was
> encouraging at first. . . . It was easily seen that their simple hearts
> . . . were hungry, starving for peace and happiness. In a few months
> a community would be transformed. But when I left it and crossed
> the mountain into another valley, the old trouble would break out
> afresh. Some reckless boy would start a fight and then the feud
> would rage again. (*op. cit.*, 52)

This is also shown particularly in the pardons granted in the fifteenth century in the territory ruled by Philip the Good, Duke of Burgundy. In nearly every case we find that the summary of these cases indicates that "peace with the family of the victim" was one of the pre-requisites of pardon (remission of sentence).

The interesting thing about these cases is the different evaluation that is put upon the actions of members of the domestic household (sons, fathers, wives, adolescent children, and relatives by degree of relation specified), simple relatives (*parens*), and friends, retainers, companions, and more distant relatives (*amis*). The tendency throughout these cases, which cover the period from 1438 to 1467, is to appease the household relatives and to force the others to fall in line with public order. In the case of the pardon granted Robin Bon Enfant in Flanders in 1456, there was difficulty in finding any members of the domestic unit of the person killed. In this case a simple pardon was granted with the provision that the guilty person serve one year in a projected crusade.

All this indicates that the actual relations in the domestic house-hold are the chief inciting emotional forces in the larger family feuds. Once these members find a substitute way to settle difficulties by ap-pealing to the church or to the ruler, we find within them psychological forces that lead to the growth of the sovereignty of the public forces over the trustee family. The powers of the religious and public forces are strengthened and the more powerful they become, the more they grow of themselves.

In summarizing this matter of the "causes" for the rise of the domes-tic family to the modal type, it should be pointed out that four concepts have been introduced. These are: religion, government, excesses of the trustee family, and the desire of the domestic unit for more equitable treatment than that afforded by clan rule. When all of these combine together for any length of time under forms favoring the domestic family, this type of organization becomes dominant in society. However, the very combination of these four elements indicates some integrating force which would bring all of them together at the same time in a system for promot-ing the domestic family unit. This leads to the problem of a more ultimate social causation. Movements in one phase may be integrated with others so that the whole thing evolves together. However, our specific problem is to clarify the first steps in causation; this has been done above.

Domestic Family—Cause of Decline in Modality

As already pointed out, the domestic family has repeatedly retreated from the modal type, to be superseded by the trustee type. This has already been explained in terms of specific situations when disturbances in the society make the domestic family no longer able to survive except under the protection of a clan organization. The religious, moral, and governing agencies that previously protected the domestic family in its intrafamily relationships no longer seem able to function. In such a situation the domestic unit falls back upon clan solidarity.

However, the specific situation which needs further examination is the development of the domestic family into the atomistic type. This situation evolved rapidly after the fifth century B.C. in Greece, after the first century A.D. in Rome, and after the seventeenth century in our modern Western world. On this particular problem the following observations seem important.

We cannot think of the domestic family as being the agent of its own decay. It cannot go into excesses of familism, as the trustee family with its blood vengeance has done. Neither can it go into excesses of antifamilism such as arise in the philosophies of atomism, where race suicide can and has become the dominant trait. Domestic familism leads to trade, commerce, migration, and modern society. Nevertheless, the domestic family is itself capable of consuming most of the gains from this increased economic efficiency. When trade increases, the family system can use the economic advantages for itself. It can provide for its members more adequately. In general it is impossible to think of clear-cut internal developments in the domestic family that would bring it into such disrepute as to menace the integrity and continuance of the unit itself.

Primarily, we have to think of the decay of modal dominance of the domestic family as arising from external and not internal systems of causation. Changes in the state and the religious, moral, and economic institutions are the important factors that make the domestic family give way to a new type. New religious institutions appear or the old ones are changed and give way to new ideas. The state seeks to gain power by taking over the functions of many of the religious institutions. We have seen this occur in the Middle Ages when state control over marriage was increasingly substituted for religious control. The same happened in Greece and Rome, where state legislation regarding marriage and the families was more or less substituted for former religious control. Economic institutions antithetical to the family system arise with the aid and connivance of the state. Slavery based upon the introduction of millions of war captives into the households and farms of Rome was a great economic institution that menaced the domestic household. The farmer with a household of his own was in competition with the great estates manned by slave labor. These were well described by Cato the Censor in his *De re rustica*. When slavery became dominant in the country districts of Italy the possibilities of slave revolts became imminent. These bloody rebellions made living in the countryside dangerous for the Roman family. The only alternative in the districts capable of being farmed on a large scale by slaves was for the Roman people to go to the cities. There, instead of being left to carry on as self-supporting, domestic, economic units, the state began to feed them with corn allotments from the provinces. This corn was taken from the conquered slave laborers in the Valley of the Nile.

We may illustrate this from the study by Ferlet. He always couples the decay of the Roman family with the increase of foreign slaves and with the depopulation of the country districts. Before the development of slavery as a state-supported economic institution in Rome, it possessed that middle class of common people, "which she was to lose later." With the successful completion of her wars for the domination of the Mediterranean world, great estates were set up in Italy and particularly in the conquered provinces economically near the Roman cities because of the cheapness of water transportation over cart transportation from the rural districts in Italy.

> Under these conditions, the small farmer, with whom the state
> entered into unfair competition instead of helping him to sell his
> products, was quickly reduced to destitution. His personal labor
> no longer yielded him any profit, because the water freight of the
> wheat from Sicily or Sardinia cost less than the overland carriage
> into Latium of cereals from Etruria, Campania or Northern Italy. He
> was obliged to abandon his land, and to take refuge in the obscurity
> of the slums of Rome. (Ferlet, *L'abaissement de la natalité à Rome
> et la dépopulation des campagnes*)

Cereals were replaced in Italy by livestock production on great estates.
This required few men, and these could be slaves without families. Many
other economic, social, political, and religious changes came about.

> Under such conditions, celibacy and childless marriages had become
> frequent. Marriage was regarded as a burden, and we observe, in the
> upper classes, even with Cato and those who shared his sentiments, the
> general acceptance of the maxim to which Polybius, a century earlier,
> had attributed the decay of Greece: namely that the duty of a citizen is
> to avoid scattering his fortune and to avoid having a child. (*Op. cit.*)

All of these manifestations continued for some time in the Roman
Empire before the domestic institution of the family was replaced by
the atomistic. However, we introduce them to show that the chief causal
agent in the change was largely external to the family. The domestic
family exists at either its upper or lower range until external conditions
make its survival impossible.

The same general type of external change brought about the decay
of the domestic family and the development of the atomistic as the modal
type in Greece. The people to whom Pericles spoke in his funeral oration
about 429 B.C. had no intention of giving up the domestic family institution to which they were attached. It was external conditions in the next
century that made childlessness popular, divorces frequent, and *manus*
and *potestas* dead legal powers. When every street was filled with female
brothels, and when the courts were filled with lawsuits over possession
of male prostitutes, one could not expect any great number of men or

women to stay home, have children, or follow the formula of *proles, fides,* and *sacramentum*. Since slaves and immigrants could be imported by the thousands to do the work and to fill the gaps in society left by childlessness, the domestic family institution could not maintain itself.

These external changes were also facilitating factors in the decline of the domestic family in modern Western society. We have recited here how the political, religious, economic, and other conditions effect changes from a profamily to an antifamily attitude in the modern societies. The people who became famous as social philosophers in modern society were the ones who were fundamentally opposed to the family—Erasmus, Francis Bacon, Rousseau, Comte, Marx, and others. At first the domestic family unit and system opposed these changes. Even at the time of Isaeus in Greece, the appeal he made to the Greek courts to give the decision to his client in order to save the client's family had more meaning than an appeal to justice or economic right. The familistic people of Rome welcomed the Augustinian attempts to reform the family system and preserve the domestic unit. It was the domestic family system that was shocked by the Cromwellian reforms in England, the revolutionary changes after 1793 in France, and after 1936 forced the Russian government to give up antifamilism. What remains of the modern domestic family affords the sole support to the forces opposing the use of the state to destroy family mores.

Conclusion

This chapter shows that domestic familism is one of the universal conditions of man. There are strong periods in the development of civilization in which domestic familism is the modal type of all families. In the earlier trustee periods and in the later atomistic times, domestic familism, in spite of its subservience to the clan or the state, is still the mainstay of those societies. In trustee family periods, much greater attention is paid to domestic family attachments than to the relations between the local family and the wider group of relatives and kin. In atomistic family times, domestic family relationships are not very popular with the mass of "public" men. They wish to live their lives untrammeled by familistic "hostages to fortune"; this trend can continue only so long as there are others who do bear these "hostages" to carry on the basic social burden, and who constitute a group largely unhonored, unwept, and unsung.

Within the domestic family we have a semi-independent system of social regulation which differs considerably from the changing body of laws and ethical rules imposed upon the society by the outer ruling groups. This is due to the fact that the domestic family is always adjusting itself to a variant and changing group of human natures. The personalities of the domestic family vary not only from family to family, but also from time to time within the family, due probably partly to inheritance, but also to environment and growth. To these mixed personalities the domestic family has to adjust as best it can. Therefore, it must necessarily be equipped with a very broad system of apparently contradictory rules, so there cannot be any one inflexible system of regulation. Moralists may moralize, legalists legalize, and psychologists psychologize, but members of the domestic unit must still do their best to get along with each other. They go by their own variant system and are, for the most part, unchallenged unless unable to control their own internal affairs. Then, and only then, does the external system of rules attempt to control the family. An explanation of this is to be found in the adaptation of the domestic unit to human nature. While there tend to be certain recurring family types and norms of behavior, these cannot be depended upon. Nevertheless, the domestic unit must continue to function.

This chapter also examined the "causes" of the appearance and disappearance of the domestic family as a modal type. It rises from trustee family conditions partly because of external causes and partly because of the very nature of familism. The trustee family is not as compatible with the peace and security of the domestic family as this unit desires. In its cruder form it constantly uses up the energy of the domestic family by its constant interclan quarrels and disputes. The Homeric family picture is never beautiful until it depicts domestic family conditions. Ordinarily it gives a picture of the domestic family completely disrupted by quarrels between the clans. The excesses of the trustee family, the desire of the domestic family for a more fundamental independence than it possesses under the trustee family, the rise of outside agencies of a moral, religious, or political nature to keep peace and order between families, the extension of trade, commerce, and economic pursuits—these are the fundamental causal factors in the rise of the domestic family to a modal type. The change from trustee to domestic familism is partly internal, partly external. The backward change from domestic to trustee is largely external. The breaking-up of the agencies that support the domestic family externally is generally a cause of this change. The domestic family cannot survive unaided by any external force. When these aids disintegrate, the trustee family reemerges to fill the breach left by decay of the external forces.

The change from a modal domestic type to the atomistic is due largely to external forces alone. There is nothing within the domestic family to cause its own breakdown. Individual domestic families, of course, have abnormalities which cause them to break up. But as a social institution of the modal type, there is no general cause within this family type which is antithetical to it. Consequently the change from domestic to atomistic family modality moves the whole system of social causation, at least temporarily, from forces within the family itself to larger social and cultural movements. These larger cultural movements are decided by nonfamily sociologists. These larger social forces are those which dominated later Greece, later Rome, and our own society from the eighteenth century onward.

15

THE ATOMISTIC FAMILY SYSTEM—

CAUSAL ANALYSIS

IT IS CUSTOMARY FOR PEOPLE with very decided opinions to take opposite points of view about the atomistic family. Many place it as the high point of civilization, the peak of human development. Others speak just as seriously of the decadence of the times.

This bivalent attitude toward the family also exists in other times and under other types of families. The trustee family puts *fidelitas* on a very high basis, and the days of chivalry, "when knighthood was in flower," are long remembered. But the plebs and the common people do not hold the same opinion. The common clients of the Homeric family, who were treated without mercy or justice by the members of the great clans, did not think highly of the trustee family. Neither do the men who love decency and justice in relations between families idealize this type of family. Gregory of Tours, Burns of the Mountains, Henry II of England, and the religious, moral, ethical, and political leaders of all times have been extremely shocked at the exaggerations of human behavior brought about by this trustee family system. Tacitus admired the trustee family of northern Europe because, from the standpoint of fidelity and lack of adultery, it was morally clean, and because it was antagonistic to homosexuality and vice, but he recognized that Roman civilization with its atomistic family and its individualism also had its good points.

The people who are close to the clanlike trustee family admire its capacity to secure elementary justice and protection in a society where no other social system is capable of functioning. They admire its contributions to social solidarity and hate its excesses. The people removed from the trustee family admire it sometimes for the same things and sometimes for others. They also make fun of its ineptness in certain social systems. There are songs of praise for the Homeric and Beowulfian characters; there is hatred for the ignorant hillbilly and his blood feuds.

In times when the trustee family is no longer the main type, we also have our remembrances of the older "aristocratic" days when real familistic leaders were supposed to dominate the situation. The background of much of the idealization of the old, pre–Civil War South is partly an unrealized tribute to the better phases of trustee familism, now allegedly "gone with the wind."

The domestic type of family has both idealizers and detractors. Christian theories of the Middle Ages set forth this type of institution as one of the basic prerequisites for man's salvation. They held out for this ideal system and tried to deal sternly with schismatics and heretics who set up opposing ideas. Nevertheless, the very existence of schismatics and heretics showed the existence of well-founded criticisms of the domestic family. As a matter of fact, many of the implied familistic ideas of Erasmus are a substantial criticism of the domestic conceptions held by the canon law doctors and Christian divines. For earlier arguments against the Christian family views, see St. Jerome, *Against Jovinianus.*

This divergence of opinion applies equally well to the atomistic family. People praise its freedom, its streamlined characteristics, its mobility, its lack of nuisance value. But there are also the St. Jeromes, the Salvians, and others who damn these times and these families (or the lack of them) with the strongest vitriol. The memory of the free atomistic family among the old Romans was carried over into the Middle Ages. The people who had known this freedom from family domination idealized it after it was gone.

The Government of God, written by Salvian, Bishop of Marseilles, about 450 A.D., is a very vitriolic attack upon the atomistic family system of the last days of Rome. Salvian is often accused of exaggeration because other writers of the same period give a more optimistic picture. My own personal opinion is that he exaggerates very little. He speaks of the Roman commonwealth as now "drawing its last breath" and points out that "relations do not preserve the bond of kinship." He asks the rapacious at least to "spare the members of their own families." He asks "who now honors his wife by faithful observance of the marriage vow?" He shows that the stronger family system among the barbarians is not greatly affected by the Roman society, and describes in detail the common acceptance of sex perversions (see the translation by E. M. Sanford, Columbia University Press, 1930).

There are really two types of detractors of the atomistic family times. One may be illustrated by the Jovinianus type of mind and the other by St. Jerome. Jovinianus wrote a book on the family in late Rome in which, among other things, he attacks the Christians for putting the state of virginity higher than marriage as a condition for the ideal Christian. This Jovinian quoted the Bible to prove his point, using such passages as:

> Be fruitful, and multiply, and replenish the earth. (Gen. 1:28)

> Therefore shall a man leave his father and his mother, and shall cleave unto his wife: and they shall be one flesh. (Gen. 2:24)

With these and numerous other Biblical quotations he attacks the atomistic family of late Rome because it is unfamilistic and implies that the Christians by their excessive emphasis upon asceticism and virginity are adding fuel to the flames of unfamilism.

St. Jerome takes up his cudgels to defend Christianity and attacks Jovinianus with vitriolic fervor. The church, according to Jerome, divides virtue and sin into many categories, of which virginity is one of the highest virtues. It does not despise marriage because marriage as an institution produces virginal children. He gives the other side of the argument and summarizes the criticisms which ascetic Christianity made of any marriage as opposed to complete renunciation of social life.

Causal Analysis of the Rise of Atomism

There should be no question of the fact that the present period is one of widespread domination by the atomistic family. Present family relations are almost as completely individualized as it is possible to have them and still retain any familism at all. Every day the gossipy press brings out fresh evidence in startling cases where the individuals openly and knowingly suppress the family in the interest of the individual.

An example is reported by the United Press from Carson City, Nevada, as of December 2, 1945:

> District Judge Clark J. Guild granted divorces to Mrs. Delbert G. Faust and Mrs. Roy O. Preisler, both of East Orange (N.J.), late yesterday, and immediately thereafter he performed the double marriage in which Faust wed the former Mrs. Preisler and Preisler married the onetime Mrs. Faust. . . . The court awarded custody of the youngsters to their respective mothers.

Here all the known familistic and social defenses of the family were openly violated by all parties concerned, including even the judge. Here was collusion and connivance on a wholesale scale. There was no guilty or innocent party (recrimination) or, if so, condonation was evident. In other words, the family is considered, *de facto,* a private contract of a very brittle nature and one having not even a mild public significance. Here we have achieved very easily what the revolutions in France and Russia brought about in their most violent and antisocial periods.

When we turn to the causes of this, it is necessary to repeat a statement made in the last chapter: The change from domestic family modality to atomistic moves the whole system of social causation, at least temporarily, from forces within the family itself to larger social and cultural movements.

In other words, the whole system of causation has moved from the family itself into the larger culture. The individual is free to do largely what he wishes as long as the state and public have no workable objections. Religious and moral views have no role in reinforcing familism. The external "spirit" integrating the culture is not a familistic one at all.

What becomes of the family is no longer a matter for family ethics but is rather a matter for cultural drives and outward determinism.

This type of family arises first as an extension of the ideas of freedom of the individual, a theory which takes its foundation in the surplus moral strength of an earlier and stronger familism. If we leave the individual completely alone, as Erasmus suggested, Folly will make him both good and familistic. Thus the individual is left more and more alone to do as he wishes. At first the freedom becomes an incentive to economic gain, the type of freedom emphasized by Hesiod in his *Works and Days*. But sooner or later the meaning of this freedom changes. The individual, having no guiding moral principles, changes the meaning of freedom from opportunity to license. Having no internal or external guides to discipline him, he becomes a gambler with life, always seeking greener pastures. When he comes to inevitable difficulty, he is alone in his misery. He wishes to pass his difficulties and his misery on to others. Consequently he continually helps to build up institutions to "remedy" his misery. He willingly follows any prophet (and they are mostly false ones) who comes along with a sure-cure nostrum for the diseases of the social system.

Thus we witness the peculiar anomaly in that atomistic people, who seem to have given all for "this freedom," are the ones who create the most violent and bloodthirsty dictatorships. A cardinal example in the present century is the Hitlerian one by which, for the first time in some centuries, people were killed on a wholesale scale without apparent cause. Class revolutions kill and starve millions. Much of the starving is inadvertent; most of the killings are based upon the belief that the victims are enemies, class opponents, or counterrevolutionaries. But in the Hitlerian dictatorship apparently no logical rules of killing were followed. Sadistic persons did as they chose.

This is the type of thing that arose during the extremely atomistic period at the end of the Roman Empire. Each new emperor had new nostrums for his people. He killed until he was satiated; then he himself was killed, to be replaced by new killers. If there were longer periods of relatively stable peace, these seemed merely to be times when society became temporarily exhausted from its orgy of killings.

From the time of Hesiod to Pericles, freedom had one meaning; from the time of Pericles to Demosthenes, another. In the first period, it meant the creation of a great civilization; in the second, it meant lawsuits over possession of homosexual favorites and similar matters (Hyperides, *Against Athenogenes*; Lysias, *Against Simon*; Aeschines, *Against Timarchus*; Demosthenes, *Against Neaera*).

There simply is no positive workable causal system within the remaining atomistic family itself that can control this situation, either to promote it or to hold it down. What real familism is left in society is found among a minority of the people and is largely of an informal domestic type. These people possess considerable insight into the difficulties of the social system, but they are a relatively silent or futile minority. Their experiences are not shared by the world at large, chiefly because most of their knowledge is gained only through personal experience. The religious and moral agents that once supported their system of familism are largely out of favor with the masses or are inwardly corrupted by a lack of knowledge of their real functions in society. Thus the system of atomistic familism is carried by its own momentum to its extinction, largely unchecked by anything other than the total dispersal of the biological, psychological, and social resources of the society.

This corruption of the religious agencies is seen in the sanction of the Hollywood type of marriage by the agents of the church. Historically, Christianity was very violent in its opposition to this use of marriage as a conventional cover for temporary sex liaisons. Now many of the agents of what was once Christianity sanctify these changing pseudomarriages.

Thus the "cause" of the rise of the atomistic family to dominance is the extension and elaboration of concepts, ideals, practices, and beliefs which made the domestic system take precedence over the trustee until, in due time, these beliefs (freedom, individualism, private right, etc.) and practices no longer permit the system of faith of the domestic family to be dominant. The Periclean Greek psychology was an extension of the system of ideas antagonistic to old Greek beliefs, which had set in by the time of Solon. The basic sociological conceptions of the Roman Empire were an extension of the freedoms within the Roman social system already emerging at the end of the Punic Wars. Modern eighteenth-century atomism in social beliefs was a development from earlier ideas of the Renaissance and the Reformation.

When the atomistic family overtakes the domestic family system, there is a change of meaning of the variables. At first, when rainwater is added to soil, it yields an increase of productivity. Later, this addition of more and more water can sour the soil and cause a decrease in productivity. Too much water floods the crops. This change of meaning-relations between two variable systems is evident in most social and even physical phenomena. In particular, under given external possibilities the atomistic family can develop from the domestic, but when this stage occurs the whole social system, including the family, takes on new meaning.

The Progress of Atomism

Once atomism becomes the dominant mentality in family relations, slowly at first, and then more rapidly, it moves forward to a more and more individualistic world. There is nothing within the experience of the society to check this and there are many things in its favor. The atomistic family cannot, does not, will not, and has not stopped at the stage of a civil institution. As shown earlier in this chapter and elsewhere, the next step from civil institution is *private* contract. The difference between civil institution and private contract (registered for purposes of proof, like a bill of sale or a real estate deed) is profound indeed. On the one hand and in an earlier period, there is the conception that marriage and familism is a civil responsibility and can be so regulated, an attitude common among the more conservative philosophers of the eighteenth century. Hume's statement that "men know that these notions are founded on the public interest" is an example of this. (See the section on "Chastity and Modesty" in volume II of his *A Treatise of Human Nature*.) Hume and others substitute the "public interest" conception for the earlier post-Renaissance philosophy that the family is, like the state, a "natural" group. But following this the idea arises that marriage is a private arrangement and what people do about marriage and family relations is distinctly their own business (as long as they pay a lawyer to fill out the papers and a clerk to register them and do not stir up immediate public resentment).

The Hollywood type of marriage, for instance, is not a civil marriage. It is a private agreement between persons who have no intention of doing anything other than cohabiting sexually without observing further the implications in terms of the family. They register the marriage and go through the normal divorce procedures not because of the recognition of any civil responsibility, but simply because they are afraid that scandal will hurt the sales of movie admissions to the adolescent and "momship" audiences.

This is not true only of Hollywood. Hollywood has been mentioned only because large audiences hear about their sexual combinations and permutations under the guise of familism. If the rector of one church refuses sanction to people in the spotlight and another gives it, it becomes international news. But the same attitude is prevalent among the bourgeoisie and intellectual groups. Hollywood presents merely the more brightly colored and visible aspects of this "generation of vipers." The hillbilly, the war-worker, the masses of the people are but one step behind the Hollywood, bourgeois, and Bertrand Russell conceptions of familism as a private rather than civil or religious affair.

This comes about because almost the entire control of the family is determined by external causation—by the dominant fashion or cultural coloration of a given time. Since that is sensate, to use Sorokin's terminology, marriage must go on to sensate levels of experience. And since the limited, purely sensate conception of familism and love is antithetical to almost any family life at all, marriage must go. At first the expense and notoriety of breaking a marriage operates somewhat as a check. At all times many persons are too lethargic to change. A small proportion have children and feel some responsibility to these. A number become senile (decay bodily and sexually) very rapidly and can no longer find other suitable mates. Fundamentally, except for that small percentage who want simple decent family life (because they either understand it or want it as a foil for their outer creative work), those who retain familism are engulfed in it more or less blindly and accidentally. There are no accepted moral philosophies, religious dogmas, public laws, social sanc-

tions, or conceptions of decency to restrain people. The nonfamilistic
have no faith. Perhaps they need it and use some of its basic hypotheses
(to paraphrase William James, *Varieties of Religious Experience*), but no
such infinite beliefs exist for them consciously and effectually as a series
of historic and accepted dogmas of truth.

If there is any possible power that can stop this movement, it must
be found in the exterior environment of the society. It will consist chiefly
of antagonistic forces arising from the decay of previous social conditions.
This decay can be temporary, like the panic of the 1930s or the civil wars
preceding Augustus, or more permanent, as in the Dark Ages after the
decline of the Roman Empire. Conditions arise in which it is difficult
for even the civilized domestic institution of the family to survive. Then
the family system changes and in time (at least in the past) recovers some
of its familism. But it was a rough and brutal road leading from Rome
to the Renaissance.

The Roman Atomism

The situation at the end of the Roman Empire should be very instruc-
tive. At the time of this great breaking-up, the family according to St.
Ambrose was such that:

> Women are in a hurry to wean their children;
> If they be rich, they scorn to suckle them;
> Poor women expose their children;
> And if found, refuse to take them back;
> The rich, rather than see their fortune divided,
> Use murderous juices to kill the fetus within the womb;
> Men have not the affection of crows for their little ones.
> (Adapted from *The Life and Times of St. Ambrose*, P. de Labriolle,
> St. Louis, 1928, 172–74)

The reaction to this situation was extremely violent. No longer were the people dealing with men of the character of Augustus, who, at his best, sought to control familism by "economic" sanctions.

> For all nations you have made a fatherland. (Tacitus on Augustus)

No longer were men of the type of Marcus Aurelius in control:

> Of my grandfather Verus I have learned to be gentle and meek,
>   And to refrain from all anger and passion.
> (*The Golden Book*, first two lines)

The men who came into control in regard to the family were violent and had not the slightest objection to using extreme force to see that familism was regulated according to what they conceived to be a new or a more workable system. The rural landlord who was now becoming increasingly important as trade, commerce, city life, and industry declined sought to and did dictate both personally and by law the character of marriage and family life among the *coloni* on his estate or small principality.

> By combining management of production with powers of government on their estates, the landlords forced the peasants into a position of greater subservience and made themselves quite as much petty lords as property owners. . . . The imperial bureaucrats, [seeking] more revenue for the state, winked at new agrarian abuses. (Ralph Turner, *The Great Cultural Traditions*, vol. II, New York, 1941, 944 *et passim*)

Law changed its character. This point has been reviewed in previous chapters, but it is worth noting again that men no longer looked at the law as an attempt to find a fundamental workable truth, but more and more adopted the new spirit announced by Modestinus. According to him the function of the law was "to command, forbid, allow, punish."

However, the change occurred not only in the economic and governing aspects of society, it also affected the religious organization. In the period of the decay of the Roman Empire a new religious class, the Christian official, or agent of historic Christianity, rose to power. This class of Christian priests helped to reorient the elements of society in a new manner. Fundamentally this meant a return toward familism. The church also shared this same "command, forbid, allow, punish" spirit toward the family. Thus the whole culture—economically, governmentally, and religiously—took a severe repressive attitude toward antifamilism. The "cause" for change in the atomistic family had to come from without. The family itself was too weak to institute this change by internal familistic causation.

St. Basil, as well as other influential leaders of the Christian church, illustrates the commanding, forbidding, allowing, and punishing technique characteristic of the age, which was to be found not only in the feudal manors, in the local administration, in the public law, but also in the rapidly increasing bureaucracy of Christian leaders, priests, bishops, and other divines. The society was conscious of the fact that something was wrong. The pagans blamed the Christians for a long period, as we see from the defense of Christianity given in St. Augustine's *City of God* as well as the claim that it was not responsible for the sacking of Rome in 410 A.D. The Christians in turn blamed the situation on the moral decay of the period and were attempting to reconstruct the family as one step toward preventing further moral decay. They were willing to use strong measures to prevent any antifamilism except of the ascetic type—celibacy in the desert or in the monastery.

This idea fit well into the psychology of the landlord and the public administrator—either local or in Constantinople. They wanted a good supply of Romanized soldiers, workers, farmers, artisans, and taxpayers. By law and administration—some legal and some extralegal—they also developed this commanding-punishing technique. The result demonstrates that when the family is completely atomized, familistic reform seemingly must come from extrafamilistic forces in the culture. Men do not seem to turn back willingly toward the familism necessary to preserve the social system. That is a point with which "liberal" antifamilists do not seem to reckon. None are so blind as those who will not see.

The Mechanics of Atomistic Extension

The atomistic family arises in a domestic world. Its basic drives are the forces that gain headway through the destruction of trustee familism. These forces are, of course, integrated with other drives in the culture. The culture is integrated more and more in a "logical-meaningful" manner against familism. It has fuel to fan its flames if there are familistic peoples available, but not yet quite integrated, within the social system. These are the barbarians, the immigrants, the slaves, the war captives, or children from the unsophisticated fringes of the great cultural universe. These fill the gaps left by families that are decaying. St. Jerome mentions some Romans who represent ancient lines, yet we know these were exceptions, few in number. As Marcus Aurelius had already indicated more than a century before, every day someone was buried who could have had put on his gravestone that he was the last of his line.

The first rise of the system seems justified because now sons may take over fathers' professions and wealth. Representative firms and going businesses need not be split among many children. No one has to go to the hinterland or to the colonies and establish new connections. Competition among the older families is not great, for positions are made available by deaths. Life becomes generally easier in such times. The "attrition of the ordinary base entrail," which was the definition of coitus by Marcus Aurelius, could go on now without profound social consequences in terms of children to bear, rear, provide for, educate, and launch into life. Then as now, to use the Ogburnian terminology, the family could give up its "other functions" and concentrate upon "affection."

This development of the atomistic family was aided by the rise of involuntary sterility. No system of birth control works quite so well and with so little worry as one that is associated with a high probability of involuntary sterility. The Romans had their sex-hormone stimulants (love philters), their Soranus who wrote the perfect birth control system, and also their involuntary sterility.

They also had immigrants to back up their social system so that, no matter what the basic family concepts in Roman culture, it could carry on seemingly endlessly. Greece declined quickly and easily. Two centuries after his time, Pericles could not have made his "Unknown Soldier" speech because the heterogeneous peoples then in Athens, the slaves and immigrants, would not have understood his appeal. They spoke a babel of tongues. But the Roman social order was constantly nourished by the northern Europeans who came into this wonderful social system. Rome drained northern Europe as the modern Western European powers and America have constantly drained the excess peoples from the more familistic regions into the less familistic ones.

The atomistic system arises and develops because it emphasizes a system of superficial, discernible values. The values of atomism as opposed to the fundamental values of familism are like the values of energy-giving foods as opposed to the values of the protective and facilitating foods. Calories—sugars, starches, fats—are tempting foods. Vitamins, minerals, vegetables, amino acids, and "protective" foods are not so tasty and discernible. The growth of atomism is inevitable and seemingly inherent in society, once it gains headway and as long as relative conditions of the outside world are not absolutely inimical to it.

This system spreads to the rural districts and to the outer fringes of the cultural universe. The *concubinatus* form of marriage worked its way into the Egyptian colony. As Procopius reports in his *Secret History* of the excesses around the Court of Justinian, the cities were all alike. The boast of Justinian's wife that she had had sexual intercourse (without becoming pregnant) in every conceivable manner was not her boast alone. It was the boast of a high proportion of the women of the Roman Empire. This is not a diatribe against a "generation of vipers." It is simply a statement or description of the fact that the social system—much like ours will shortly become—had reached a situation in which the majority were unwilling to carry on the burden of providing for posterity. The delights of Rome in its last days were not different from those of the "heroes" of Homer. In later Rome everyone wanted to be a "hero"; no one wanted to be a parent. Even Plutarch's letter to his wife ("you loved your children") could no longer be written generally of either the lowborn masses or the more fortunate highborn.

This social system develops its own methods of extension and its own *agents provocateurs*. They are those who accept atomism as the *ne plus ultra* of civilization and seek economic, social, or pseudointellectual reasons to extend the system. They are insidious and they are everywhere. In other words, when in Rome, do as the Romans do. Don't be like you used to be or as you were taught; instead, be modern, streamlined, and up to date.

This, however, eventually has to end, as the basic, moral, and ideological population sources of the strength of the culture dry up. The rise of resentment against this overextended atomism is the next step. The lack of familism becomes a source of antithesis. It plays a negative creative role. This is the final step in the causal role of the atomistic family, when it creates, purely negatively, conditions that lead to a new synthesis and reaction.

Atomism in Its Final Stages—Negative Causation

The previous discussion shows how the atomistic family is established and how it extends itself. General cultural determinism takes over and the family system gradually loses its significance in the total social scheme. The system of atomism grows and grows, until finally it creates strong currents of resistance. By commanding, forbidding, and punishing, these new forces seek to put over a new social system. A part of this new system may consist of stoical negation. Endure life, avoid it, or do nothing about it. But another part is a reintegrated family system, consisting of doctrines often called new but really so ancient that the people do not recognize them. For instance, the family in the *Laws* of Plato goes way back to the family of Greece at the time of Solon. The family system of the church fathers harks directly back to an ancient domestic family system. It could be found in Scipio's Rome, in Solon's Greece, or in the Code of Hammurabi. Our final problem is to discuss what forces bring about this new orientation of family philosophy. Is it a reaction to divorce, to childlessness, to adultery, to sex perversions, to juvenile delinquency, to all of these things, or to what? The problem is important.

In general when a social system reaches the later phases of developed atomism in family relations, it reaches a state where the following forms of behavior gain great prominence. These are forms of action and thought that are identical with those during the high periods of atomism in Greece, Rome, and the modern world. They are as follows:

1. Increased and rapid easy "causeless" divorce. (Guilty and innocent party theory became a pure fiction.)

2. Decreased number of children, population decay, and increased public disrespect for parents and parenthood.

3. Elimination of the real meaning of the marriage ceremony. (*Manus* and *potestas* have no great implications.)

4. Popularity of pessimistic doctrines about the early heroes.

5. Rise of theories that companionate marriage or a permissible looser family form would solve the problem. (*Hetaera* relations in Greece and the *concubinatus* marriage form in the whole Roman Empire.)

6. The refusal of many other people married under the older family form to maintain their traditions while other people escape these obligations. (The Greek and Roman mothers refused to stay home and bear children.)

7. The spread of the antifamilism of the urbane and pseudointellectual classes to the very outer limits of the civilization. (Even the Egyptian peoples in contact with Roman society took up the *concubinatus*, contrary to their earlier family system.)

8. Breaking down of most inhibitions against adultery. (The adulterer now felt that his act should be looked at as no worse than *stuprum* or at most a tort.)

9. Revolts of youth against parents so that parenthood became more and more difficult for those who did try to raise children.

10. Rapid rise and spread of juvenile delinquency.

11. Common acceptance of all forms of sex perversions.

All these forms of behavior reach great heights of popularity in the final atomistic period. They become accepted as the things to do. Consequently, they themselves cannot be the cause of the rise of any antagonistic system. The question is what can cause the rise of antithetical systems of family behavior, forbidding and punishing these popular forms of conduct. To answer this question we must ask what these forms of behavior represent. What is lacking in the social system of which these forms are symptoms? What is the fundamental disease? This involves the basic question as to the real nature of the family as a social organization.

Those who have followed this analysis thus far will see that two fundamental attributes of human life are closely connected with familism and are largely inherent in its organization. These may be called *fides* and *sacramentum*, to use two Latin words familiar in the Christian doctrine on the nature of the family. Essentially *fides* means *loyalty in human relationships*. *Sacramentum* means that basic human relations are considered as *products of a system of values coming from the infinite world*; it means that loyalty between peoples in their basic relationships is a *way* of life without which there cannot be long continued order in the social universe. Both separately and together, *fides* and *sacramentum* mean that *other persons* are considered human beings like us. Unless there are strong reasons to the contrary, they are to be treated as a special class, very different from the physical, botanical, and animal forces in the universe. All social life is built upon these basic assumptions. Self-sacrifice for group interests, the recognition of contracts, legal and moral norms, and the inviolability of standards of international law depend upon the acceptance and preservation of this conception of humanity. The belief that human beings and human relations are sacred is the cornerstone upon which the total social structure is built.

The two main hypotheses may be stated as follows:

1. *The decay of the family into extended atomism gives rise to antagonistic forces because it weakens the fundamental value systems and natural infinite beliefs upon which society is built.* The disease is not divorce, adultery, homosexuality, etc. These are but symptoms of the final decay of the basic postulates upon which the "human" part of society is built. This leads to another and very important postulate.

2. *Family sociology is the field in which, under certain conditions, the social thinker can get closest to absolute and basic cause.* Family sociology, in many of its ramifications, comes the closest to infinite cause demonstrable in a finite universe.

Any causal analysis refers always to a preceding or associate set of conditions. Philosophers always seek a basic set of conditions, beyond which empirical experience can probe no further. In the field of family sociology, and largely only in that field, it is possible for man to penetrate into the basic field of finite causation. Beyond this, we go into unexplainable and uncontrollable infinite causation, a subject not very amenable to empirical development. The rest of this chapter seeks to demonstrate the validity of these two postulates. It is an analysis of the process of negative causation rising from extreme atomistic family conditions.

Exposition of Working of Atomistic Negative Causation

The previous section pointed out that the quintessence of familism is a scheme of loyalty in human relations that requires self-sacrifice of the individual. He does this because he considers this loyalty in accord with a system of values arising in the infinite world. What else can make a parent or child sacrifice for the family as he must? The familistic person considers that he must carry on the purpose of the family and make sacrifices for the group, to the neglect of his own selfish ends, because of some infinite reason. It is right to marry, have children, and rear those children properly, rather than to expose them or give them away. It is right to do as one's parents suggest. Thus he begins to consider other persons—wife, children, and kin—as part of himself and sacrifice for them becomes sacrifice for himself. He trades his worldly or finite opportunities for his infinite self.

From this gradually arises the idea of the fundamental oneness of people, or to put it in purely philosophical language, the idea of the fundamental dignity of the human being. That being the case, the source of human social organization and its motivation is the family relation. When this family relation is disrupted, society loses its basic social motivation. The value systems and infinite beliefs upon which society rests are weakened until the resultant disorder and selfishness weaken or break up the social system. An understanding of this takes us back to "basic cause" in humanism or social relationships. From this we can see that atomism in family relations is *not important because of its symptoms* but primarily because of the *decay of the basic components of social life.* Thus atomism becomes the negative cause for releasing the forces antagonistic to it by removing from the social system the elementary force that enables the greater society to work.

Durkheim, in his *Elementary Forms of the Religious Life*, gives philosophical insight into the basis of this phenomenon. Religion is "more than the idea of God or spirits" and the unifying of "man to a deity." Religion is a differentiation of objects, practices, and beliefs into those that are "sacred" and those that are "profane." The sacred is the "collective" or social thing. Religion "has given birth to all that is essential in society" and hence the social idea "is the soul of religion." The "living source" from which religion is nourished is "in society." Thus there is "something eternal in religion" and every society has the need of "upholding and reaffirming at regular intervals the collective sentiments and the collective ideas which make its unity and its personality."

This leads us to inquire into the close relationship between the family and religion, or the relation between a system of family values in the finite world and that interpretation of the infinite system of values which is known as religion. Breasted, who deals exceedingly carefully with the "emergence of a moral order" in this thing called modern civilization, says:

> I have been not a little surprised how (the materials from the earliest pyramid age of Egypt) unmistakably disclose the family as the primary influence in the rise and development of moral ideas. (The maxims of Ptahhotep, c. 5,000 years ago, illustrate this.)
>
> Take to thyself a wife as the heart's mistress;
>
> Fill her body, clothe her back;
>
> Make her heart glad as long as thou livest;
>
> Have children; rear them right; that is correct living;
>
> Be not avaricious toward thy kin;
>
> Treat other families as if they were yours;
>
> Conjugal infidelity means death;
>
> Never practice the corruption of boys.
>
> (See *Dawn of Conscience*, New York, 1935. The above is adapted from 116–17 and 133–36)

Breasted concludes:

> The thing which was long called the "moral consciousness of mankind" has grown up with each generation out of the disciplines and emotions of family life, supplemented by the reflection and teaching of experienced elders. (410)

It is unnecessary and confusing to go into the voluminous literature on religion or to give citations to back up these statements. To do so would lead us into the basic doctrines of Confucianism, Hinduism, the Vedic Hymns, the Zend Avesta, the Old Testament, the Koran, and post-Roman modern Christianity. It would also lead us into the factors influencing Jainism, Buddhism, and all other great religions. Anyone with the slightest perspective on all these sacred books and religions will know immediately that familism and domestic practices form their main central core. Taoism, as a turning away from the world, is a doctrine that arose in antagonism to Confucianism; it was not unlike the ascetic movement in the early Christian church. Neither Taoism nor this ascetic movement became dominant in the two great religious bodies that finally developed from these conflicting times and philosophies. By the time of St. Isidore, *familism* was *the theme* of Christianity. Rather than enter such a devious discussion, let us look at the close correlation between familism and types of religion or collective ideas. The trustee family periods are essentially polytheistic ones, whether we consider the gods of pre-Confucian China, of Homer, of druidical northern Europe, or of camp-meeting days in Kentucky. Essentially, each family has its own gods and religious beliefs which, given time, can be raised to polytheism. The coming of the domestic family institution is always associated with a drawing-in of the number of godly beliefs, because "all men are one" outside of the domestic family and must have a common denominator in a god and a moral code. Periods of atomism of the family are always periods of disbelief in that one god. James's *Varieties of Religious Experience*, a description of individualism in infinite conceptions, and the atomistic family conditions are but opposite sides of the same eternal page. Fustel de Coulanges understands this when he places side by side the family change in Greece and Rome with changes in religions and the conception of god. Atomism in Greece began to develop rapidly from the time of Pericles; it was at the same time (416 B.C.) that the young men of Athens committed the greatest sacrilege by pulling down and defacing the statues of the gods. This very sacrilege happened again several centuries later in Rome. Atomism in Rome was closely connected with disbelief, whether we view it from Mommsen's standpoint or from that of Augustus. According to Mommsen, the first profanation of the Vestal Virgins began in Rome, when the famous Clodius, who was trying to have an affair with some girl, was caught in a house where the Vestal Virgins were meeting. Augustus tried to remodel both the family and religion.

The whole historical development of Christianity is major and decisive proof of the relationship between religion and the family. The Roman family had disintegrated as an institution. The church diagnosed the trouble as a lack of *fides* and *sacramentum* in social relationships. As religion became more powerful—at about the time St. Isidore was its chief philosopher—the church finally realized that the best way to overcome the lack of *fides* and *sacramentum* in the total social system was to emphasize *proles*, or the childbearing function of the family, as a first step toward increasing the social force. The church sought by *proles* to inculcate an infinite system to back the finite belief of *fides*.

This "correlation" between religion and the family ultimately leads to an unavoidable statement of social causation. Religion is a doctrine of the infinite. The chief, and largely the only basic, agency translating infinite and inescapable doctrines of human behavior into the finite is the familistic system. Religion has never succeeded without a familistic doctrine. (Cf. Taoism and Western asceticism which were short-lived.) On the other hand, familism has never succeeded without a system of infinite faith, which is simply the acceptance of a basic religious code of values. As shown, attempts to "buy children" (the Roman caducary laws and the widespread modern family aids) have not produced many children. Mothers will not bear the pains of childbirth nor fathers the worries of parenthood for economic rewards alone. Fundamentally, people are familistic because they think it right and for no other reason.

Conclusion

This leads, then, back to our main idea. *Atomistic familism causes a dispersal of the infinite faith underlying the family system.* This lack of faith leads inevitably to the breaking-up of familism. The symptoms of this, or rather the alternative forms of behavior—from adultery and divorce to homosexuality—cannot be the "causes" of an antagonistic movement. Once established, these practices become accepted and are an end in themselves. Underneath these symptoms lies a basic system of negative causation—the lack of faiths and beliefs in the social system strong enough to enable the social system to continue to function. Paraphrasing the famous statement by Marcus Aurelius ("that which is not good for the beehive is not good for the bee"), we may say that the antifamilism of times of high atomism is not good for society and hence inevitably becomes antithetical to the individual.

Thus this analysis leads to the reaffirmation of two conclusions. *In familism we can approach closely that dream of the philosophers, determining the "first" cause in social systems.* Beyond the primary cause, which is always held to be an infinite god of nature, this is the closest approach to real causation we can have. The atomistic family brings about a resurgence of familism by its negativistic spewing of antisocial doctrines into the social order. These doctrines are directly connected with the unwillingness of people to do things just because they are "right," whether in business, farming, industry, government, or the family. Thus when we speak of the "fall" of great civilizations, like those of Rome or Greece, in which an inner decay is the main agency, we are justified in giving an absolute causal analysis. For soil erosion and history, deforestation and history, hay and history, centralization and history, bad government and history, malaria and history, barbarians and history, we can substitute a basic and primary causation—*familistic decay and history.*

This single-factor statement of historical cause does not preclude all the other "causes" set forth by the philosophers of history. It simply points out that the final outcome in numerous great historical changes is decided by changes in the family. It gives the family a unique main-index place in judging historical change; it also makes family change the final decisive force. A certain type of society—largely a limited type—can exist under the trustee family. There are wider possibilities of types of civilizations under the domestic family than under the trustee type. Civilization must be held to a certain level of order and public decency or there can be no domestic family. On the other hand, the domestic family permits a certain level of decency in civilization. While the atomistic family is not a complete prerequisite to the first flowering of a great civilization, it seems necessary to its final culmination. When the atomistic family is carried too far it inevitably tends to limit the possibilities of expansion of the civilization and (through its negative causation) seems to force the processes of decay.

This is the basic theme of family and civilization. Civilization grows out of familism; as it grows it loses its original connection with the basic spring which furnished the essence of civilization. When this process has gone too far, the civilization soon exhausts its inventory of social "material." Then occurs a reaction or decay. The amount of reaction and decay and the length of these "Dark Age" periods seem to depend upon how quickly the culture finds its way back to the fundamental mother-source—familism.

16

THE FUTURE OF FAMILY AND CIVILIZATION

Now what about the future of the family? This also involves the
future of our civilization. The previous analysis has shown the close
relationship that exists between family and civilization.

Western society, of which America is the most extreme present
manifestation, has gone through two great family crises during its history
and is about to reach the maximum development of a third. An understanding of these crises and the difficulties they present should be very
helpful in contemplating the future.

The first part of this analysis has been historical and descriptive.
The last part is analytical and "cause-seeking." The great family changes
described here seem in large part peculiar to Western society and so
far seem to have been inherent in its very social processes. Other great
civilizations of which we have a record have had none of these great
family crises. They have changed, but neither so greatly nor so violently
as in the West.

In all of China's family history there has been only one major standard of reference, one "family Bible"—the Confucianist system of *li*, or
moral behavior. In Hindu society, practically from its beginning until
now, the Ramayana epic has been the Bible of the masses.

Near Eastern society (Persian, Babylonian, Egyptian, Semitic, and Arabic) also followed almost the same family patterns for thousands of years, as is indicated by the astonishing similarity between the family and the legal, religious, and moral codes that have dominated that region and the interrelations between these codes.

The Greek Family Crisis

The first of these Western family crises developed in Greek civilization after the time of Pericles and the Peloponnesian War (430 through 400 B.C.). In the space of two centuries the family system described by Pericles in his funeral oration for the unknown soldier (429 B.C.) was completely broken. Pericles talked to his audience of how the strong Athenian family system could withstand the shocks of the wars among the Greek nations and re-create a great culture once the civil wars were settled. He was sure that those parents who had lost sons in the wars, and who were still fairly young, would return home and have more children to replace those lost.

The picture of what actually took place in the following two centuries is recorded concisely in the legal cases left by the Greek orators, in the numerous defenses of Socrates by Xenophon, Plato, and others, and in the analysis by Polybius of the process and the causes whereby the upstart country of Rome became master of the Mediterranean. We see the complete disruption of a family system, similar to that occurring about us now, with equally disastrous social consequences. The orations of Demosthenes and his group against the "collaborators" with Macedonia would fit our modern period very well. Only a change of names and dates is necessary. The trial of Senator Timarchus by Aeschines and the scandalous *Against Neaera* by Demosthenes would not be entirely out of place today.

Plato was probably the person who brooded most over this situation. Many of his later writings were an attempt to understand and to suggest a remedy for this broken family situation. The family was disrupted. The most typical picture is given in the court-martial trials of the younger

Alcibiades, who was the grandson by adoption of Pericles. "Like father, like son," except that here grandfather set the pace. The tragedy of the decay of Greece is mirrored in the collapse of this one great family from Aspasia to the two trials of Alcibiades the Younger.

The complete story of the disruption of that great civilization and its social consequences was somewhat disguised in history by the influx of peoples from below the Mediterranean who filled up some of the depleted Grecian ranks. It was prevented from reaching a maximum of destruction by the rise of Rome, which preserved the Mediterranean society of that time from anarchy. Nevertheless, the picture of Greece is not a pretty one from the period of the death of Aristotle until the time, about 90 A.D., when Plutarch gave his "family sociology" lectures in Rome.

Judged even by our contemporary value systems and the emphasis we place upon the preservation of the benefits of civilization, it is a bleak account of great decay. Plutarch's "moral lectures" indicated that none of the values that either we or the early Greeks considered basic to civilization then existed in Hellenistic society. By the time of Plutarch, virtue, chastity, fidelity, having and rearing children, and even the loyalty of brother to brother had disappeared among all classes of Greece. Only those who had a personal preference for family values kept to the older standards. While Plutarch indicates in his *Lives* that he knew of an earlier and familistic Greece, as a sophist, his "moral" lectures were a constant deprecation, even a sneer, at those old values.

Plutarch, as a character, would feel more or less at home in American society as it is now developing. As a matter of fact, many of our sophisticated writers of today are of the Plutarchian type. They defame the old heroes of our Western society by picking out the real or alleged worst sides of their lives and presenting these as the entire picture. They constantly criticize, either directly or by implication, our earlier systems of accepted moral behavior.

This breaking-down of the Greek family system is extremely interesting reading. For one thing, the Greeks never hid the facts from view. The reason Greek family decay is not well known and understood today is because the students of that culture have preferred not to give us the real tale, or because they did not dare tell all.

The Greeks of the third century B.C. were not the parents to whom Pericles spoke so seriously at the funeral of the unknown soldier. They were rather the type of person who wanted the navy restricted so that they could have more public feasts (*Lycurgus Against Leocrates*). They were farmers who wanted to participate in the demoralized sensualism of the city (*Hyperides Against Athenogenes*). They were businessmen who cared more for sex than for business or for honor (*Lysias Against Simon*). They were politicians whose private lives were utterly scandalous (*Aeschines Against Timarchus*). They were the unscrupulous lawyer or the woman who had at the most only one or two children (*Demosthenes Against Neaera*).

The Roman Family Crisis

The second great crisis of the Western family system was that of Rome in the second and third centuries of our era. Prior to that time the Roman family had reenacted early Greek family history, having gone through a Homeric period and a Hesiodic stage. Although the leading families in Rome were demoralized by the wealth that followed the development of empire and the civil wars leading up to Augustus, the common family was still fairly strong. Augustus, who was Emperor-Dictator at about the time of Christ, used rather strong measures against decadence in the leading families, and by this ruthlessness helped preserve the "Roman tradition" among them for more than a century.

After that period, the Roman family approached a crisis almost identical to that of the earlier Greek family and that facing us today. Very little is known about it by the public today because most persons stop reading Roman history after Julius Caesar and Nero. However, if we read the Roman interpretations themselves (Aulus Gellius, Martial, Juvenal, Lucian of Samosata, Dio Cassius, Ammianus Marcellinus, and Procopius, for instance), we get a well-defined picture of family decay. This family decay is reflected in their family law. They turned gradually from economic sanctions for familism, as instituted by the Augustan reforms, to the severest physical punishments. These physical punishments became common and accepted after 400 A.D. The situation in Justinian's time, described in the *Secret History* of Procopius (about 535 A.D.) was, as he himself indicates, to be found in every center of the empire.

We can see here the reason why the early Christian fathers took such a firm stand against family decay and why a man like St. Augustine, in his *City of God* and many of his letters, apologized for the Romans and compared them unfavorably with the more moral behavior of the warlike and crude barbarians. (This is also the attitude of Tacitus in *Germania*, of Salvian in the *Government of God,* and of many others.)

The only difference between the Greek and Roman family decay was that the Roman family crisis overspread a much wider territory and involved many more people. At first its effects did not have severe social consequences because it took a long time for the social anarchy to consume all the country people in the north. These were the "good barbarians," who constantly entered the empire and filled up the gaps left in the social system by the decayed Roman families. By the third century, the supply of good barbarians had dwindled, and "all Gaul," as well as most of Western Europe, had decayed just as seriously as Rome and Italy itself. Salvian in 450 A.D. mentions the decay in Spain, France, Germany, Switzerland, Italy, and North Africa. The evidences of this family decay were the same in Rome and in Greece.

The Recreation of Familism

Decay of the Roman family system was a phase of a general decline, of which the breaking of the family was partly a cause and partly an effect. When finally consummated and spread throughout the subject peoples, the immigrants, and the country people of the empire, it became the "causal" or vehicular agent in the collapse of that civilization. Three or four new agents or forces, each with its own ideas for a new kind of family, struggled for supremacy within the remnants of the empire. The Christian emperors, who wanted sufficient people to carry on the former social processes, were one agent. Another was the Aurelius Augustinian type of Roman, who was sick at heart of the awful physical, social, moral, and spiritual decay, and who set forth a recreated philosophy of the domestic family in *fides*, *proles*, and *sacramentum*. A third agent was the great landlord or feudal lord who came into prominence now that trade, industry, and city living were precarious. He wanted his people (*coloni*) to stay on their farms, get along together, neither marry nor divorce without his permission, and above all have children to provide a future labor supply. He wanted a surplus of children so that he could supply drafts for the armies and still keep his estate running. Finally, there were the new barbarian groups and barbarian rulers from the north and east, who did not want their people to abandon the old trustee family system or the law institutionalized in the barbarian codes. All these forces wanted a recreated family system. The only differences lay in the kind of system they strove to recreate.

The struggle between these groups lasted for some centuries. At first the barbarian system won because the Roman rulers came more and more often from barbarian stock and because the great landlords preferred the barbarian system to the Christian. Furthermore, the great landlords held the reins over the rulers because they ran the local districts and became increasingly responsible for paying taxes and furnishing men for the armies and the government. The church also was more deeply influenced by the barbarians because it found them better subjects for Christianization. From the sixth to the ninth centuries of our era, the family actually became more like the Homeric organization than anything Rome had seen from the end of the Punic Wars to the third century A.D. Later the church system won, and the domestic family became dominant in Western Europe from the tenth century until after the Reformation. This was due to the growth in power, influence, and ingenuity of the church and the decay of the feudal lords and the ruling powers. The church learned to use the feudal lords and rulers, as well as the kin-clan organizations, in its control of the family system. Later when the states and rulers began to become more powerful, they joined forces with the church because they were naturally opposed to the local powers and administration of justice by the clan-groups and feudal rulers.

The net result of these changes, achieved after several centuries, is that our medieval family again became the same type of organization as that which existed in Greece after Homer and before Pericles and in Rome when she first became mistress of the civilized Western world. The church had changed the order of its three family precepts from *fides*, *proles*, and *sacramentum* to *proles*, *fides*, and *sacramentum* (the Isidorean-Acquinian order). Society was reinvigorated and ready to march forward again. Its leaders had forgotten most of the earlier family experience in the Greek and Roman days and no longer thought the family needed any public guidance.

Gradual Development of the Third Family Crisis

The third family crisis, like the earlier ones, began slowly, moved imperceptibly through several centuries, and finally, as in Greece and Rome, advanced quickly toward a grand finale. One of the outstanding earlier documents is the *Praise of Folly*, by Erasmus. Here he set forth the theory that the family really needed no oversight because men were foolish enough to be virtuous, to prefer to marry virgins, to have children, and to be "good" citizens. His work is outstanding for its clarity as an early statement of the theme that would reach a climax in the nineteenth century.

Most writers praise or blame the Protestant leaders for the philosophical steps that led to the modern atomism of the family. Neither praise nor blame is deserved. The original Protestant leaders, from Huss through Luther and Calvin to those of the eighteenth century, really wanted a stricter and more puritanical family than actually existed in the Middle Ages. The founders of the modern philosophy that the individual is God were not the religious leaders but the intellectual sophists. The Reformation leaders were profamilistic.

Nevertheless, in the field of philosophy there was a gradual development of new ideas concerning the nature of man and his family. These ideas started in the humanist period prior to the Reformation and evolved eventually into the concepts of the nineteenth century. The "new" ideas were essentially the same as those found in Greece in the fifth and fourth centuries B.C., as brought out in the trial and defense of Socrates. Socrates was accused of destroying the Greek family system; his defense by Xenophon and Plato was simply their efforts to exonerate Socrates from this responsibility. The same system of "new ideas" about the family was also used later to bring about the decrease of the power and meaning of the Roman family system.

The approaching climax of the modern family crisis was evidenced by four "revolutions"—two political, one peaceful, and an international sit-down strike. The two political revolutions in the family were the family law changes of the French government from 1791 to 1816 and those of the Russian government from 1917 to 1936. In these two unique episodes, whole national legal systems were changed overnight so that marriage, parenthood, and familism completely lost public sanction or legal meaning. During the English revolution of the Cromwellian period the whole Western world was shocked simply because the revolutionary government required marriage before a state rather than a religious official. That Milton escaped beheading for advocating divorce was afterward pointed out as "miraculous." But one hundred and forty years later in the French Revolution, as one of the speakers in the Assembly pointed out, the marriage fee became simply a tax on prostitution. Divorce was established at the will of either party without the consent or even the knowledge of the other. The same changes were brought about in Russian family law after 1917 and lasted until the countermovement of 1936.

The peaceful revolution was achieved in the United States following 1820, largely under the guise of succulent phrases and legal technicalities. Two of these phrases were *feme sole* legislative conceptions and omnibus divorce clauses. But the fundamental changes were achieved through the development of ideas regarding split jurisdiction. Marriage and divorce no longer had to take place in, or according to the regulations of, the actual place of residence or jurisdiction (the *proprius parochus* idea of the Council of Trent). Thus a North Carolina couple could, according to a Supreme Court case (*North Carolina v. Williams*) drive to Nevada, live together six weeks in a tourist camp, divorce their respective spouses, marry each other, and return to North Carolina to live as a respectable married couple. While this particular couple was finally penalized after two decisions by the U.S. Supreme Court, millions of others have done and are doing the same thing without being penalized, as the minority report on the case (Justice Black) brought out. The governor of North Carolina later pardoned the couple.

One phase of the American revolution in family control is the inclusion of two different conceptions of the meaning of marriage under one system of family law. From the time of Pericles on, the Greeks tried to separate somewhat antithetical family ideals into an extremely secluded private family based upon *manus, patria potestas,* and parenthood, and a public relation with a *hetaera,* in which few legal and social consequences were involved. In other words, they moved toward the oriental conception of polygamy, except that the second partner seldom undertook any domestic, parental, or familistic obligations. They developed a public and a private wife system. This did not work because the private wives never became institutionalized into a family system. Toward the end of the Hellenistic period in Greece, marriage and familism became simply a farce.

The Romans experimented with this problem and developed two distinct forms of marriage law. If the couple chose the marriage of *dignitas*—meaning *manus, potestas,* mixing of estates, and procreation—they were supposed to abide by it. If the couple preferred a less binding relationship, they could enter a simpler type of marriage, not involving *manus, potestas,* mixing of estates, or children. These looser family ties were sanctioned under the *concubinatus* family law and procedure. However, this system failed simply because few men or women were willing to choose or abide by the marriage of *dignitas.* Toward the end of what the French call the *haute empire* period (c. 300 A.D.), marriage and familism in Roman society also became farcical—a grand vulgarization—with extremely devastating social consequences.

Due to very clear historical reasons, in the United States we have tried to cloak both forms of marriage and familism, or the lack of it, under one general legal system. Here also we seem to be coming quickly to a farcical climax because the legal bulwarks of the total family system are adjusted only to its weakest units. As a result, in our culture the parental unit has no real backing or workable public support in law. Parents must now try to rear a family under a social and legal system adjusted to those couples who do not want the paraphernalia of familism—common income, expenses, children, union for perpetuity, or serious familistic obligations. In our modern Western society the forgotten person is the man or woman who honestly and sincerely wants to be a parent. This affects our whole social system; it affects all the practicalities of life, from renting a house to economic advancement under our different forms of bureaucracy. If there are children, renting a house is difficult, changing jobs is difficult, social activities are difficult. In the words of Bacon, to have children is to give "hostages to fortune," and one is no longer a free bargaining agent.

The fourth modern revolution, the sit-down strike on having and rearing children, brings the family to another crisis. The birth rate has dropped rapidly to a negative amount through a movement that began in the various European countries in the last third of the nineteenth century and has spread throughout all Christendom.

This is exactly what happened in Greece and Rome. Once again, as in those cultures, the social consequences were delayed by the immigration of peoples from the more familistic districts. There is also a further identity in that when the sources of immigration (what the Romans called the "good barbarians") also became exhausted, the family crisis reached its grand finale within one or two generations. Between 1820 and 1920, the United States imported forty million immigrants from Europe. These are now no longer available. When the United States has exhausted the surplus population of the French-Canadians and the Mexicans—almost the only fertile peoples of the Western world now available to us—we too will begin the grand finale of the crisis.

Predictions as to the Future of the Family

Current writers on the family have made numerous direct or implied predictions as to the future of the family. The most prevalent idea is that the family has merely to achieve the freeing of the individual to arrive at its "ideal." The attitude is somewhat bivalent—we want to retain the family, but it must not interfere with our love affairs, either hetero- or homosexual.

Sorokin takes up the family as a part of his general analysis of the changes in Western culture and gives us very specific statements as to the future of this system. He states very definitely that the culture which has dominated Western society for the past five centuries is breaking down. The present difficulty is not "local" or "superficial," but is one of the "deepest crises of its life." For the family he holds:

> The family as a sacred union of husband and wife, of parents and children, will continue to disintegrate. Divorces and separations will increase until any profound difference between socially sanctioned marriages and illicit sex-relationship disappears. Children will be separated earlier and earlier from parents. The main sociocultural functions of the family will further decrease until the family becomes a mere incidental cohabitation of male and female while the home will become a mere overnight parking place mainly for sex relationship. (*Social and Cultural Dynamics*, vol. IV, 776)

In other words, Sorokin predicts a further and further breakdown of the family until the relations between husband and wife and between parents and children will become incidental and chaotic. Sorokin does not set any foreseeable limit to this gradual breakdown of the family relation and the attendant dispersal of social values.

No one can deny that Sorokin has the facts to support his conclusions. In no single one of the value systems holding the family together is there any retention of former standards. L. M. Terman, in his study of premarital chastity among women entering marriage, found it was 82 percent for the group born before 1890 and only 32 percent for those born after 1910. If the trend continues, he pointed out, premarital chastity of males would vanish from the group born after 1930 and of females for the group born after 1940. This in itself is merely an illustration. As shown earlier in this work, *all forms of behavior associated with familism have declined in the same specific fashion.*

There is little left now within the family or the moral code to hold this family together. Mankind has consumed not only the crop, but the seed for the next planting as well. Whatever may be our Pollyanna inclination, this fact cannot be avoided. Under any assumptions, the implications will be far-reaching for the future not only of the family but of our civilization as well. The question is no longer a moral one; it is social. It is no longer familistic; it is cultural. The very continuation of our culture seems to be inextricably associated with this nihilism in family behavior.

This process of atomization is hastened by the Pollyanna stories and pseudohistories given by the family sociologists. They believe that the family is getting better and better all the time. In ancient society, it was a large patriarchal unit. In medieval society, it became the small patriarchal unit. Only modern society after the industrial revolution achieved the democratic, companionate unit.

Analytical and Predictive Conclusions

This ends the historical and descriptive part of the subject and lays the groundwork for a few pointed remarks of another character.

1. The United States, as well as the other countries of Western Christendom, will reach the final phases of a great family crisis between now and the last of this century. By that time the social consequences of this crisis will approach a maximum. This crisis will be identical in nature to the two previous crises in Greece and Rome. The results will be much more drastic in the United States because, being the most extreme and inexperienced of the aggregates of Western civilization, it will take its first real "sickness" most violently.

2. Efforts to meet this situation in the United States will probably be very exaggerated. We will probably try all the "remedies" suggested or tried in Greek and Roman civilization, profiting perhaps but little from the mistakes already made in those periods. The violence and abruptness of the changes will probably be extreme indeed.

3. Very little public knowledge of the nearness, the inescapability, or the seriousness of this impending crisis exists. The intellectuals almost completely avoid discussion of it. When they do touch upon it, they hide their heads in the sands of "cultural determinism," holding that the inevitable crisis will approach us very slowly, will be met with the proper remedies at the proper time, and will have no serious social consequences. No thoughtful analysis of the problem and its implications exists.

4. In the past these family crises have been associated with changes in the vehicular agents which interpret the general social system to the family. The three great vehicular systems which mitigate between family and society are the clan, the religious institution, and the national state. Each major change in the family system in Western society has been associated with a shift in power between these three vehicles. The dominant vehicular agents of Western society by periods have been as follows:

CHIEF FAMILY CONTROL AGENT IN WESTERN SOCIETY
(OMITTING GREECE)

Agent Controlling Family	*General Period of Most Powerful Influence of Agent*
Clan	Italian society to period of the Twelve Tables
Religion	From the Twelve Tables (450 B.C.) to Augustus (28 B.C.–14 A.D.)
State	From Augustus to Constantine (after 300 B.C.)
State and Religion	From Constantine to 6th Century, A.D.
Clan	From Gregory of Tours (6th) to 11th centuries
Religion	From 11th to 17th centuries
State	From 17th to 20th centuries

5. The most devastating social changes have occurred when the state relinquished its control of familism. This is probably due to the extremely "utilitarian" idea in state control of familism and the "totalitar-

ian" nature of its relation to familism. In the pure clan-control system, there is always great opposition to the excesses of those in control. The masses and the weaker clans turn to religious and state agencies to appeal for help against the stronger clans in the name of justice (Hesiod in Greece; the plebs in Rome; the common people who entered the feudal system in the early Middle Ages to avoid the excesses of the local "Homers"). In the pure religious control, the religious body uses the clan and the state (after "Christianizing" them) as agents to control and direct familism (for example, the castigation of Louis at Aix la Chapelle by Pope Nicholas I, in the Lothaire II divorce case. It was contended that he and Lothaire had set a bad example for all Christendom). But when the state assumes control, it brooks no interference, nor calls for any aid until it has exhausted familistic resources. Even Augustus, when he used the religious appeal to rebuild Roman familism, made the emperor "God." Instead of appealing to religion, he tried to *be* religion, making the state plan a religious one.

6. Since the forthcoming struggle over familism will be one in which the national states seemingly will have exhausted their ability to direct and preserve order in the family system, we may speak of the impending social disarrangements and confusions as a "crisis" rather than as one of the normal slower changes always going on within the greater family system.

7. The failure of the state control of familism lies partly in its method—or lack of same. As contrasted with clan and religious control, the state never sets up any ideal of familism. In such documents as Homer and Beowulf, which illustrate extreme clan control, there is an imperishable and inescapable ethical ideal. When Beowulf makes his last statement before death, he reiterates that he had never turned against his kinsmen and reemphasizes an ethical ideal: "Kinship true can never be marred in a noble mind." Religious control of familism is based upon an unchanging ethical idealism. Confucius, Ramayana, and St. Augustine set ideals which are cast aside only with the breaking of the influence of the ethical bodies bounded by their philosophies. However, state law is a constantly changing conception of the family, whether it be from the Roman Twelve Tables to the Novels of Justinian, or from the elev-

enth- century Anglo-Saxon barbarian code (*Leges Henrici*) to the recent case of *North Carolina* v. *Williams,* heard by the United States Supreme Court in 1944.

8. Social work agencies and other meliorative bodies which represent public and state attempts to strengthen and preserve familism will find themselves increasingly inadequate to deal with the problem as the crisis becomes more acute. The state will step in with increasingly drastic measures or different attempts at control. Unless these state measures are wisely considered, they will only make the situation more confused and difficult.

9. If the national states profit from the past experience of the agencies dealing with the family, they might turn to the other vehicular agents that have in the past been influential in the family and earnestly seek their help. The success of this method will be partly influenced by the earnestness and sincerity of the appeal. No halfway measures will suffice. No agency is willing to make itself merely a "cat's paw" for the state, to be discarded as soon as the situation shows improvement.

10. A drastic need exists for some broad research agency to study the problem of the impending crisis of the family. At present there is none in existence with adequate vision of the problem. Most of our present agencies are still thinking in terms of Erasmus and blind cultural determinism.

A Theory of the Family and Civilization

If we look back over the road followed by the family and civilization, we are led to some interesting conclusions. We might state that in general the most important contribution of the family to great civilizations has been made by the domestic unit. This type seems essential to high civilization. The trustee family never produced anything greater than the heroic epic. It belongs to the primitive formative periods of civilization. It is too decentralized, too localistic, for great civilization. The atomistic family, when it attains complete dominance, is the accompaniment of dying cultures. The creative periods in civilization have been based upon the domestic type. The end of a creative period is always one in which the domestic type is submerged in the atomistic. This seems due to the fact that the domestic family affords a comparatively stable social structure and yet frees the individual sufficiently from family influence to perform the creative work necessary for a great civilization.

A second corollary between family and civilization is that speculation about the family and the future course of civilization arises only when the atomistic type of family is coming into full control of society. The speculations of Socrates, Plato, and Aristotle coincided exactly with the period of rising atomism in Greece. These men wrote in the century following Pericles. They preceded the century which led to the final appraisal by Polybius of the great Greek civilization. The same correlation took place in Rome. During the third century, the historians of Rome began to report family decay on a wholesale scale. At the same time there arose a group of educated and sophisticated men—Basil, Jerome, and Augustine, for example—now called the Church Fathers, who raised the same fundamental questions regarding the social problems of Rome. They finally concluded that the trouble lay in the decay of human character. The Greeks perceived the relation between family and civilization only dimly; the Church Fathers saw the connection far more clearly.

We are again today confronted with the same crisis. The same problems, the same family type, and the same questions are facing us. Will we reach the same answers to the basic problems as did the Romans and the Greeks, or will our advance over the first Roman solutions be comparable to that of the Romans over the Greeks? As explained in the previous chapter, my own personal opinion is that the basic trouble has always been the family. I believe that the Greeks realized this only partially, the Romans more completely. I think it is possible, if there is anything more than blind cultural determinism and accident in history, that in this period we can clearly recognize and act upon this fundamental relation. However, this may be an overestimation of human intelligence.

A number of other questions also come to the forefront. One of these is, have these great swings of the family and civilization been inevitable? A few suggestions that might help answer this question follow.

In Western society, the upward swings of the family and civilization appear to have been inevitable. They were motivated by the eternal desire of man for the benefits of civilization. Pericles thought that the Athenians had something worth keeping, something that had been achieved slowly and at great cost. Every great culture has started with the feeling that it had a mission to perform. Each step the Romans took seemed forced upon them, in order that they might keep and extend the cultural gains of their earlier years. To do this they pacified Italy, then the Western Mediterranean, then the known world.

No sooner had the modern world achieved a stable social system, founded upon the domestic family condition of canon law, than it began to move forward. When the men of the Renaissance began to learn of the great civilizations that had preceded them, their eagerness to promote learning knew no bounds. Society seemed to leap forward in its eagerness to retrace the earlier classical steps to greatness. What society had, it wanted to keep and to promote. No antiquated family system must be allowed to prevent the rise and improvement of Western culture.

In the earlier period it had been the humanitarianism of Roman society that furnished the ethical documents of Christianity. These ethical conceptions were what finally enabled men to achieve the humanization of the earlier trustee family. It was Christianity that finally forced barbarian practices of blood vengeance and family rule to give way to compulsory public composition and amend. There was always the feeling that the "civilized" way of doing things was the "right" way, and one worth working for.

I do not believe that the downward swings have been so inevitable. If Alexander had lived in Greece during the first Peloponnesian War and had led the forces of either Athens or Sparta, the situation might have been entirely different. Pericles was not a good military strategist. He was a defensive fighter who wanted the Athenians to come within the city walls and leave the other forces to wear themselves out, instead of taking the initiative and being aggressive. Before the war was well started, typhus had decimated the crowded Athenians. If Athens and Sparta had gotten together to rule the Greek world, the story would have been entirely different. If Macedonia had stopped with the pacification of Greece, instead of wasting resources in the attempt to unite all the Eastern Mediterranean world at once, the story might have been different. In every case, a few individuals made the decisions. These individuals were dealing with matters concerning which they had little known historical experience to guide them. Philip wanted to consolidate Greece and might have stopped successfully at that. It was Alexander who formulated the plan of, and took the final steps for, an Asiatic campaign. In the same way, the fundamental decisions that will affect modern civilization and its family system will be made by a relatively few individuals.

What would have happened in the Roman Empire if the members of the Claudio-Julian line who followed Augustus had been the best of the family instead of the worst? What if Germanicus had ruled for several decades after Augustus? What if Agrippina the Elder, his wife, had become queen instead of her dissolute daughter Agrippina the Younger? If Commodus and Caracalla had been strangled or exiled to barren islands, what would have been the course of Roman history? What would have happened if at the start Christianity had had an established and clearcut doctrine of the family and a transition had been made immediately from the Augustan reforms to a familistic-moral doctrine backed by an intelligent understanding of its historical validity?

I do not believe that we know as yet the total influence of clearly established social ideas. We are facing the problem now in another field. This is in the field of atomic war, about which the physicists are unanimously agreed on one idea—avoid atomic war, or else!

I do not believe that all social change is of the drifting type—that it is "culturally determined," as the sociologists say. This denies the validity and usefulness of all knowledge in the social sciences. If this is so, every philosopher in the social sciences, from Socrates to the present, has been nothing but a troublemaker and a useless parasite.

This raises one fundamental question. Christianity arose from the decay of the family at the end of the Roman Empire. Prior to that time it was one of a number of faiths struggling for the mastery of the minds of the people within the Roman Empire. The finite uniqueness of its answer was in terms of familism. It is a potential storehouse of practical experience. Now, was Christianity a product purely of its period, and is it to pass away when modern civilization faces a similar devastating decline of familism? When the Greeks got into trouble with their family system, the only historical recourse available to them was the code of Solon. Homer did not help them meet this problem. When the Romans got into trouble, they gradually evolved the Christian doctrine of the family. It was a long road from Tertullian to Isidore. The question now is, has all this thinking been wasted? The low level of understanding of this problem in modern books on the family would indicate that it has. On the other hand, this need not be so.

In other words, have we Westerners evolved into a permanent civilization, finally catching on after the third attempt to arrive at the basic social realities? Or must there be another cataclysm? The garden variety of thinker, by his emphasis upon cultural determinism and his fatalism, seems to favor the cataclysm. He is more dangerous than a thousand Spenglers because it is his cynicism, his avoidance of the real issues, his willingness to be popular rather than scholarly, which makes it difficult for others to face the real issue. He wants to teach a family sociology composed entirely of invalid and unexamined clichés. "Divorce is but an escape from an already broken marriage." "The family is getting better and better every day." "If your boyfriend cries at the cinema, he will make a good husband." "Don't scold your wife at the breakfast table." (How about "Don't scold your husband at the breakfast table," too?) It is this type of thinker who rushes hotly to the defense of Freud. He is the modern Plutarch.

There seems some possibility that we have finally gotten safely on the bright side of the "dawn of conscience" and will remain there. But whether we have or not, the struggle over the modern family and its present rapid trend toward a climactic breakup will be one of the most interesting and decisive ones in all history. So much is at stake. Social processes are now so much more integrated than in previous crises. And, finally, the forces of both rejuvenation and decay are well armed. On the one hand we have the great Western historical experiences; on the other the antifamilistic pathway is made so easy for the masses (at least at first) and so popular among our modern Plutarchs.

However, all of this is largely problematical. The only thing that seems certain is that we are again in one of those periods of family decay in which civilization is suffering internally from the lack of a basic belief in the forces which make it work. The problem has existed before. The basic nature of this illness has been diagnosed before. After some centuries, the necessary remedy has been applied. What will be done now is a matter of conjecture. We may do a better job than was done before; we may do a worse one.

The Future

Theoretically the family might stay where it is now, it might decay further, or it might show a resurgence of Victorian morality. The probabilities are nil that the family system will remain in *status quo*. At no time in history has the family lain dormant for any length of time. This petrification is particularly unlikely when the family and the entire social fabric is changing rapidly. One of the salient characteristics of our whole society is rapid change. The family will probably keep on moving, in one direction or another. One of the reasons it cannot stop now is that it is already so completely atomized that it produces no stable social body in which to solidify. Its human products, children, are not sufficient to reproduce the society of which it is a part. Its psychological product, the human stuff of society, discussed in the last chapter, seems insufficient to give the society a workable, stable moral code widely enough accepted to enable the great society to hold together. Outside of a few limited circles, there simply seems to be no strong established systems of social belief. This phenomenon and its relation to the weakened atomistic family have been discussed in the previous chapter. It seems evident that the family cannot and will not stand still.

That the family of the immediate future will move further toward atomism seems highly probable. Except for the Christian church—which at present is not popular among the directive forces of Western society—no agency or group of persons seems fundamentally interested in doing anything other than facilitating this increasing atomism. New names for the decaying atomistic family, seeking to give it the prestige of improvement or progress, are constantly being invented. No matter what it really means, every slogan that now commands prestige is attached to the atomistic family. It and its extension toward further atomism are called liberal, humane, democratic, free, etc. Anyone who even suggests that the preservation of the familistic system is desirable is simply considered out of his head by the modern Plutarchs.

J. K. Folsom's *Family and Democratic Society*, New York, 1943, illustrates this trend of thinking on a wholesale scale. Here we find that Frederic Le Play's ideas on preserving France by trying to save the stem-family system are "fascistic" (95). But when he analyzes the modern fascist family in Germany (193 ff.), he shows an organization that has nothing in common with Le Play's ideas, from those on divorce, bastardy, and the position of women to homosexuality. The fascist type of family is really the dissolution of the family into a state institution, for the breeding of cannon fodder, along "Brave New World" conceptions. Fascism is a product of the atomistic personality and not of the Le Play type of mind. See also 237, where Folsom classifies Le Play and the Christian conception of the domestic family as military fascism. The fascist conception of the family is that of state regulation of the family entirely for state-military purposes. Le Play seemed more than anything else to favor the preservation in Europe of a few highly modified and domesticated trustee families. The church has always favored the domestic tradition. Folsom, who seems to favor extended atomism (until public order can be secured only by the "commanding, forbidding, allowing, and punishing" technique) calls every social institution antithetical to extended and decadent atomism "fascism." Hence, Folsom illustrates *par excellence* how many of the agencies of modern society are working day and night to extend atomism.

While Folsom's work has been singled out for discussion, it must not be reckoned as the only book of its type. With few exceptions, all modern books on the family are of this type, if we look beyond the lip service given to familism. The most common technique in reaching this point of view is to neglect the history of the family, so that the student has no well-documented intellectual background to hamper his wholesale acceptance of the glorification of present atomistic trends. The student who reads the modern book on the family is never given access to *any source* that would show him that mankind has trod this path before. When he reads the modern argument for dual marriage systems, or *alpha* and *beta* marriages, or for the conception that sex is "only another drink of water," he simply does not have adequate information available to realize that this is a reappearance of a family decay, *identical* to that which preceded the complete nihilism of the great cultures of Greece and Rome. No modern work on the family ever suggests this.

Consequently, we are directly bound to reach the conclusion that unless some unforeseen renaissance occurs, the family system will continue headlong its present trend toward nihilism. There is as yet no force with sufficient power, knowledge, and interest to prevent this current trend. National states, except when urgently in need of supplies of cannon fodder, have seemingly little interest in preserving the family. Their social processes are in the hands of the bureaucrats and the atomists. What knowledge exists of the family and its fundamentals is strictly limited to these two social classes and consists solely of a variegated amount of misinformation.

Furthermore, apparently we cannot relapse into a semiprotected decay as did the Greeks, who were sheltered under first the Macedonian and later the Roman umbrella. Greece could sink into its Hellenistic or twilight silver age under the aegis of these neighboring disciplinary powers. But Western society will find no such protection. There are no "hands that stretch across the sea" to comfort and protect us in our old age. We, product of "dragon seed," as Mommsen called us, will go as dragons when we go.

The Revival of Familism

Must we face this Spenglerian end? This is the fundamental question of the twentieth century. Is it not possible that social intelligence can mean something? Are history and sociology a futile record—merely an expensive accompaniment of the later stages of a predestined course? There seems to be little comfort in the answers to this question given by the cultural historians and the philosophers of history, whether those by G. Hansen, Brooks Adams, Corrado Gini, W. E. Flinders-Petrie, Arnold Toynbee, P. A. Sorokin, or others.

In sociology we sometimes speak of a theory of limits. When a movement goes so far in one direction, it seems to stir up antagonistic forces that bring about a return toward an old idea or a revision of an old idea. We have already discussed in the previous chapter how, in the field of the family, the atomistic family has already entered into the negative causation stages. The decay of the family system is forcing purely negatively into the social system those things which seem to make the society so weak that it cannot carry this atomization much further. In the past, this has eventually stirred up currents of resistance against atomism and these have finally overwhelmed it. However, this process has always taken time. It took so much time in the later Roman Empire that the people gave way to barbarian rule and control. Must these blind processes of social change carry on again? Must we propagandize for centuries for asceticism before we find that the real need is for children and familism?

In a theoretical sense, this need not be the course of modern society. We have the intelligence, and powerful enough educational and propaganda agencies, to bring about a revision and the more or less permanent reinstatement of familism. Public opinion could bring this about, once we were convinced of the truth of the causal analysis so elaborately proved in this book. There need be no communist, fascist, totalitarian, pseudodemocratic, or other kind of dictatorship to achieve this renaissance. All we really need is to educate our Plutarchs. Then they would shout for familism—and against antifamilism—with all the vehemence with which they take up other "causes."

One cannot tell whether such educated literati will arise. If such a group did emerge, they could make it extremely uncomfortable for the *agents provocateurs* of atomism whenever these appeared in modern society. The literary classes possess peculiar mental qualities of dogmatism and a pervasive pressure upon public opinion unknown to any other social class.

However, this Plutarchian class is at present unsure of itself. It feels the social situation to be grave but does not know what the answer to the problem should be. Most of its members are now convinced that the family is the hobgoblin of society. Most of them are in the enemy's camp. Many of them work on the problem, but turn up universally with the wrong answers.

The solution of the problem, other than in terms of the "commanding, forbidding, allowing, and punishing" technique, lies in the hands of our learned classes. They must understand the possibilities of a recreated conception of familism and its basic meaning to society. The commanding, forbidding, allowing, and punishing technique is probably no answer at all. It seems to be merely something that "Christian Emperors" and other reformers take up when the greater social system is already in a decadent and weakened state.

The answer to the problem may lie in scholarship and teaching. There is greater disparity between the actual, documented, historical truth and the theories taught in the family sociology courses than exists in any other scientific field.

When the answer to this great social problem is finally discovered, it will be found to lie in the making of familism and childbearing the primary social duties of the citizen. This will have to be voluntary—not compulsory. The solution will prove to be not in *fides* alone but in the strong union of *proles-fides*—children and familism.

Family and Civilization:
Carle Zimmerman Confronts
the West's Third Family Crisis

Bryce Christensen

T HE STRUGGLE OVER THE MODERN family and its present rapid trend toward a climactic breakup will be one of the most interesting and decisive ones in all history. So much is at stake.["] So writes Harvard sociologist Carle Zimmerman in his classic *Family and Civilization*, first published in 1947. Sixty years later, residents of the United States and other Western democracies do indeed find themselves in the midst of a climactic breakup of family life in which much is at stake. And few books offer more much-needed insight into our current social crisis than Zimmerman's remarkably prescient work. Even the book's most notable weakness—its faith in secular scholarship as a remedy for the family disintegration it both describes and anticipates—actually underscores the reasons for our current social crisis and further exposes the cultural forces that have produced it.

For many Americans the reality of that crisis might seem so obvious that we need no Harvard scholarship to recognize it. After all, as a prominent demographer acknowledged in 2006, "the share of children residing with two biological parents has been steadily declining [in recent years], and the proportion of children residing in stepfamilies or families formed outside of marriage, including single-parent and cohabiting families, are at all-time highs."[2]

The overall pattern of social statistics would indeed seem to signal a crisis in family life. Though the divorce rate has moderated a bit since the eighties, it remains more than 30 percent above that recorded in 1970.[3] Meanwhile, the national marriage rate has plummeted to an all-time low, more than 40 percent lower than it was in 1970.[4] The drop in the marriage rate, of course, helps account for the sharp rise in the illegitimacy rate: only one in twenty American births was out of wedlock in 1960; now more than one in three American births is out of wedlock.[5] While out-of-wedlock fertility has skyrocketed, overall American fertility has languished since the early 1970s, remaining below the zero population growth level of 2.1 births per American woman, so creating what some observers have called "the Birth Dearth."[6] The American population has continued to grow only because of immigration.

Even the social statistics indicating upward trends suggest a crisis in American family life. Americans see problematic growth in, for example, the number of couples cohabiting outside of wedlock. Once a relatively rare and scandalous occurrence, nonmarital cohabitation is now a widespread practice accounting for the unions of at least 5 million American couples.[7] Even more problematic growth is now evident in the number of homosexual couples whose unions are officially recognized as civil unions in some states and—defying every lexical tradition—as "marriage" in the state of Massachusetts.[8]

Given such a litany of social statistics, why do Americans need Zimmerman's 1947 scholarship to recognize a crisis in the nation's family life? We need Zimmerman's powerful book to help immunize us against the sophistry with which many elite Americans have explained—or rather, explained away—the disintegration of American family life. Such sophistry has been fully evident in America's public life since at least the mid-sixties, when Daniel Patrick Moynihan issued a federal report expressing deep concern about the way family life was unraveling among the nation's inner-city blacks. Moynihan worried about a "family structure [that had become] highly unstable, and in many urban centers

[was] approaching complete breakdown."⁹ For his trouble, Moynihan was lectured by sociologist Herbert Gans, who opined that "the matriarchal family structure and the absence of a father" was "a viable solution" to the problems blacks faced in urban life.¹⁰

Gans was joined by leftist Frank Reissman, who complained that Moynihan had myopically ignored the "powerful coping endeavors" blacks had developed within "the extended, female-based family."¹¹ In the same vein, feminist Laura Carper defended female-headed households among American blacks as one more instance of the "matriarchy" found among "many oppressed peoples throughout the history of Western civilization."¹² Some commentators reduced Moynihan's concerns about the disintegration of the black family to no more than his being "hung up on middle-class family norms."¹³ It is no wonder that one journalist has remarked that "there was seemingly no untruth to which some would not subscribe" in their attack on the Moynihan report.¹⁴

Unfortunately, the mendacity of antifamily sophists would continue long after the 1965–66 attack on Moynihan. It continued when the sexual revolutionaries of the sixties and seventies began spreading their family-killing poisons of pornography, fornication, and licentiousness. From the very beginning of their crusade against family-reinforcing moral principles, sexual revolutionaries found numerous sophists in academe, journalism, and the judiciary willing to support their cause. Professors and activist journalists helped swell the choir that praised Alfred Kinsey for publishing dishonest sexology scholarship, lauded William Masters and Virginia Johnson for converting sex into the relentless pursuit of the perfect climax, responded to *Hair*—that sixties paean to nudity and sex—with thunderous ovations, and marshaled arguments justifying the salacious activities of Hugh Hefner and other pornographers intent on what they themselves called "the Rape of the American Puritan Ethic."¹⁵

Typical of the nation's liberal intellectuals, sophist and sexologist Isadore Rubin explained in 1965 why he and professional colleagues had turned against marriage and family life: "The beginning of wisdom for educators is the recognition of the fact that the old absolutes are gone; that there exists a vacuum of many moral beliefs about sex."¹⁶ A great many college and university professors endorsed Rubin's dubious line of thought. It is thus in "the college community of the late 1960s and early 1970s" that author Carl Danzinger sees "the changing of norms and values" governing sexual behavior.[17] This change in norms and values accelerated under the influence of academics such as psychologist Lawrence Casler, who attacked "the ideal of sexual fidelity" and advocated a society of "transitory pairings" in which people would "certainly have a greater chance for sexual happiness, no longer restricted in their choice of bedmates by a set of artificial and outmoded social prohibitions."[18]

Though Casler might seem extreme, scores of professional therapists gathered in Chicago in 1978 to discuss "healthy aspects of extramarital aspects of extramarital relationships."[19] No wonder that the president of the American Association for Marriage and Family Therapy declared, "I wouldn't say that marriage and self-actualization are *necessarily* mutually exclusive. But they are difficult to achieve together."[20] With good reason, sociologist Robert Bellah discerns the emergence among such professionals of a "therapeutic attitude [that] denies all forms of obligation and commitment in relationships" and that "not only refuses to take a moral stand [but] actively distrusts 'morality.'"[21]

During the sixties and seventies, antifamily sophistry so pervaded "elite attitudes toward sex, marriage, divorce and parenthood" that sociologist Christopher Jencks recognizes it as a potent reason that during that era the marriages of "couples with neither money nor education" began to fail in record numbers. Disadvantaged couples who looked to the cultural elite for cues as to acceptable behavior saw little to encourage deep family or marital commitments.[22] And unfortunately, in recent years the middle class has begun to look to the antifamily sophistry of the elites almost as much as the underclass did in the late sixties and seventies. Middle-class vulnerability to sophistry thus helps explain why the marital, divorce, and illegitimacy statistics for the nation's white majority are now just as bad as those for blacks at the time Moynihan issued his prescient but much-derided report on the Negro Family.[23]

Nor have the antifamily sophists now working their malign magic on the white middle-class been any less vehement than those who helped destroy the families and marriages of blacks in the sixties and seventies. Indeed, like their predecessors these sophists have been particularly vocal in attacking those who dare to express concerns about contemporary trends in family life. Their response to *Marriage in America*, a 1995 warning from a distinguished group of historians, legal experts, and social scientists worried about the harmful social effects of an increasingly pervasive "culture of divorce and unwed motherhood," was typical.[24] Like an aroused hive of bees, academics, journalists, and judges have responded to this and similar warnings by attacking marriage and the family with even greater mendacity and shamelessness than did their predecessors in the sixties and seventies. Feminist Stephanie Coontz, for instance, has accused scholars who worry about family decline of falling into "the nostalgia trap," indicting them for a lack of "tolerance for alternative family forms."[25]

In the same spirit, psychologists Louise B. Silverstein and Carl F. Auerbach dismiss as fraudulent "the claim that there is one family structure, that is, the two-parent heterosexual married family, that [is] best for children," complaining that such a claim helps generate "a pseudoscientific rationale for defining nontraditional families as deficient."[26] And social scientists Mary Jo Bane and George Masnick recognize only one reason for "resistance to changes in our households and families": ignorance. They assert that such resistance can only reflect a "genuine lack of understanding of what is happening and why."[27]

Meanwhile, twenty-first century journalists manifest the same sophistic impulse when they continue to celebrate the sexual revolution as the liberation of a nation previously "hobbled by Puritan roots" and now finally awake to the joys of "sexual freedom."[28] These sophists of the popular press urge sexual libertines to "claim their own sexuality" by jettisoning the outmoded "Puritan value system."[29] Journalists giving modern sexual anarchy a cover of deceptive rhetoric will naturally view "the sexual revolution as a necessary liberation of the human body and spirit."[30]

Social scientists who have sounded warnings about family decline can only marvel at the fury of academics and journalists intent upon discrediting them. Sociologist Noval Glenn, for instance, sees in their writing "a vehemence uncharacteristic of most intellectual and academic debate."[31] The reasoning of the antifamily crowd has made sociologist Da-

vid Popenoe grieve that his colleagues would go to "sad, even heartrend-
ing . . . lengths . . . to distort the evidence and undeniable truths" about
the family as they "serve their own agendas."[32] But the sophistry that has
distressed and grieved sober social scientists such as Glenn and Popenoe
has simply confused many Americans, so weakening their commitment
to the moral principles that sustain successful marriages and families.

Recent clashes between realists such as Glenn and Popenoe on the
one hand and antifamily scholars such as Coontz and Bane on the other
would not have surprised Zimmerman. "Disagreement over the family,"
he comments in his landmark work, "is not new. On the contrary, it is
one of the oldest arguments of history" (2). Fortunately, Zimmerman's
great book helps twenty-first century Americans recognize where truth
collides with falsehood in this argument. The massive scholarship of
Family and Civilization unmistakably identifies recent changes in family
life as social decay and exposes the mendacity and illogic deployed by
those trying to explain away that decay as social progress or individual
liberation. Indeed, Zimmerman specifically warns his readers against "the
Pollyanna stories and pseudohistories" promulgated by sophists trying to
persuade the public that "the family [is] getting better all the time" (274).
Zimmerman identifies such mendaciously cheery-minded whiggism
as one of the influences through which "this process of atomization is
hastened" (274).

In scholarship that is impressively wide in its sweep (probing historical social patterns in Hindu, Chinese, Mediterranean, and European
societies), Zimmerman establishes beyond a reasonable doubt that family
breakdown poses a grave threat to modern Western civilization. Formi-
dable scholarship identifies "familism" as "the basic spring that [has]
furnished the essence of civilization" (262). In permissive modern social
attitudes, Zimmerman recognizes the emergence of "the idea of atomistic
man as the only unit in society,"[33] an idea whose cultural prominence
can only mean that "the Western world has entered a period of demoralization comparable to the periods when both Greece and Rome turned
from growth to decay" (174). Indeed, as he surveys social life in modern
America, Zimmerman catalogues various "forms of action and thought
. . . identical with those during the high period of atomism in Greece

[and] Rome" (255). This catalogue includes social characteristics all too familiar to twenty-first century Americans:

> Increased and rapid early "causeless" divorce . . .
> Decreased number of children . . .
> Elimination of the real meaning of the marriage ceremony . . .
> The spread of the antifamilism of the urbane and psuedointel-
> lectual classes . . .
> Breaking down of most inhibitions against adultery . . .
> Revolts of youth against parents so that parenthood bec[omes]
> more and more difficult . . .
> Common acceptance of all forms of sex perversions. (255)

Such family-destroying developments, Zimmerman warns, must ultimately prove "devastating to high cultural society" (19), underscoring his warning with analyses of how "the development of the atomistic family" helped bring low ancient Greece and Rome.[34] Comparing America's twentieth-century social trends with those evident in the histories of decadent Greece and Rome, Zimmerman hazards a prophecy: "This crisis will be identical in nature to the two previous crises in Greece and Rome. The results will be much more drastic in the United States because, being the most extreme and inexperienced of the aggregates of Western civilization, it will take its first real 'sickness' most violently" (274).

Some twenty-first century observers might question this prophecy, pointing out that Zimmerman expected "the final phases of [America's] great family crisis" before "the last of [the twentieth] century" (274). But this quibble counts for little. For even if the American family crisis had not yet reached its "final phases" by the end of the twentieth century, it had indeed grown very severe. The intensification of that crisis in the twenty-first century only makes Zimmerman's prescient analysis of our circumstances even more valuable.

The value of Zimmerman's work clearly manifests itself in the way it helps readers to understand that recent changes in family life constitute a civilization-threatening crisis. These readers realize that many of our most threatening social problems originate in family disintegration. Zimmerman well understood that "the antifamilism of times of high atomism is not good for society and hence inevitably becomes antithetical to the individual" (261); consequently, those who study his work recognize much of today's social and individual distress as the consequence of family decay.

Americans schooled by Zimmerman will know, for instance, the reason that American psychologists have in recent years been lamenting "an epidemic of mental disorders" and have been worrying in particular about "an earlier onset of depression through the twentieth century," resulting in "a sharp rise in rates of depression among adolescents and young adults."[35] Zimmerman's perceptive twenty-first century readers will discern the malign psychological consequences of family breakup even without reading the professional literature confirming the linkage between family breakup and clinical depression.[36]

In the same way, students of Zimmerman know very well precisely what social changes have incubated the criminality threatening modern America, especially the inner cities. The upsurge in crime in the second half of the twentieth century will puzzle few observers who recall that Zimmerman linked family breakdown to the "rapid rise and spread of juvenile delinquency" (255), that he perceived a grave danger to "the very continuity of our culture" in the rising tide of "nihilism in family behavior" (274), and that he predicted that the family crisis of the late twentieth century would affect American society "violently" (274).

Those familiar with Zimmerman fully anticipated the findings of recent scholarship identifying "the decline of stable two-parent families and the institution of marriage" as a "root cause of the wave of black inner-city male violence that began building during the 1960s and 1970s and rose again in the late 1980s and early 1990s."[37] Just as unsurprising for students of Zimmerman is criminological research showing that living in a broken home puts many children on a trajectory of criminality through adolescence and young adulthood,[38] that adolescents who watch their parents divorce are particularly vulnerable to the temptations of illegal drugs and alcohol,[39] and that the prevalence of single-parent households in an area predicts its crime rate more reliably than does its racial makeup.[40]

And while others may wonder why many of today's adolescents fail in school or today's adults shrink from the burdens of citizenship, students of Zimmerman recognize that academic achievement and civic virtue must wane in a society losing its families and marriages. After all, within Zimmerman's perceptive vision, familism constitutes "the basic spring which furnishe[s] the essence of civilization" (262).

No one who shares Zimmerman's vision will marvel at the findings of research showing that family disruption and maternal employment both result in lower academic attainment among the children affected.[41] Schools, after all, can hardly perpetuate the essence of civilization when its "basic spring" has been broken or weakened.

Of course, a family breakdown that weakens society's "basic spring" harms society in ways that show up outside the classroom. Sociologists thus merely confirm what students of Zimmerman already know when they report that high divorce rates predict "low rates of participation in community politics, recreation (e.g., YMCA), and educational activities."[42] Zimmerman's pupils know that a crisis in family life must inevitably translate into a decline in "social civility"—as evidenced in low rates of "volunteering, civic association membership, voting, and religious participation."[43] And when twenty-first century sociologists worry aloud that family disintegration means the loss of "the essential glue of a moral society," Zimmerman's students hear but an echo of his sobering voice.[44]

Zimmerman's students hear their teacher not only when honest scholars acknowledge the harmful effects of family disintegration but also when candid political philosophers question policymakers trying to compensate for family failure by building larger government bureaucracies. After all, Zimmerman predicted that as the nation's family crisis deepened, "social work agencies and other meliorative agencies . . . [would] find themselves increasingly inadequate to deal with the problem" (277). Zimmerman further anticipated that as social work agencies foundered in their attempts to deal with the family crisis, "the state w[ould] step in with increasingly drastic measures or different attempts at control" (277). But Zimmerman recognized that "unless these state measures are wisely considered, they will only make the situation more confused and difficult" (277).

Oxford scholar Basil Mitchell is thus not breaking new ground but simply validating Zimmerman's concerns when he points out that government policies that ignore or attack the family must invariably "weaken the moral ties which bind society together," resulting in "an increasingly heavy burden on the State apparatus." Mitchell compellingly explains the statist pathology that Zimmerman anticipated:

> [T]he greater the number of marriage breakdowns, the greater the number of one-parent families in need of support; the greater the number of sexual relationships in which no definite responsibilities are assumed, the greater the insecurity of any children born to them; while in turn, the official acceptance of such relationships, combined with an emphasis on the needs of children as the sole consideration tends inevitably to diminish the standing of marriage. . . . So there are more casualties for the State to rescue, and the more single-mindedly it concentrates on this task, the more unmanageable the task becomes.[45]

Popenoe joins Mitchell in validating Zimmerman's prescient concerns about misguided government responses to the family crisis. Surveying decades of attempts to rescue the family through welfare-state policies, Popenoe concludes that "the inherent character of the welfare state by its very existence help[s] to undermine family values or familism—the belief in a strong sense of family identification and loyalty, mutual assistance among family members and a concern for the perpetuation of the family unit."[46]

If twenty-first century Americans still entertain doubts about Zimmerman's views after reading Mitchell and Popenoe, they can dispel those doubts by turning to the growing statist disaster evident in the nation's government policies on foster care and child-support collection. Though their motives are often laudable, the government leaders responsible for these policies have amply validated Zimmerman's prediction that the nation's family crisis would swamp social-service agencies and would prompt state officials to enact "drastic" measures that would only make a bad situation "more confused and difficult." Because they have shrunk from the task of combating illegitimacy and divorce, government officials have engineered a massive but failing foster-care system that looks more and more like "a bureaucratic concentration of [the] problems . . . of family decay," including child abuse and mental illness.[47] Similarly, government policymakers who refuse to reinforce wedlock but who want to compensate for its failures are making life "more confused and difficult" for millions of bewildered Americans. For in creating a huge computerized system for collecting child-support from fathers, they have increasingly treated innocent fathers as "quasi-criminals, perpetually under corrective supervision" within an error-prone but perilously intrusive judicial system.[48]

Academics and intellectuals have been slow to recognize the political and social dangers in the "drastic" measures that state officials increasingly rely on to compensate for family failure. But then, much to his credit, Zimmerman detected the peril in the modern "alliance" between a secular state and the deracinated intellectual. Tracing the history of this alliance, Zimmerman limns the history of this alliance and explains its origins, noting how "the state . . . [had] become jealous of the joint control it [had previously] exercised with the church over the family and social systems. Slowly and surely the state broke this alliance in favor of a new unity with the intellectual and reasoning type of man, as opposed to the traditionalist with his emphasis upon the former system of values" (117). Zimmerman puts his readers on guard against this "new hybrid, a cross between the questioning intellectual and the growing state," by indicting this "union between the state and the intellectual" as an essential part of the strategy through which "the atomistic family was achieved" (118). Just where the new intellectual must place his primary loyalty is all too apparent to Zimmerman, for this is a new social type who can "continue to function [only] as long as his actions [are] work[ing] to the benefit of the state" (118).

Zimmerman's monitory analysis of the dubious collaboration between the modern intellectual and the modern state counts for more and more as a growing army of intellectuals undermine the family while justifying "expanding surrogate family services by welfare, police, and public health officials."[49] The state grows as the family withers.

Indeed, many of the statist intellectuals about whom Zimmerman expresses concerns have been passionate admirers of the ideological social visions advanced in utopian works such as Edward Bellamy's *Looking Backward: 2000–1887* (1888), William Morris's *News from Nowhere* (1891),

H. G. Wells's *A Modern Utopia* (1905), Charlotte Perkins Gilman's *Moving the Mountain* (1911), and B. F. Skinner's *Walden Two* (1948). Though these blueprints for utopia differ significantly in their details, all propose the creation of the ideal society through the weakening or outright abolition of marriage and family.⁵⁰ Not content with contemplating mere literary depictions of such a society, the kind of intellectuals Zimmerman saw in dubious alliance with the state have done much to translate the antifamily tenets of utopian ideology into real-world government policy. Writing in 1963, political theorist George Kateb conceded that "a sufficient anti-utopian case could be made to rest on the sanctity of the family," but he nonetheless considered "anti-utopian positions on the nature of government" to be "out of touch even with what had already become part of the political life of the United States, the British Commonwealth, and Scandinavia."⁵¹

Remarkably immune himself to the utopian virus that has infected so many modern intellectuals, Zimmerman decisively parts company with social reformers traveling "the antifamilistic pathway" (281): these are his foes, people "in the enemy's camp" (286). Such intellectuals view "the family [as] the hobgoblin of society" (286) and so fail to guide society "back to [its] fundamental mother-source—familism" (262). Readers indeed have every reason to be impressed by Zimmerman's refusal to join other modern intellectuals in antifamily utopian fantasies and by his acute analysis of the danger in the modern alliance between the state and the secular intellectual.

But what, then, are these readers to make of Zimmerman's concluding assertion that "the solution of the problem [of social disorder] . . . lies in the hands of our learned classes" (286)? What are they to make of his claim that "the answer to the problem may lie in scholarship and teaching" (286)? What can they make of his call for "some broad research agency to study the problem of the impending crisis of the family" (277)? This assertion, this claim, and this call constitute a very dubious culmination to an analysis that has put the reader on guard against the "hybrid" alliance of the growing state and the skeptical modern intellectual. For who, after all, would sponsor such an agency if not the state? And who would most of those serving on this agency be if not secular modern intellectuals of the very sort Zimmerman sees helping to promote antifamily ideologies? And would not the very establishment of such an agency fit very neatly into the agenda of those in favor of state growth?

It can only astound many of Zimmerman's most careful readers that he somehow reaches the final page of his *Meisterwerk* believing that "our learned classes" can be brought to "understand the possibilities of a recreated conception of familism and its basic meaning to society" (286). For Zimmerman's own analysis repeatedly fosters doubt and not faith in the deracinated secular intellectuals who now make up our learned classes. This analysis shows readers that "modern thinking about the family" often entails a theoretical commitment to "the constant linear or stair-step movement toward human betterment, consist[ing] in the dropping of family bonds and the perpetual creation of new types of families" (19). Intellectuals devoted to effecting such "human betterment" will naturally consider "the old-fashioned family" as "a force holding back the general development and freedom of a people."[52] Such views lead inevitably to "the revolutionary conception that social institutions, such as the family, should be destroyed in order to further progress."[53] Utopia beckons, and modern intellectuals press toward it, smashing family ties as they go.

Despite the antifamily ideologies he finds among many modern intellectuals, Zimmerman does hold out hope for the "Institutional School" of family scholars, a school he finds "more in line [than their utopian colleagues] with the empirical world that we know."[54] It is undoubtedly these empirically minded scholars that Zimmerman believes can yet lead our "learned classes" back to family integrity and social strength. It is such empiricists that Zimmerman has in view when he contemplates the modern crisis in family life and then asserts, "Family sociology is the field in which, under certain conditions, the social thinker can get closest to absolute and basic cause. Family sociology, in many of its ramifications, comes the closest to infinite cause demonstrable in a finite universe" (256). It is thus the etiological probings of empirically minded family sociologists that embolden Zimmerman when cultural determinists predict a future of complete family disintegration. Zimmerman rejects such a prediction because "it denies the validity and usefulness of all knowledge in the social sciences" (280).

Zimmerman's own parsing of the sociological data, however, actually fosters little faith in the power of social science to cure the modern diseases afflicting the family. The very best social scientists—and this would surely include Zimmerman—deliver a convincing and timely diagnosis of our family-destroying malady, but they offer nothing like a cure.

The impossibility of using the best social science to cure the epidemic destroying modern American families manifests itself, to begin with, in its cultural impotence among the elite classes who are best situated to access it and best able to understand it. Zimmerman acknowledges that the twentieth century witnessed "prominent logicians and mathematicians writ[ing] against marriage and family," while "smart circles" so readily lent their support to cultural attacks on wedlock that the institution was "prostituted in the press, radio, [and] divorce mills" (122). It is back to "urbane and pseudointellectual classes" that Zimmerman traces the contagion of "antifamilism" (255). No wonder Zimmerman detected "contempt for familism" within America's "so-called educated circles," circles in which he could not see "even the intellectual honesty of the Greeks or Romans," who at least acknowledged the signs of decadence when their family life disintegrated (174).

Zimmerman discerned little intellectual honesty in "current writers," among whom "the most prevalent idea is that the family has merely to achieve the freeing of the individual to arrive at its 'ideal,'" as the family is transformed so as "not [to] interfere with our love affairs, either hetero- or homosexual" (273). When dependent on such purblind authors, readers can only expect what Zimmerman finds: namely, a "low level of understanding . . . in modern books on the family" (281). Zimmerman finds intellectual honesty about family disintegration absent even among "family sociologists," whom he indicts for spreading misleading but comforting "Polyanna stories" about how "the family [is] getting better and better" (274). Zimmerman even acknowledges that "there is greater disparity between the actual, documented, historical truth and the theories taught in the family sociology courses than exists in any other scientific field" (286). Far from renewing and strengthening family life, such family sociology has only helped make "the antifamilistic pathway . . . popular among our modern Plutarchs" (281).

After reading Zimmerman's own timely and well-aimed attacks on modern intellectuals, the reader can only wonder how he could repose so much trust in the nation's "learned classes," so much faith in the effects of "scholarship and teaching." After all, when it comes to family issues, modern intellectuals are substituting sophistry for good scholarship even in—perhaps especially in—the family sociology courses where such scholarship merits the closest attention. Nor will a survey of the scholarship and teaching during the fifty years since the publication of *Family and Civilization* significantly lessen the reader's doubts about Zimmerman's desperate and self-contradictory turn toward the learned classes and scholarship as an antidote to family decline. To a depressing degree, after all, such scholarship and teaching amounts to no more than repetition of the comfortable mendacities of sophists such as Coontz, Silverstein, and Auerbach.

It may seem churlish and ungrateful for readers who highly value Zimmerman's dissection of the modern crisis in family life to resist the measures he proposes as a resolution of that crisis. But in truth, it is hard to see how a serious reader can do anything but resist those measures if he takes to heart Zimmerman's own perceptive analysis of the role of the modern intellectual and elite classes in producing that crisis. In a peculiar way, Zimmerman's final reliance on the secular intellectuals and research that his own analysis cast into doubt renders his diagnosis of our civilizational crisis all the more urgent and convincing. If even a scholar as learned and profound as Zimmerman remains within the thralldom of the type of secular-statist intellectuals who have created the very crisis he diagnoses, then our situation is truly as desperate as his book indicates.

That resolving modern America's family crisis would require cultural inspiration which secular intellectuals and researchers cannot provide was well understood by one of the social scientists Zimmerman most respected and from whose work he appropriately drew. Sociologist Pitirim A. Sorokin, the first chairman of Harvard's sociology department and one of Zimmerman's closest colleagues, adduces considerable evidence—cited by Zimmerman—that family life was eroding in modern America and would surely continue to do so in the years ahead:

> The family as a sacred union of husband and wife, of parents and children, will continue to disintegrate. Divorces and separations will increase until any profound difference between socially sanctioned marriages and illicit sex-relationship disappears. Children will be separated earlier and earlier from parents. The main sociocultural functions of the family will further decrease until the family becomes a mere incidental cohabitation of male and female while the home will become a mere overnight parking place for sex relationship. (cited in Zimmerman, 273)

This part of Sorokin's dark but all-too-accurate prophecy of the future of American family life very much accords with the themes and principles of Zimmerman's analysis. Unfortunately, Zimmerman did not quote—and possibly did not even accept—the part of Sorokin's prediction that identified his hopes for the eventual renewal of America's family life. Sorokin pinned his best hopes for family renewal not to the nation's "learned classes," nor to "a broad research agency," nor to "scholarship and teaching." Sorokin interpreted family disintegration not in isolation but rather as just one of the death tremors of a failing sensate culture.

"Nobody can revive the dying sensate order," Sorokin admitted. He therefore anticipated that the collapse of the sensate culture would mean "tragedy, suffering, and crucifixion for the American people." But he envisioned a future in which a chastened and humbled people would recover strong marriages and strong family lives as they listened to "new Saint Pauls, Saint Augustines, and great religious and ethical leaders."[55]

A vision of family renewal catalyzed by "new Saint Pauls, Saint Augustines, and great religious and ethical leaders" will strike many of Zimmerman's readers as far more plausible than Zimmerman's own hopes for renewing family life through the efforts of the nation's "learned classes," the work of "a broad research agency," and the influence of "scholarship and teaching." Zimmerman's formula for resolving the looming family crisis did not seem entirely convincing even to himself. When he points to the work of the nation's "learned classes" as a source of renewal his model is revealingly tentative: "The answer to the problem *may* lie in scholarship and teaching" (286, emphasis added). And when he asserts the ability of informed modern Americans to "clearly recognize and act upon [the] fundamental relationship [between family and civilization]," he concedes that he might be indulging in "an overestimation of human intelligence" (278).

And if Zimmerman's plan for renewing family life through scholarship reflects "an overestimation of human intelligence," it quite possibly reflects an underestimation of the role of religion in sustaining marriage and family. To be sure, Zimmerman recognizes "the close relationship between the family and religion" (258). In particular, he acknowledges that in the world created by the collapse of the Roman Empire, it was "the church . . . [that was the decisive influence in] impressing upon the demoralized peoples of Europe the essence of sacrament in marriage and family life" (89). But as he looks to the future, Zimmerman questions rather than affirms the enduring power of religious faith: "Was," he asks, "Christianity a product purely of its period, and is it to pass away when modern civilization faces a similar devastating decline of familism?" (281). Zimmerman provides no clear answer to this question. Nor, as he voices his hopes in a family renewal dependent upon the "learned classes," "a broad research agency," "scholarship and teaching," does he anywhere indicate that he is waiting for "new Saint Pauls, Saint Augustines, and great religious and ethical leaders."

Zimmerman's failure to include religious leaders in his vision of the future of the family life is all the more striking given that his own trenchant analysis undercuts rather than fosters confidence in the nation's learned classes, the research agencies they control, and the scholarship and teaching they perform. Had he been less willing to relegate to the past the influence of religion on the family, Zimmerman might have realized that even the best empirical scientists will never sway secular intellectuals who, having jettisoned traditional faiths, have embraced utopian-progressive statism as a surrogate metaphysical creed.[56] Only a genuine faith can combat the temptations of a counterfeit. Only new Saint Pauls and Saint Augustines can break the family-destroying spell of progressive utopianism and fortify intellectuals and the general populace with the integrity necessary to resist the gravitation of the burgeoning secular state.

Zimmerman understood perhaps as well any twentieth-century social scientist how that gravitation had helped subvert the traditional family. After all, he highlights the way collaboration between the burgeoning state and the intellectuals serving its interests helped foster the emergence of "the atomistic family" and weaken the family-reinforcing cultural influence of church and tradition. Perhaps Zimmerman should have pondered longer the implications of his own analysis. State officials naturally grow more powerful when religious leaders lose cultural sway and inherited traditions fade into social irrelevance. Families naturally grow weaker as a consequence of this cultural displacement. But once this displacement is well advanced, even many of the best scholars find its dynamic difficult to resist.

Zimmerman's readers owe him fervent thanks for his prodigious labors in diagnosing and analyzing our current family crisis. But to deliver us out of that crisis, it is surely time to start looking for—even praying for—new Saint Pauls and Saint Augustines.

Demography is destiny:
The fate of the Western family
and Western civilization

James Kurth

Two Revolutionary Transformations in the West

During the past half-century, the family has undergone a revolutionary transformation in all of the West. What was once a common extended-family structure has shrunk first to a nuclear-family structure and then, during the past quarter-century, to a nonfamily phenomenon, i.e., a widespread pattern of no truly dense family relationships at all. We now seem to be nearing the terminal end of the traditional family, with a majority of marriages ending in divorce and reinvented as serial marriage, with most marriages issuing in only one or even no child, and with homosexual marriage or "civil unions" being legalized by an increasing number of courts and legislatures throughout the West. This transformation of the Western family has alarmed and appalled social and cultural conservatives, particularly Christian ones; at the same time, it has been promoted and applauded by social and cultural liberals and progressives, particularly by feminist ones.

The decline, perhaps even the death, of the Western family is thus a principal topic of concern among a large section of conservatives. It is very appropriate, therefore, that this topic is discussed at length in the essays by Allan Carlson and Bryce Christensen that are part of this volume.

At the same time that the Western family has undergone this transformation, Western civilization itself has undergone its own revolutionary transformation. What was once a common conception, even a grand alliance, among the nations of Western Europe, North America, and even Oceania (i.e., Australia and New Zealand) has broken apart into conflicting conceptions. This division has occurred not just between the United States and the other nations but also within many of these nations and especially within the United States. The political, intellectual, and cultural elites of the West for the most part no longer believe in the values and principles that used to be ascribed to Western civilization, particularly those which were held by two of the traditions which shaped the West, the classical culture and the Christian religion.[1] Rather, these elites believe in the values of multiculturalism, universalism, feminism, and "postmodernism," which also can be seen as "post-Western" ideologies. Moreover, they believe that this transformation of Western civilization into a post-Western, or multicultural and universal, civilization represents the steady, seemingly inevitable progress toward the fulfillment of the values and principles of that third tradition which has shaped the West, i.e., the Enlightenment.[2]

The Islamic Transformation in the West

Unfortunately for these contemporary believers in the Enlightenment doctrine of progress, something important has happened within Western Europe in the past two decades, which is now challenging their complacency. This is the steady, seemingly inevitable growth of alienated and even anti-Enlightenment communities composed of Muslim immigrants and also their offspring who have been born within the European countries.[3] These Muslim communities are not just post-Western like our political, intellectual, and cultural elites; they are consciously anti-Western. Like Islam itself, these communities have always rejected Western civilization, and they now wish to replace it with some kind of an alternative Islamic civilization.

This Islamic transformation has not exactly been promoted and applauded by liberals and progressives in Western Europe (where they often call themselves social democrats or socialists). However, such people have certainly been confused and feckless about what to do about this transformation. They have been intellectually and morally disarmed by their own ideologies of universalism and multiculturalism, which they derive from the Enlightenment.

The Enlightenment, especially in its French but also in its Anglo-American version, has been especially committed to the idea of universality, and with it a disdain for the particularities of time, place, culture, and religion. Indeed, the Enlightenment worldview does not take either the classical culture or the Christian religion seriously (its French version actively despises Christianity); it holds that religious or cultural traditions provide no good reason to exclude anyone from immigrating to an enlightened society. Similarly, the Enlightenment thinker has not traditionally taken the Muslim culture or the Islamic religion seriously, but rather has tended to assume that a Muslim who is exposed to or immigrates to an enlightened society will eventually give up the Islamic faith and become an enlightened, universal individual like everyone else. Thus, what the Enlightenment tradition takes seriously is the imperative of universalism. Accordingly, the indiscriminate admission of immigrants, including Muslim immigrants, into Western nations has not only been permitted by this particular, and peculiar, Western tradition; it has been seen as its fulfillment.

Conservatives in Western Europe have not been intellectually and morally disarmed by universalism and multiculturalism in the same way as liberals and progressives. Many have been alarmed and appalled by the Islamic transformation; however, they too have been confused and feckless about what to do about it. They have been intellectually and morally disarmed not so much by their own ideologies, as is the case with the liberals and progressives, but by the economic interests of one of their largest and most important sectors, i.e., businesspeople. These people want the cheap labor force that immigrants provide. Together, the cultural ideologies of the Left and the business interests of the Right have formed a grand coalition in favor of admitting large numbers of Muslim immigrants, and therefore, in effect, in favor also of the Islamic transformation within the Western European nations.

The Connection between the Western Family and Western Civilization

Most social and cultural conservatives in the West have not put the two dynamics, or two declines—that of the Western family and that of Western civilization itself—together. Conservatives of course see each as a problem, but most tend to focus on only one of them to the exclusion of the other. In fact, however, these two dynamics are now, have been, and will continue to be causally related. It is therefore amazing that Carle Zimmerman saw these dynamics and their connection and that he wrote a great book about it sixty years ago—*Family and Civilization*.

Today, when social and cultural conservatives look back upon the time in which Zimmerman wrote, the late 1940s, they often see it as a sort of golden age. Although in the America of that day there was already a great deal of concern about the increasing incidence of divorce, the nuclear family still seemed to be strong and largely intact. In Europe, divorce was rare and not only was the nuclear family strong, but even the extended family was common. And both America and Europe were just beginning a great baby boom that would banish for decades any discussion of the declining birthrates that Zimmerman expected. This robust nuclear family and robust baby boom would last in the West for most of the next two decades, until the mid-1960s. Overall, the condition of the Western family seemed to be very good.

Of course, the condition of Western civilization was a matter of great concern in the late 1940s. Europe had nearly destroyed itself in two world wars over the preceding three decades, in what had amounted to a new and terrible Thirty Years' War (1914–45). Moreover, the Soviet Union and international communism posed a great threat to the nations of the West.

James Kurth

Although some sophisticated commentators saw communism as a sort of heresy of Western civilization, for almost everyone else Soviet communism seemed to be very much an Eastern—and anti-Western—ideology and even to be a kind of barbarism, an anti-civilization.

However, the very clarity of this Eastern, barbarian threat wonderfully concentrated the minds of the American elites of that era and motivated and energized them to take the lead in the formation of a grand alliance of Western nations (particularly the North Atlantic Treaty Organization, or NATO). They also took the lead in legitimizing this grand alliance by constructing a broad, deep, and shared conception of Western civilization. This robust Western alliance and robust Western ideology would last for most of the next two decades, until the mid-1960s.

The Zimmerman Vision

Carle Zimmerman looked beyond those next two decades and saw the longer run and the deeper forces that would eventually shape the future of the Western family and Western civilization. Moreover, these forces have decisively shaped the realities of our own time, and they will continue to shape them. Indeed, what Zimmerman saw then very well may reveal our end and our fate.

Zimmerman could see so far into the future because he could see so far into the past. He looked back in particular to the original predecessor of Western civilization, the classical civilization of ancient Greece and Rome. He also examined medieval Europe and the modern West.

The Stages of Family Structure and Civilization

Zimmerman traced the evolving dynamics of the family through three successive stages, which he termed (1) the "trustee" family, whose ideal type is the tribe or clan bound by dense and intense ties of blood and honor and which is commonly found in pastoral and agrarian societies;

(2) the "domestic" family, whose ideal type is the extended or nuclear family bound by deep ties of faith and fidelity and which is commonly found in societies that have become partly urbanized and commercialized; and (3) the "atomistic" family, whose ideal type is simply a couple of individuals and perhaps a child or two, who are bound by contractual but changeable ties of self-interest—a very thin nuclear family or even a nonfamily—and which is commonly found in highly urbanized, commercialized, and educated societies, such as those in the modern (and now postmodern) West.

Zimmerman also traced the evolving dynamics of civilization through successive stages. The different stages of pastoral, agrarian, urban, and commercial development obviously will have a shaping effect upon family structure and will help to bring about the different stages of trustee, domestic, and atomistic development. Different stages of economic development offer different kinds of incentives and disincentives to the different members of a family, influencing the transformation of families from one type into another. However, the reverse cause-and-effect pattern also operates. The different stages of trustee, domestic, and atomistic development will have their own shaping effects upon the character of civilization and will help to bring about not only the different stages of pastoral, agrarian, and urban/commercial development but also different qualities and degrees within these stages.

By the 1940s, Zimmerman concluded, Western civilization had largely arrived at the stage of the atomistic family and indeed at a rather late phase of that stage. The atomistic or individualistic family especially tends toward being no family at all and particularly to having few or no children. The fall in reproduction rates and population levels characteristic of the atomistic family eventually brings about the fall of the civilization itself.

Zimmerman's extensive description in 1947 of the consequences of the atomistic family will sound familiar to observers of our own society today:

> In general when a social system reaches the later phases of developed atomism in family relations, it reaches a state where the following

forms of behavior gain great prominence. These are forms of action and thought that are identical with those during the high periods of atomism in Greece, Rome, and the modern world. They are as follows:

1. Increased and rapid easy "causeless" divorce. (Guilty and innocent party theory became a pure fiction.)

2. Decreased number of children, population decay, and increased public disrespect for parents and parenthood.

3. Elimination of the real meaning of the marriage ceremony.

4. Popularity of pessimistic doctrines about the early heroes.

5. Rise of theories that companionate marriage or a permissible looser family form would solve the problem.

6. The refusal of many other people married under the older family form to maintain their traditions while other people escape these obligations. (The Greek and Roman mothers refused to stay home and bear children.)

7. The spread of the antifamilism of the urbane and pseudointellectual classes to the very outer limits of the civilization. . . .

8. Breaking down of most inhibitions against adultery.

9. Revolts of youth against parents so that parenthood became more and more difficult for those who did try to raise children.

10. Rapid rise and spread of juvenile delinquency.

11. Common acceptance of all forms of sexual perversions. (255)

Although the next two decades seemed to represent a reversal of the Zimmerman cycle and even a restoration of a robust Western family and robust Western civilization, with the 1960s both the family and the civilization regressed back to the downward trend of the cycle. They have continued in this downward direction until today.

Demography Is Destiny

Demographers observe that, in order for a particular population to sustain its numbers at its current level, it should have an average reproduction rate of 2.1 births per woman. The reproduction rate for almost every Western nation has fallen beneath 1.5 during the last couple of decades (and for Italy and Spain, formerly the European nations with the highest birthrates, it is now beneath 1.2). Although the United States has a growing population, that population growth is entirely due to immigration and to the higher reproduction rates of peoples of non-European origin. Among most European-American groups, the reproduction rates are also beneath the level of sustainability. When one projects these demographic statistics forward, it would appear inevitable that, in half a century, most European nations or peoples will have only two-thirds or half the population that they have today. Furthermore, a much larger percentage of that population will be old and no longer able to work.

The reproduction rates of most Western peoples began their decline in the 1960s. At the beginning of that decade, after almost two decades of a baby boom in all Western nations, almost no one expected the imminent end of that boom and its replacement with a baby dearth. What brought about this sudden and surprising fall in the birth rate?

Certainly technological changes contributed to the demographic change. The great expansion in access first to contraception (the Pill) in the 1960s and then to abortion in the 1970s obviously meant that women (and also, in their own way, men) experienced a great expansion in their capacity to choose not to have children. Moreover, there were underlying sociological and economic changes going on. First, in the 1950s there was within all Western nations a great increase in urbanization, a great migration from the farm to the factory. Urbanization historically had been associated with the (eventual) lowering of the birth rate—the well-known "demographic transition"—and so it was now. Second, in the 1960s there was within the urban centers of the West a great increase in clerical and technical workers, and these office workers were disproportionately women. The result was a different kind of great migration, one from the home to the office. In short, from the 1950s to the 1970s the nations of the West underwent a great increase first in industrialization and then in post-industrialization. Children, who had been economic assets for their parents when they were on the farm, ceased to be so when the parents were in the city, and indeed for women working in the office they became actual inconveniences or even burdens.[4] The 1950s–70s also was the time of the great transformation from a producer economy to a consumer economy, with the concomitant development of a consumerist ideology ("consumer sovereignty") whose central value was self-gratification.

These vast technological, sociological, and economic changes of the 1950s–70s affected everyone, of course, but their impact was greatest upon the young, i.e., upon the baby-boomer generation as it entered adolescence and then early adulthood. The natural, but paradoxical, result was that many baby boomers chose not to have babies, and thus it was that the generation of the baby boom brought about the generation of the baby dearth.

The Final Conclusion of Individualism

Looking back now from the vantage point of several decades, we can see that these technological, sociological, and economic changes were probably inevitable and therefore that some kind of ideological and cultural changes were probably inevitable too. However, the specific and radical changes in ideology and culture that actually occurred were probably not inevitable; there is a good deal more contingency and choice in regard to changes in the mental realm than in the material one. In particular, traditional theologies and ideologies that put family obligations at the center of life came under attack and were replaced with new and radical ideologies like "expressive individualism." Familism was replaced with feminism. The adoption of these new ideologies was a matter of personal choice.

By itself, however, the logic of unconstrained individualism leads to demographic decline. Persons who see themselves first and foremost as freely choosing individuals will normally choose to have few children. They also will normally choose to minimize the sacrifices that they make for these few. Rich individualists (and there are many of these in contemporary Western societies) will be able to sacrifice money (since they have a lot of it), but they will be much less likely to sacrifice time (of which they have much less, and certainly not enough to expend on more than one or two children). This partly explains why, for so many such children in the West (or post-West) today, childhood is a *faux* paradise filled with expensive consumer goods and fragile human ties. Poor individualists (and there are also many of these in contemporary Western societies) will be both unable to sacrifice money and unwilling to sacrifice time for their children. This partly explains why, for so many poor children in the West today, childhood is a disaster area, a howling wilderness. In any event, be they spoiled rich children or deprived poor children, they are likely to become even more compulsively individualist than their individualist parents.

Individual Choice: The Abandonment of the Christian Faith

Hypothetically, the atomistic family system and its individualist value system could be overcome with different value systems that put the family, including children, at their center. As Zimmerman shows, this historically was the case with value systems based upon tribal membership, religious faith, or communal identity. He sees religious faith as especially important in establishing and maintaining the "domestic" family system, which to him is the most solid base for a robust civilization. (As a slogan familiar in the 1950s put it, "the family that prays together, stays together.") It is no accident that in the United States today the people with the highest birth rates are those who are members of traditional religions, especially those with dense communal ties (i.e., evangelical Protestants, traditional Catholics, and, especially, Mormons and Orthodox Jews).

In the West during the modern era (beginning in the sixteenth century and culminating in the early twentieth century), tribal identity was left behind, but religious identity remained strong. This was true in most Western nations even as late as the 1950s. The Christian religion provided its believers with an origin in the past, a role in the present, a vision of the future, and a cosmic meaning in one's children, who were integral parts, as Edmund Burke put it, of the great "contract between the living, the dead, and the yet to be born."

However, all that was half a century ago, and we are now in the West of the postmodern era. In Europe especially, there is virtually nothing left of the Christian faith. As visitors to Europe can readily observe, what most Europeans now believe in most is individualism and hedonism.

The story of the decline of the Christian faith in Europe is complex. But the main reason that the Europeans of the baby boomer and later generations have abandoned Christianity is that it explicitly stood in the way of their expressive individualism, their self-centered desire to be free of any religious and communal restraints. In short, Europeans have abandoned the faith of their ancestors not because of the force of historical events, but because of a free act of will (or of willfulness).

In any event, the only peoples in Europe who now seem to hold views and values that encourage large families (e.g., those based upon tribal membership, religious faith, or communal identity) are the communities that are formed by Muslim immigrants. And of course, these are the only peoples in Europe whose birth rates are high enough to sustain or increase their populations.

In the United States, the decline of the Christian faith has not been nearly as pervasive as it has been in Europe. However, it has certainly declined within the professional class, and it has virtually disappeared within the academic sector. These two groups, of course, have very low reproduction rates. More generally, as we have noted, most American groups which are of European origin have a reproduction rate that is not high enough to maintain their current numbers. They too are following the Europeans on the path of population decline.

What Is to Be Done?

Can anything be done to reverse this population decline among the Western peoples? Hypothetically, there are a number of pro-family and pro-natal policies that governments can enact. However, such policies were undertaken by various European governments at various times during the twentieth century, and they rarely did much to raise birth rates. This was true even when the policies were enacted within a traditional ideological and cultural context, e.g., at a time of strong Christian religion. They are hardly likely to be effective today, when the ideological and cultural context is defined by expressive individualism and triumphalist feminism, which are positively hostile to family structures that would encourage having several children. In any case, government policies can have only a marginal effect against such massive sociological and economic forces as the movement of families from the country to the city, the movement of women from the home to the office, the movement of the economic center of gravity from production to consumption, and the consequent transformation of children from economic assets into economic burdens.

From the secular perspective, therefore, the prospects are for a continuation of low reproduction rates among Western peoples and therefore for a steady and severe decline in their populations. Conversely, there will be a continuation of high immigration of non-Western peoples into the Western nations, a continuation of higher reproduction rates among the non-Western communities in the West than among the Western peoples themselves, and therefore a steady and substantial rise in the populations of these non-Western communities.

Europe: A Tale of Two Civilizations

The most dramatic political consequences are likely to occur in Europe. There, most of the non-Western communities will be Muslim. These Muslim communities already perform functions essential to the economic system, and they are poised to become within the next decade an important part of the political system, including the exercise of political power within the context of democratic elections, multiparty politics, and coalition governments. Many European countries will become two nations, and Europe as a whole will become two civilizations. The first will be the Western civilization or more accurately, given its rejection of many Western traditions, the post-Western civilization, descended from European peoples; it will be secular, even pagan, rich, old, and feeble. The second will be the non-Western civilization, descended from non-European peoples; it will be religious, even Islamic, poor, young, and vigorous. It will be a kind of overseas colony of a foreign civilization (a familiar occurrence in European history, but this time the foreign civilization will be the *umma* of Islam, and the colonized territory will be Europe itself). The two civilizations will regard each other with mutual contempt, but in the new civilization there will be a growing rage, and in the old civilization there will be a growing fear. They will provide the perfect conditions for endemic Islamic terrorism, or at least for terrified Western people.

The United States: Two Nations or a New Civilization?

Analogous, but less dramatic, developments are likely to occur in the United States. Here, the most numerous of the non-Western communities will be Latin-American in their origin. Latino immigrants obviously already perform functions essential to the American economic system, and Latino-Americans are steadily acquiring political power, including a kind of veto power on many issues where they have a concern. It is possible that the United States also might become two nations, or even two civilizations (although this is not as likely as in Europe). The first will be the Anglo nation, descended from European peoples; as in Europe, much of this nation will be secular, even pagan, rich, old, and feeble. The second nation will be the Latino nation, descended from Latin-American peoples; much of it will be religious, particularly Christian (evangelical and Pentecostal Protestant, as well as Roman Catholic), poor, young, and vigorous. The two nations will regard each other with mutual suspicion and, in a few aspects, with contempt. It is probably too much to predict that in the Anglo nation there will be a widespread fear of some kind of Latino terrorism, although young Latinos in the United States may learn from their Islamic counterparts in Europe. However, it is certainly likely that there will be a widespread fear of Latino crime. The gated communities of Anglos, which are already widespread in the Southwestern United States, are likely to become an even more central part of the Anglo way of life, the distinctive architectural style and urban design of the Anglo nation.

Progeny, Fidelity, and Sanctity

Zimmerman would not have been surprised by these demographic developments in the West—the sharp decline in the birthrates of the national populations and the large growth of the immigrant communities. He accurately forecast their essential dynamics in *Family and Civilization*. He did not forecast where the particular external and internal threat to Western civilization would come from, but he anticipated that it would come from a civilization (or a barbarism) where the prevalent family structure was domestic or even trustee, extended/nuclear or even tribal/clan. Today, the extended or nuclear family is prevalent in Latin American culture and in Asian cultures. The tribal or clan family is prevalent in Muslim cultures. And over the long run, demography is destiny. A civilization that is characterized by an atomistic family (or a nonfamily) structure—which is a structure also characterized by very low reproduction rates—will succumb to one or more of the civilizations that are characterized by a more robust family structure and therefore by a more robust reproduction rate.

Is there a way for Western civilization to escape this demographic destiny? Zimmerman observed that when classical civilization reached a state of awareness of the connections between family and civilization (i.e., during the Roman Empire), it developed a clear conception of what made for a robust and healthy family and civilization. This conception was nicely summed up by Christian thinkers in the three-part formula of *proles, fides,* and *sacramentum*, which we might paraphrase as progeny, fidelity, and sanctity (58, 67, 72). This meant that the family would have children and many of them and that these would be the fruits of a close and continuing tie between husband and wife and also of a religious foundation and inspiration for the family.

Seen from a different aspect, this meant faith in one's God, faithfulness in one's marriage, and faith in the future of one's next generations. In other words, at that most fundamental of bases of family and civilization was that most intangible of human motives—faith.

James Kurth

The Condition for a Revival

Zimmerman observed that there had been efforts to revive the family and the civilization in the past and that some of these had been successful. From his historical review, we can draw certain conclusions.

A successful revival of family and civilization obviously must entail a revival of the reproduction rate, i.e., a return to progeny, the first element in the Christian formula. When confronted with the problem of population decline, governments have often tried to encourage more births by instituting pro-natalist policies. However, such policies by themselves have almost never been sufficient to bring about the desired rise in reproduction rates. The incentives and disincentives that governments can offer are too thin and superficial to change human decisions about something so fundamental as childbearing.

Consequently, a successful revival of family and civilization must also entail a return to fidelity, the second element in the Christian formula. Individual calculations of self-interest have to be replaced by mutual understandings by both husband and wife of their joint and shared identity. In other words, not only the ideology of feminism but also that of individualism must be replaced by an ideology of familism. However, even fidelity and familism by themselves have not been robust enough to counteract the inevitable temptations and centrifugal tendencies toward self-interest and individualism.

Consequently, a successful revival of family and civilization must also entail a return to sanctity, the third and the most fundamental element in the Christian formula. In particular, the notion of contract has to be replaced with something more like the notion of covenant. Moreover, this covenant has to be not just between the husband and the wife but between several human generations, between "the living, the dead, and the yet to be born." And indeed, historical experience seems to show that this covenant has to be not just between these successive generations of human beings in this world, but it also has to be a covenant with a spiritual power, a God, in the other world.

In *Family and Civilization*, Carle Zimmerman demonstrated from history that only a revival of religious faith had ever brought about a reversal of population decline. Only the reestablishment of the "domestic" conception of the family could overcome the entropy toward few or no children that is inherent in the "atomistic" family, and only a robust religious faith could overcome the many economic disincentives to having children in an urban setting. Such a revival of religious faith and reproduction rates had occurred in late antiquity with the rise of Christianity. It had happened again in the modern era with such religious revivals as the Protestant Reformation, the Catholic Counterreformation, the American Great Awakenings, and the Christian moral revival of Victorian times. Zimmerman's analysis implied that it could happen again in the West in the late modern era with some new kind of religious revival.

As it turned out, the revival of Western reproduction rates—the baby boom—had begun in 1946, at the very moment that Zimmerman was completing his book. Most demographers did not attribute this reproductive revival to a religious one; however, religious values were generally more pervasive in the West during the two decades of the baby boom han they were during the two decades before or than they have been during the four decades since.

And so there will be an integral and intimate connection between the West's faith and its fate. Religious revival, however, is not something that scholars can or should predict, or that governments can or should legislate. This is not a matter for Caesar, but for God, and it will not happen according to the world's timing, but according to the Lord's. The true answer to the question of what is to be done about reviving the Western family and Western civilization is that God only knows.

NOTES

Family and Civilization:
Carle Zimmerman Confronts the West's
Third Family Crisis
Bryce Christensen

1. Carle C. Zimmerman, *Family and Civilization* (this edition), 281. Henceforth, all quotations in this essay follow by parenthetical page numbers are from this book. Quotations from other sources are designated by footnote.

2. Susan L. Brown, "Family Structure Transitions and Adolescent Well-Being," *Demography* 43 (2006), 447.

3. United States Bureau of the Census, *Statistical Abstract of the United States:* 2001, Table 117. http://www.census.gov/prod/2002pubs/01statab/vitstat.pdf.

4. *Ibid.*

5. See United States Bureau of the Census, *Historical Statistics of the United States: Colonial Times to* 1970 1, 20, 64. See also United States Bureau of the Census, *Statistical Abstract of the United States:* 2004–2005, Table 80. http://www.census.gov/prod/2004pubs/04statab/vitstat.pdf.

6. United States Bureau of the Census, *Statistical Abstract of the United States:* 2004–2005, Table 77. See also Ben J. Wattenberg, *The Birth Dearth*, (New York: Pharos, 1987).

7. United States Bureau of the Census, "Number of Cohabiting Couples, Based on Two Indirect Measures: 1977–1997." *Current Population Survey,* July 16, 1999. http://www.census.gov/population/documentation/twps0036/tab01.txt.

8. See "Full Text of Mass. Gay Marriage Ruling," MSNBC. http://www.msnbc.com/news/995055.asp?cp1=1.

9. Daniel Patrick Moynihan, "The Negro Family: The Case for National Action," in *The Moynihan Report and the Politics of Controversy*, Lee Rainwater and William L. Yancey, eds. (Cambridge, MA: Massachusetts Institute of Technology, 1967), 51.

10. Herbert J. Gans, "The Breakdown of the Negro Family: The 'Moynihan Report' and its Implications for Federal Civil Rights Policy," in *The Moynihan Report and the Politics of Controversy*, Lee Rainwater and William L. Yancey, eds. (Cambridge, MA: Massachusetts Institute of Technology, 1967), 450–51.

11. Frank Reissman, "In Defense of the Negro Family," in *The Moynihan Report and the Politics of Controversy*, Lee Rainwater and William L. Yancey, eds. (Cambridge, MA: Massachusetts Institute of Technology, 1967), 475.

12. Laura Carper, "The Negro Family and the Moynihan Report," in *The Moynihan Report and the Politics of Controversy*, Lee Rainwater and William L. Yancey, eds. (Cambridge, MA: Massachusetts Institute of Technology, 1967), 471, 474.

13. David T. Courtwright, *Violent Land: Single Men and Social Disorder from the Frontier to the Inner City* (Cambridge, MA: Harvard University Press, 1996), 230.

14. Philip Gailey, "'A Generation Lost' Series," *St. Petersburg Times*, February 9, 1992, 2D.

15. Allan Carlson, "Sexuality: A Litmus Test for Culture," *The Family in America*, May 2001, 1–8.

16. Quoted in Allan Carlson, *Family Questions: Reflections on the American Social Crisis* (New Brunswick, NJ: Transaction, 1988), 84.

17. Carl Danziger, *Unmarried Heterosexual Cohabitation* (San Francisco: ER, 1978), 76.

18. Lawrence Casler, *Is Marriage Necessary?* (New York: Human Sciences Press, 1974), 161–65.

19. Philip L. Elbaum, "The Dynamics, Implications, and Treatment of Extramarital Sexual Relationships for the Family Therapist," *Journal of Marriage and Family Therapy* 7 (1981), 493–96.

20. Quoted in Martha Weinman Leir, "Staying Together," *Ladies' Home Journal*, Sept. 1991, 60–4.

21. Robert Bellah, et al., *Habits of the Heart: Individualism and Commitment in American Life* (Berkeley: University of California Press, 1985), 101–102.

22. Christopher Jencks, "Deadly Neighborhoods," *New Republic*, June 13, 1988, 28–9.

23. Bryce Christensen, "Time for a New 'Moynihan Report'? Confronting the National Family Crisis," *The Family in America*, October 2004, 2–3.

24. Council on Families in America, *Marriage in America: A Report to the Nation* (New York, 1995).

25. Stephanie Coontz, *The Way We Never Were: American Families and the Nostalgia Trap* (New York: Basic Books, 1992), 1–3, 225.

26. Louise B. Silverstein and Carl F. Auerbach, "Continuing the Dialogue About Fathers and Families," *American Psychologist*, June 2000, 683–84.

27. Mary Jo Bane and George Masnick, *The Nation's Families: 1960–1990* (Cambridge, MA: Joint Center for Urban Studies of MIT and Harvard University, 1980), 1–2.

28. Lynn Elber, "Eternal Playboy Hefner Gets into Bed With His Own Reality TV Series," *Augusta Chronicle*, August 7, 2005, G8.

29. Kate Flatley, "From the Waist Down: Men, Women, & Music," *Wall Street Journal*, August 6, 2001, A11.

30. Leonard Pitts, "Baby, I Want You! (But First, Sign a Pre-Sex Agreement)," *Houston Chronicle*, January 12, 2004, 2.

31. Noval Glenn, "A Plea for Objective Assessment of the Notion of Family Decline," *Journal of Marriage and Family* 55 (1993), 543.

32. David Popenoe, "Ideology," *Disturbing the Nest: Family Change and Decline in Modern Societies* (New York: Aldine de Gruyter, 1988), 679.

33. Cited in Zimmerman, Carle C., *Family and Civilization* (New York: Harper, 1947), 55.

34. Cited in Zimmerman, Carle C., *Family and Civilization* (New York: Harper, 1947), 774–75.

35. Gerald L. Klerman, "The Age of Youthful Melancholia: Depression and the Baby Boomers," *USA Today*, July 1988, 69, 71.

36. Cf. Robert H. Aseltine Jr. and Ronald Kessler, "Mental Disruption and Depression in a Community Sample," *Journal of Health and Social Behavior* 34 (1993), 237–51. Also Kelly J. Kelleher, et al., "Increasing Identification of Psychosocial Problems: 1979–1996," *Pediatrics* 105 (2000), 1313–21.

37. David T. Courtwright, *Violent Land: Single Men and Social Disorder from the Frontier to the Inner City* (Cambridge, MA: Harvard University Press, 1996), 242, 272–80.

38. Birgitta Medrick, Robert L. Baker, and Linn E. Carothers, "Patterns of Family Instability and Crime: The Association of the Family's Disruption with Subsequent Adolescent and Young Adult Criminality," *Journal of Youth and Adolescence* 19 (1990), 215–18.

39. William J. Doherty and Richard H. Needle, "Psychological Adjustment and Substance Use Among Adolescents Before and After Parental Divorce," *Child Development* 62 (1991), 334–37.

40. Douglas A Smith and Roger Jarjoura, "Social Structure and Criminal Victimization," *Journal of Research in Crime and Delinquency* 25 (1988), 49–52.

41. Cf. Barry D. Ham, "The Effects of Divorce on the Academic Achievement of High School Seniors," *Journal of Divorce & Remarriage* 38.3/4 (2003), 180–84; Wendy A. Goldberg, Ellen Greenberger, and Stacy K. Nagel, "Employment and Achievement: Mothers' Work Involvement in Relation to Children's Achievement Behaviors and

Mothers' Parenting Behaviors," *Child Development* 67 (1996), 1523–25; Wendy D. Manning and Kathleen A. Lamb, "Adolescent Well-Being in Cohabiting, Married, and Single-Parent Families," *Journal of Marriage and Family* 65 (2003), 889–91.

42. Robert J. Sampson, "Crime in Cities: The Effects of Formal and Informal Social Control," in *Communities and Crime*, Michael Tonry and Norvel Morris, eds. (Chicago: University of Chicago Press, 1987), 280–307.

43. Corey L. M. Keyes, "Social Civility in the United States," *Sociological Inquiry* 72 (1972), 400–08.

44. Howard M. Bahr and Kathleen S. Bahr, "Families and Self-Sacrifice: Alternative Models and Meanings for Family Theory," *Social Forces* 79 (2001), 1245–56.

45. Basil Mitchell, *Why the State Cannot Be Morally Neutral: The Current Confusion About Pluralism* (London: The Social Affairs Unit, 1989), 5–15.

46. David Popenoe, *Disturbing the Nest: Family Change and Decline in Modern Societies* (New York: Aldine de Gruyter, 1988), 72.

47. Cf. Bryce Christensen, *Divided We Fall: Family Discord and the Fracturing of America* (New Brunswick, NJ: Transaction, 2005), 66–7.

48. *Ibid.*, 48–9.

49. Bryce Christensen, *Utopia Against the Family: The Problems and the Politics of the American Family* (San Francisco: Ignatius, 1990), 29. Cf. Bryce Christensen, *Divided We Fall: Family Discord and the Fracturing of America* (New Brunswick, NJ: Transaction, 2005), 137–40.

50. Cf. Bryce Christensen, "The Family in Utopia," *Renascence* 44 (1991), 33–43.

51. George Kateb, *Utopia and Its Enemies* (London: Free Press, 1963), 209, 232.

52. Cited in Zimmerman, Carle C., *Family and Civilization* (New York: Harper, 1947), 24.

53. Cited in Zimmerman, Carle C., *Family and Civilization* (New York: Harper, 1947), 24.

54. Cited in Zimmerman, Carle C., *Family and Civilization* (New York: Harper, 1947), 40.

55. Pitirim Sorokin, *Social and Cultural Dynamics: A Study of Change in Major Systems of Art, Truth, Ethics, Law and Social Relationships*, revised and abridged edition, 1957 (reprint: New Brunswick, NJ: Transaction, 1985). Cf. Bryce Christensen, "Pitirim A. Sorokin: A Forerunner to Solzhenitsyn," *Modern Age* 38 (1996), 386–90.

56. Cf. Bryce Christensen, "The Family in Utopia," *Renascence* 44 (1991), 32–40.

Demography is Destiny:
The Fate of the Western Family and Western Civilization
James Kurth

1. James Kurth, "Western Civilization: Our Tradition," *Intercollegiate Review* (Winter/Spring 2004), 10–18.

2. Samuel P. Huntington, *Who Are We? The Challenges to America's National Identity* (New York: Simon and Schuster, 2004), 264–73.

3. Philip Jenkins, "Demographics, Religion, and the Future of Europe," *Orbis* (Summer 2006), 519–39; James Kurth, "Europe's Identity Problem and the New Islamist Threat," *Orbis* (Summer 2006), 541–57.

4. Pavel Kohout, "Population, Prophets, Pensions, and Politics," *Orbis* (Fall 2005), 731–42.

Index

A

abortion, 62, 70

active solidarity, 26, 28

adultery, 33, 43, 51, 83, 100, 150, 242, 255, 261

amend, 52, 154, 204, 206, 219

America. *See also* American familism: family sociology in, 189–92; immigration and, 187, 190; marriage and, 190–91

American familism: Appalachian-Ozark, 142, 205–10; blood vengeance and, 28; divorce and, 145–46, 168–71; family control and, 269; feuds and, 28; legitimacy and, 32–33; marriage and, 168–71; private contract conception of family and, 7–8; Puritanism and, 103–4; social control of, 162, 165, 168–71; state-family theory and, 145–46; trustee familism and, 28

Anglo-Saxon family, 96–97, 107–10, 113–15, 231

antifamilism, 140, 145, 148, 200, 238, 251, 255, 285

anti-institutionalism, 110–13

Appalachian-Ozark familism, 142, 205–10

atomistic familism. *See also* domestic familism; Greek family; Roman family; trustee familism: anti-institutionalism and, 110–13; causal analysis of, 241–62; criminal responsibility and, 36; cultural integration and, 192–93, 244–45; decline of, 254–57; divorce and, 28, 39, 100–101, 150–53, 162–63, 255; eighteenth-century, 105–7; family, decay of and, 51; family, social control of and, 176–77; family and civilization and, 277–78; freedom and, 245–46; individualism and, 12, 30, 31, 46, 242, 244–45; involuntary sterility and, 252; *manus* and *potestas*, nullification of and, 158–62; marriage and, 31–32, 34, 158–62; meaning of, 30–34, 35–36; mechanics of extension of, 252–54; model of, 176–77; modern family and, 93–122; negative causation of, 254–60; nineteenth-century, 140, 141–63, 166–67; nullification and, 158–62; personality and, 181; private contract conception of family and, 33–34, 247–48; progress of, 247–49; property ownership and, 36; Puritan philosophy and, 100–105; rise of, 115–18, 244–47; seventeenth-century family conceptions and, 97–100; social control of, 166–67; state and, 23; state-family theory and, 143–46; trustee familism and, 35–36; Western society and, 35–36, 43

B

Babylonian family, 264
Balkan family, 40
barbarian family, 31, 40, 47; abortion and, 62; canon law and, 35; Christian church and, 52; clan and, 75; composition and, 4; family, origin of and, 9; family life and, 48–49; feuds and, 62; marriage and, 4–5; Roman Empire and, 3, 4; solidarity and, 62; tribal mores of, 60; trustee familism and, 4–5, 48–49, 63, 70, 181
Beowulfian family, 76, 114, 177–78, 210, 215, 242; family, history of and, 10, 14; family typology and, 22; kin-murder and, 22; parricide and, 22; Roman family and, 4; trustee familism and, 15, 54–55
birth control, 43, 127–28, 252
blood vengeance, 26, 41, 47; American family and, 28; domestic familism and, 223; Roman family and, 52; trustee familism and, 28, 41, 49

C

canon law: barbarian family and, 35; Christian family and, 6, 52; domestic familism and, 279; familism and, 195–98; family, history of and, 10;

family and, 5, 60, 64, 76, 84; golden age of, 130; marriage and, 59, 76; trustee familism and, 35
capitalism, 35
Catholicism, 71, 85–87, 161
character, 15, 185, 241
childbearing: burdens of, 18; conjugal family and, 2; familism and, 195–98; family sociology and, 18; modern family and, 272
children: *concubinatus* marriage and, 3; *dignitas* marriage and, 3; domestic familism and, 221–22; economic individual cult and, 127; family and, 1; marriage and, 59, 85; Roman family and, 3
Chinese family, 10, 60, 259, 263
Christian church. *See also* Christian family: barbarian family and, 52; canon law and, 52; Dark Ages family and, 60–64; *dignitas* marriage and, 4; divorce and, 4, 52, 59; domestic familism and, 46, 54, 75–76; familism and, 195–98; family and, 5, 58–60; family bond and, 79; family change and, 52–55; family mind of, 50–52; legitimacy and, 31; marriage and, 50–52, 60–64, 88–89; rise of, 50; Roman Empire and, 3–4; scholasticism and, 19; trustee familism and, 54, 76
Christian family. *See also* Christian church: canon law and, 6; husband-wife relationship and, 64; marriage and, 5–6; parent-child relationship and, 64; ten-principle system of, 60–64
civilization: familism and, 262; family and, 1, 14–15, 263–86; family types and, 21–36; future of, 263–86
cojuration, 154, 204, 209

English family. *See* Anglo-Saxon family.

evolutionary theories, 9, 17–20, 124, 135–37, 138, 148

F

familism. *See also* atomistic familism; domestic familism; family; trustee familism: birth rate and, 197; canon law and, 195–98; character and, 185; childbearing and, 195–98; Christian church and, 195–98; civilization and, 262; as closed social-value system, 185–89; cultural integration and, 192–95; dynamics of, 185–201; family, causal analysis of and, 13; law and, 13; nineteenth-century, 123–40; recreation of, 267–69; revival of, 284–86; social consequences of, 186–89; social control of, 165–78; society and, 11; state control of, 275–77

family: analytical and predictive conclusions about, 274–77; behavior and, 13; breaking-up of, 13–14; canon law and, 5, 60, 64, 76, 84; causal analysis of, 10–14; changes in, 13; changing roles in, 1; changing functions of, 2; character and, 15; children and, 1; Christian church and, 5, 58–60; as civil contract, 5–6; civilization and, 1, 14–15, 263–86; conjugal, 2; decay of, 198–201; dominant-submissive, 16–17; evolutionary theories of, 9, 17–20, 135–37, 138; future of, 2, 15, 263–86; government and, 11, 211; history of, 10, 14, 16–17; origin of, 2, 9; parenthood and, 60–64; private contract conception of, 6–8, 19; proper

behavior and, 2; religion and, 258–61; as sacrament, 5, 31, 46; secularism and, 60, 97–98; society and, 1, 11, 37; third crisis of, 269–72

family bond: atomistic familism and, 39; Christian church and, 79; domestic familism and, 38, 93; fluctuation of, 37–44; husband-wife relationship and, 37; parent-child relationship and, 37; trustee familism and, 38, 93

family sociology: in America, 189–92; causal analysis and, 256–57; childbearing and, 18; evolutionary theories and, 18, 19; family, causal analysis of and, 12–13; family, history of and, 16–17, 137–39; individualism and, 20; modern family and, 19; negationism and, 16–17, 19; nineteenth-century familism and, 124; private contract conception of family and, 19; progress and, 17–20; purposes of, 179–83; rise of, 8–9; Roman Empire and, 52; Western society and, 179–83

family typology: atomistic familism and, 22; Beowulfian family and, 22; domestic familism and, 23; Greek family and, 21, 24; Homeric family and, 21; individualism and, 24; Roman family and, 24; trustee familism and, 21–25

family vengeance. *See* vengeance.

feme sole, 7, 145, 154, 156, 225, 269

feudalism, 46, 47–48

feuds: American family and, 28; barbarian family and, 62; Dark Ages family and, 62; domestic familism and, 233–34; Kentucky trustee familism and, 208–10; trustee familism and, 26, 28, 48, 204, 210, 215, 218–19

fidelitas, 31, 54–55, 241

K

Kentucky trustee familism, 208–10

L

legitimacy, 31–33, 283
lex talionis, 209
localism, 5, 44
love: romantic conception of, 43; sacrifice and, 38

M

Manichaeism, 5, 40–41
manus, 7, 29–30, 33, 64, 70, 140, 154–58, 166, 170, 172, 203, 221, 224, 271
marriage: American familism and, 168–71, 190–91; atomistic familism and, 31–32, 34; barbarian family and, 4–5; canon law and, 59, 76; Catholicism and, 85–87, 161; children and, 59, 85; Christian church and, 4, 50–51, 52, 60–64, 88–89; Christian family and, 5–6; as civil contract, 3, 94; clandestine, 87–88; *concubinatus*, 3, 4, 7, 32, 87, 95, 142, 153, 197; conjugal family and, 2; consent and, 89; *dignitas*, 3, 4, 32, 70, 87, 148, 153, 173, 174; domestic familism and, 65–69; dual system of, 284; feudalism and, 47–48; freedom and, 61; French family and, 105–7; Greek family and, 64; husband-wife relationship and, 65; indissolubility of, 86, 105–6, 109–10; inter-, 60–64; *manus* and, 7; nineteenth-century familism and,

168–71; nullification and, 68, 72, 83, 146, 151, 158–62; parental consent and, 59, 85; purpose of, 86; religion and, 61, 85–86; Roman familism and, 69; Roman family and, 3, 60–64; Russian family and, 96; as sacrament, 6, 51, 60–64, 65, 79, 81–82, 85, 90; secularism and, 98; status and, 34; trustee familism and, 60–64, 65; as unity of equals, 66–67
matricide, 25
medieval familism, 7, 118, 151
modern family, 115–18; anti-institutionalism and, 110–13; atomistic familism and, 93–122; changes in family conceptions in, 118–22; childbearing and, 272; Council of Trent and, 85–87, 90; crisis in, 269–72, 274–75; divorce and, 100–101; domestic familism and, 75–91; family sociology and, 19; Humanists and, 78–81; Hume, David and, 107–10; Puritan philosophy and, 100–105; reformationists and, 81–84, 90; seventeenth-century family conceptions and, 97–100; sixteenth-century family conception and, 87–89; Western vs. Eastern Europe and, 77–78
monogamy, 85, 109–10, 139, 142

N

nationalism, 18
Near Eastern society, 264
negationism, 16–17, 19, 146
nihilism, 23, 97, 121, 148, 223, 274, 284
nineteenth-century familism: American, 168–71; atomistic familism and, 140, 141–63, 166–67; divorce and,

P

R

4; divorce and, 2, 60–64; domestic familism and, 35–36, 40, 44; family, causal analysis of and, 11, 12; family change and St. Augustine and, 52–55; family typology and, 24; feudalism and, 46; Greek vs., 179–83; legitimacy and, 31–32; marriage and, 3, 60–64, 69; social control of, 173–75; trustee familism and, 25, 27, 28–29, 32, 35–36, 40, 44, 180, 204

ruralism, 77

Russian family: divorce and, 7, 96; marriage and, 96; private contract conception of family and, 7; Russian Revolution and, 94–96; will of the parties and, 7

S

sacramentum, 72, 91, 148, 196, 197, 238, 256

sacrifice, 38, 256

scholasticism, 19

secularism, 5–6; family and, 60, 97–98; marriage and, 98; private contract conception of family and, 89

Semitic family, 264

slavery, 42, 47

Slavic barbarian family, 10, 40, 48

solidarity, 26; barbarian family and, 62; domestic familism and, 28; trustee familism and, 49, 204

Sophism, 35

state: atomistic familism and, 23; domestic familism and, 28; familism and, 275–77; family as agent of, 6; nineteenth-century familism and, 130–35; trustee familism and, 23, 26

statism, 130–35, 140

status: family and, 1; marriage and, 34

stoicism, 185

T

transaction, 52, 154, 204, 206

trustee familism. *See also* atomistic familism; domestic familism: American family and, 28; Anglo-Saxon family and, 113; Appalachian-Ozark, 49, 205–10; appearance of, 203; atomistic familism and, 35–36; barbarian family and, 4–5, 48–49, 63, 181; Beowulfian family and, 15, 54–55; blood vengeance and, 28, 41, 47, 49, 204, 213–14, 216; canon law and, 35; causal analysis of, 203–20; character and, 241; Christian church and, 54, 76; common responsibility and, 25–26, 49; continuance of, 203; criminal responsibility and, 36; in Dark Ages, 57–73, 181; divorce and, 28, 38, 150; domestic familism and, 35–36, 232–33, 239–40; family, causal analysis of and, 12; family and civilization and, 277; family typology and, 21–25; feudalism and, 48; feuds and, 26, 28, 48, 204, 210, 215, 218–19; Greek family and, 15, 21, 24, 35–36, 40, 204; Homeric family and, 21, 24, 35, 54–55, 63, 218; home-rule and, 5, 6; individual and, 26; individualism and, 30–31; instability of, 213; justice and, 49, 207–8, 216–17, 242; Kentucky, 208–10; localism and, 5, 44; marriage and, 60–64, 65; meaning of, 25–27, 35–36, 142, 214–16; private contract conception of family vs., 7; property ownership and, 36; rights

Index

and, 26; Roman family and, 25, 27, 28–29, 32, 35–36, 40, 44, 180, 204; solidarity and, 25–26, 49, 204; state and, 49

V

vengeance, 26, 28, 41, 47, 49, 204, 213–14, 216, 223

W

wergild, 154, 204, 216
Western European family, 2, 40; domestic familism and, 88; Eastern European vs., 77–78; trustee familism and, 216–17
Western society: atomistic familism and, 35–36, 43; changes in family conceptions in, 118–22; domestic familism in, 35–36, 238; economic catastrophes and, 5; family, social control of and, 177–78; family and

civilization and, 279; family sociology and, 179–83; third family crisis in, 269–72; trustee familism and, 35–36
wife-purchase theory, 12–13
women: Amazonian, 9; *feme sole* conception of, 7, 145, 154, 156, 225, 269; wife-purchase theory and, 12–13

About the Contributors

CARLE C. ZIMMERMAN was an eminent professor of sociology at Harvard University and the founder of the subdiscipline of rural sociology. Among his many other books are *The Changing Community* and *Marriage and the Family: A Text for Moderns*.

JAMES KURTH is the Claude C. Smith Professor of Political Science at Swarthmore College and co-chairman of the Foreign Policy Research Institute's Center for the Study of America and the West. He is a frequent contributor to the *National Interest, Foreign Policy, Orbis: A Journal of World Affairs*, and other periodicals.

ALLAN C. CARLSON is president of the Howard Center for Family, Religion & Society and the author, most recently, of *Third Ways: How Bulgarian Greens, Swedish Housewives, and Beer-Swilling Englishmen Created Family-Centered Economies—And Why They Disappeared*.

BRYCE CHRISTENSEN is director of the English Language Study Center at Southern Utah University. The former editor of *The Family in America*, he is a contributing editor to *Modern Age* and has written for the *Wall Street Journal, USA Today*, the *Chicago Tribune, New York Newsday*, and the *Baltimore Sun*.